Economic Reforms
and
Rural Development
in India

ECONOMIC REFORMS

AND

RURAL DEVELOPMENT

IN INDIA

G. PARTHASARATHY

EDITED BY

G. NANCHARAIAH

Academic Foundation

New Delhi

Reprint 2004

Published in 2003 by

ACADEMIC FOUNDATION
4772-73 / 23 Bharat Ram Road,
(23 Ansari Road), Darya Ganj,
New Delhi - 110 002.

Phones : 23245001, 02, 03, 04.

Fax : 011-23245005

e-mail : academic@vsnl.com

www : academicfoundation.com

ECONOMIC REFORMS AND RURAL DEVELOPMENT IN INDIA
by G. Parthasarathy; edited by G. Nancharaiah
ISBN 81-7188-293-5

Laser-Typeset at AF's DTP Division.
Printed at Print Perfect, Mayapuri, New Delhi.

THE AUTHOR

G. Parthasarathy (born May 19, 1928) did his M.A in Economics from Madras University (1949) and Ph.D in Agricultural Economics, University of Wisconsin, Madison, USA, 1958.

G. Parthasarathy was Professor and Head, Department of Applied Economics, Andhra University; Director, Institute of Development and Planning Studies, Visakhapatnam (1992-2001); was on the State Planning Board, Government of Andhra Pradesh (1989-92); was Consultant FAO and UNDP. Presently, he is President, Indian Society of Agricultural Marketing.

Prof. Parthasarathy has published a number of books and articles.

THE EDITOR

G. Nancharaiah, currently Vice-Chancellor of Babasaheb Bhimrao Ambedkar University, Lucknow, did M.A. and Ph.D in Economics from Andhra University. He has taught post-graduate students for 26 years at different universities (Andhra University, University of Hyderabad, and Bombay University). He was Professor and Head, Department of Economics, University of Hyderabad; was a Fulbright scholar and also worked at University of California, USA.

Dr. Nancharaiah authored a book entitled "Land and Caste" and has a number of monographs, and research papers to his credit. He is on the Governing Body of Giri Institute of Development Studies and on the Academic Council of Rohilkhand University.

Contents

Editorial Introduction

G. NANCHARAIAH

THIS book comprises various research papers written by Prof. G. Parthasarathy, a distinguished senior Professor of economics who significantly contributed in the area of agriculture and rural development with reference to rural poor.

Since 1991 onwards Indian economy has been exposed to economic liberalisation and globalisation in line with structural adjustment and stabilisation policies initiated by Brettonwood institutions such as IMF and World Bank. Structural adjustment policy advocated privatisation, import liberalisation, and export-led growth while stabilisation policy emphasises reduction in fiscal deficit through withdrawals of subsidies given to industry, trade and agriculture. There has been a shift in the Indian economic policy from State oriented development strategy to market oriented development leaving the decisions of productions and distribution to the market signals. This policy became controversial as some argued in favour of it while others argued against it.

The liberal economists argued that the liberal economic policy not only releases the resources from public sector, particularly from those which are incurring losses through privatisation but also enables the State to be free from unnecessary burden so that State can use these resources for social sectors such as health, education and family welfare. It has also been argued that the restricted trade policy adopted in the post-independence period upto 1990 did not lead to any improvement in external sector but provided protection to the domestic capitalists through licensing Raj and higher rates of custom duties and quotas in India while the neighbouring countries such as South Korea, Taiwan and other Countries including China, which switched over to market oriented development policies and opened their economies, registered significant growth rates in their respective economies in 1980s. Therefore India should also go for liberalisation and globalisation emphasising market oriented development policy. On the other hand many economists argued that given the stage and structure of Indian economy, the liberalised economic policies such as withdrawal of state from the developmental activity, liberalisation of foreign trade sectors will have dampening effect on the Indian economy as it could not rise to the level of international competition and about 40 per cent of the people suffer from illiteracy and poverty due to lack of purchasing power and gainful employment. Moreover in the neighbouring countries referred above there had been agrarian and educational reform which led to egalitarian economic structures and removal of illiteracy and improved the skills of the people so that their productivities could be raised significantly whereas in India land reform could remove the intermediatory landlords but failed from the point of bringing equity in the Indian agriculture and land concentration continued in the post independence period also. As a result, the benefits of the agrarian reform did not reach the vulnerable sections of the rural India. The agricultural productivity of India is found to be much lower than the agricultural productivity in China, South Korea etc. Under these circumstances, it is argued that liberalisation policies my lead to deterioration at aggregate level in terms of growth rates and in improving the living standards of the people particularly rural poor.

In this context Prof. G. Parthasarathy, in these articles rigorously analysed the pros and cons of the structural adjustment and liberalisation policies and empirically examined its effects, at national and state level, on rural development in terms of agricultural growth, employment opportunities, wages and reduction in rural poverty. In the first article entitled 'Structural adjustments and rural development, selected issues: A survey of recent literature' he argues that higher growth need not lead to decline in the poverty particularly in the short run. Moreover when expenditure is reduced by withdrawing the food-subsidies, while procurement and thereby market prices are rising, it would adversely affect the poor. He argues that where freeplay of market forces conflict with the social objectives, there is a need for Govt. policy. He also observes that free trade of foodgrain exports may lead to 15 to 20 per cent rise in the relative domestic price which means squeeze of consumption of poor while unaffecting the relatively affluent.

The second paper entitled 'Social Security and Structural Adjustments' deals with the various forms of social security emphasising food security on the basis of NSS data. This paper brings out the extent of food insecurity in rural and urban areas. He found that about 19 per cent rural households suffered from food insecurity in 1983 in India. Erosion of purchasing power due to increase in prices and low purchasing capacity are found to be main reasons. In 1990 due to structural adjustments there was adverse effect on food security of poor. He also opines that the entry of big business increases employment insecurity particularly for women workers who work as fruit and vegetable vendors as direct transport of farm-produce from farm to factory shall take place due to vertical integration of farm and factory in the context of structural adjustments.

In the paper entitled 'Safety-Nets for Vulnerable Sections', Prof. Parthasarthy examines the impact of stabilisation policies on rural poor. In this paper Prof. Parthasarthy argues that reduction in fertiliser subsidies and rise in procurement prices of paddy and wheat caused high rate of inflation adversely affecting the poor during 1990-93 and quantity of cereal consumption also declined. This is one of the main reasons for high incidence of hunger among poor. Incidence of hunger is inversely related to income level. He argues that inflation in the context of new economic policy not only eroded the real incomes of the poor but also led to the contraction of employment opportunities in the short-run as growth of economy slowed down substantially in 1991-92. He also observes that NEP had adverse effects on handloom workers particularly in A.P. There were several starvation and suicide deaths in A.P. in the later half of 1991 as increased exports of yarn led to its scarcity in the domestic market and consequent raise in prices at high rate. He argues that cuts in the public expenditure in social sector affected the welfare of the poor in early 90s. Fiscal adjustments at state level, for example in A.P. led to withdrawal of Rs.2/- per kg. on rice and reduction in quantum of subsidised rice. All India level number of poor went up by 10.7 million in 1991-92 as compared to annual trend decline of 15.5 million between 1987-88 and 1990-91. In this context he also thoroughly reviewed the public distribution system as safety net. He found that the benefits of the PDS is mostly cornered by urban people as the per capita consumption of foodgrains from PDS in rural areas is only around 70 per cent of the corresponding per capita use of PDS in urban areas. Around one half of the quantum of cereals distributed under public distribution system

of employment at all India level was 1.78 per cent per
um for the total population while youth employment grew
1.44 per cent.

He observes that between 1993-94 and 1997, female ployment of youth received negative growth rates even in urban areas. The growth rate of female employment in al areas show a continuous slide. The negative growth of nale employment in the post-reforms period indicate that orms had an adverse effect on rural female employment. e trends in rural employment indicate that rural non-form ployment increased during the 80s but there was a decline ring the 90s.

Regarding the educated unemployment of youth he finds t in the 90s the growth rate of employment in the organised ctor was 1.58 per cent which came down to 1 per cent in 90s. The organised sector accounted for only 7.3 per cent the total workforce in 1997. The supply of labour to ganised sector comes mainly from educated. The rate of owth of the student employment in general and professional/ gher education was 4.82 per cent for the 80s and 4.47 per nt for the 90s while the demand from organised sector was creasing at 1 per cent only. It is also found that employment rates for educated aged 15 years and above e positively correlated to levels of education and rural areas perience a higher degree of educated unemployment. With e emerging pattern of foreign investment and the choice of pital intensive techniques by the MNCs dualism in the labour arket is growing with scope only for the small portion of e highly skilled persons at very high wages.

Prof. Parthasarathy in his lecture on the "unorganised sector Indian economy and public policy in the context of structural djustment" focuses on the issues of relative efficiency of the rganised vis-à-vis the unorganised sector, the exploitation o

are appropriated by the non-poor. The States with high concentration of rural poverty gain very little from public distribution and accounts for only a small proportion of total consumption. As a result its impact on food insecurity and nutrition of the poor has been uncertain for these reasons. He suggests "A sharper targeting of public distribution system along with higher ration are considered necessary for protecting the poor. A public distribution system which guarantees the food security for the vulnerable sections but does not act as disincentive to long-term growth of agriculture in the process of procurement and simultaneously does not impose burdens of food-subsidies on the state exchequer is necessary. A public distribution system linked with employment in public works is considered to have the potential to serve the objectives".

Prof. Parthasarthy examines the impact of withdrawals of subsidies on rural employment under NEP policy. The withdrawal of subsidies for inputs in agriculture would reduce employment depending upon (a) price-elasticity of input-use (b) elasticity of crop yield to input-use and elasticity of employment to yield. He observes that 30 per cent price raise in fertiliser prices given the daily status unemployment rate of the order of 8.0 per cent, unemployment rate is likely to rise by 17 per cent. At the same time even if agricultural exports are stepped up through promotion of agro-processing, their short-run effects on employment are unlikely to be favourable since the employment intensity of modern processing is likely to be less than the corresponding intensity of traditional industry. Therefore, rural development programmes, sponsored by public agencies will have to be on a much larger scale in the short and medium term of the operation of NEP. He also opines that "while the strengthening of the R-D. programmes is necessary, their success depends on an improved rate of agricultural growth, especially allied occupations, non agricultural employment in rural areas and an effective implementation of land reforms".

The paper on "agricultural exports in the context of liberalisation and globalisation of agricultural trade" examines the effects of the liberalisation of trade policy on agricultural exports during 1990-91 to 1991-93 as compared to immediate pre liberalisation period 1988-89 and 1989-90. This paper also reviews the studies on past trends in Indian agricultural trade. He observes that post liberalisation period is marked by an increase in growth rate of net-exports of agricultural commodities. But exports are marked by high instability as measured by coefficient of variation much more than instability in production and prices. In the absence of sustained growth of agricultural productivity, export promotion becomes difficult because of the competing interest of consumers and farmers and industrialists. Adhocism in exports is likely to benefit the traders much more than the producers and consumers. The short term impact of globalisation is likely to be adverse on the poor. The poor will suffer much more by the rise in food prices and their employment gains will be small due to low elasticity of employment to output in agriculture.

Prof. Parthasarathy in his paper on "Rural Poverty and Economic Reforms – Opportunities and Constraints : A case study of Andhra Pradesh" reviewed the trends in rural poverty in A.P. for the pre-economic reforms period and the opportunities and constaints of economic reform to poverty alleviation. In 1987-88 the incidence of rural poverty in A.P. shows a decline and is lower than All India. He attributes it to high agricultural growth rate in second half of sixties and eighties higher than the growth rate of labour force and population. He opines that the level of social development is critical for utilising opportunities provided by economic reforms. Literacy particularly high literacy rate among women is important as it contributes to better enrolment of children

in the schools, better nutrition and reduc
Health for all is also critical for raising the
of labour. The agricultural Production in
the years 1991-92 and 1992-93 was the lo
Since most people in rural areas are eng
the low rate of agricultural growth rate wl
the growth rate of labour force should l
reduction in incomes of the poor people.
and 90s shows a rise in terms of trade in f
Post reform period recorded a price r
commodities by 68.20 per cent as compare
period. But these favourable trends in the p
commodities may not result in gain for poo
labourers who sell only labour power but r
as the male workers suffered a loss in th
post reform period". Prof. Parthasarathy
observes that considering that the prices
consumption have increased at a faster ra
also the fact that many poor have been fo
open market as a result of weak function
1991-92 the incidence of rural poverty shou
higher than in 1990-91. The public action i
to protect the poor from displacement eff
back-wash effects of market forces. The
institutional credit is greater in the conte
the past.

Prof. Parthasarathy in his joint paper
"employment and unemployment" examine
pattern of youth employment, the extent of
regional dimensions of youth unemployme
1997 on the basis of NSSO data. He obser
cent of youth population lives in rural areas.
per cent of total labour force in rural are
cent in urban areas. During 1983 to 1997 the

unorganised sector by organised and the public support to unorganised. He also examines the adverse implications of structural adjustments for the unorganised sector. He observes that neither in Marxian theory nor in Classical Economic Theory, the unorganised sector has permanent place in the economy. But the situation in India is quite different. The share of unorganised sector in employment in Indian economy was as high as 90.66 per cent, while that of an organised sector was only 9.44 per cent in 1991. The share of employment in organised sector in 1981 was only 9.70 per cent while its share in NDP was 30 per cent. During 1980-81 to 1990-91, the share of organised sector increased from about 30 per cent to more than 36 per cent, but its share in employment declined from 9.70 per cent to 9.37 per cent.

Regarding the implications of structural adjustment, he opines that it will have adverse impact on employment both in the organised sector and unorganised sector. The organised sector is likely to witness retrenchment and casualisation of employment opportunities. The unorganised sector will be forced to accept persons released by the organised sector and in the process wage and self-employment opportunities for the unskilled and the semi-skilled are likely to deteriorate further. Safety nets and structural adjustment with human face could hardly bring solutions to their problems. "A new approach to development in which the petty producers are made the agents of social transformation through their own organisations which will bring them economies of scale of production, technology, credit and marketing will be found necessary".

It is interesting to note that the inferences drawn and predictions made by Prof. G. Parthasarathy in early 90s on the basis of the past empirical trends and theoretical analysis regarding the implications of structural adjustment and new economic policy are found to be mostly consistent with the recent trends in Indian economy particularly with reference to rural development and rural poor. Thus this book is relevant for understanding current economic problems of Indian economy particularly rural development in the context of new economic policy.

I thank Prof. G. Parthasarathy for contributing research papers for this book. I am also thankful to Dr. (Mrs.) Uma Kapila, Academic Foundation, for publishing this book.

1

Structural Adjustment and Rural Development

A Survey of Recent Literature

1. Fundamental Objective and Trade-Off between Growth and Poverty in the Short-Run

THE first and fundamental question is adjustment for what purpose (Paul Streeten, World Development, 1987, P.1470). Most fundamental objective is elimination of hunger and or elimination of poverty. Accelerating economic growth is also such a fundamental objective. These two objectives may conflict with one another at least in the short-run. Even if growth does not immeserise focus on growth, it may divert attention away from questions of poverty. In the short run it is necessary to recognise the trade off between higher growth rate and rapid reduction in poverty. The recent experiences with export trade policy of cotton yarn and its implications for the growing poverty of handloom weavers illustrate this well. Even though, the country added to its foreign exchange by exports, the handloom weavers suffered with decreased access to hank yarn and higher prices, their incomes went down sharply, raising the incidence of poverty.

The adjustment problems in the transition period will involve among others, sectoral imbalances in supply and demand manifesting themselves in unemployment combined with inflation. One has to cope with this problem.

There are again options in adjustment policies : keeping food prices down or raising them to world level of prices. Keeping, food prices down will help the net buyers but will hurt the small seller. Dantwala in his recent writings strongly argues against parity of domestic prices with international prices. Further, higher agricultural prices without action on other fronts, viz., (a) inputs, water, fertiliser, equipment, (b) innovation, technology and irrigation, (c) information through extension services, (d) infrastructure can be ineffective or counter-productive. They can be ineffective because supply response is lower without them. They can be counter-productive since the benefits of higher prices may be lost because of higher mark-up of international goods or higher money wages. Secondly, the transfer of lands of marginal farmers to large farmers could reduce the total output as productivity on large farms is lower than that on the small.

2. *Structural Adjustments : Contraction in Investment vs. Social Expenditure*

When we consider the question of adjustment by whom; the candidates are labour or capitalists. In considering the impact of adjustment policies on the poor, three things need to be noted: (i) since adjustment affects the distribution of incomes, the question of change in distribution of income needs consideration, (ii) impact on adjustments on the poor is more important than impact on income distribution, and (iii) when a cut in living standards is imposed by the need to correct a balance of payments deficit it is bound to hurt some of the poor.

Adjustments require some cuts in expenditure. But one does not want to cut investment, it would undermine long term growth. The axe will then fall on social expenditure, for instance elimination of food subsidies, cuts in social services or price increase of essentials. This will certainly hurt the poor.

Contraction of expenditure under adjustment policies should reduce inflation (Streeten, p. 1746). But in the context of rising procurement prices, rising issue prices become inevitable. Rising open market prices are associated with rising issue prices. Thus though contraction of expenditure should result in reduced prices, reduction of input subsidies followed by increase in procurement and issue prices brings about inflation that hurts the poor.

3. *Adjustment through Expenditure Switching towards Tradeables*

Adjustment normally consists of two parts: (i) expenditure reduction, and (ii) expenditure switching. Expenditure reduction tends to hit the poor unless they are specifically protected or compensated. But expenditure switching need not harm them (Streeten, "World Development", P.1476). the allocation from domestic sectors to tradeables will tend to raise incomes in the sectors. If trade is in mainly agricultural goods or non-agricultural labour intensive goods, such as garments, many poor may benefit from reallocation. On the other hand, if there is switch from labour intensive non-tradeables such as construction to capital intensive tradeables, poor will be hurt.

Further, if there is substantial mobility of the poor from the informal to formal sector, which is engaged in tradeables poor people will not be hurt. But if the mobility is limited, poor are likely to be hurt more.

4. *Structural Adjustments and Policies for Protecting the Poor*

Devaluation is injected to correct the distortions in exchange rates. If poor depend upon imports for their staple food may hurt them. Streeten suggests the following guidelines for protecting the weaker sections :

(i) Maintain a floor for minimum nutrition, health and education levels and do not permit cuts in expenditure to affect these;

(ii) Restructure production so that producers in the small scale in formal sectors are not discriminated against, give them access to credit, domestic market and source of supply;

(iii) Restructure the social services such as education, health, water and sanitation, so that the vulnerable groups are not deprived of minimum services, and

(iv) Provide international support for this type of adjustment.

Policy makers embarking on the course of rising food prices must pay special attention to protcction of the poor in the transitional period. One solution is to increase prices gradually in small steps, secondly, select subsidies concentrated on vulnerable groups, and thirdly, promotion of income subsidies to poor. Subsidies could also be combined with rations, so that the poor are guaranteed a minimum food.

5. *Structural Adjustments and the Role of the State*

The virtue of allowing the market to bring about the adjustment is that it combines signals and incentives in response to change. But where the free play of market forces conflict with the social objectives, there is a need for Government policy. The following are the areas in which public policy is needed for correcting the market failures:

(i) When workers have to be retrained for a job and have to be moved to new locations, capital is needed to finance these adjustments;

(ii) Capital markets where perfect workers could borrow their loans out of their higher earnings. But where capital markets are not perfect there is a role for Governments to finance adjustment assistance;

(iii) When adjustments are impeded by lack of knowledge or by inertia Governments have to provide information; and

(iv) If real wages are sticky and do not fall in response to decline in demand, employment will fall. Some times such unemployment may bring about adjustment more effectively than reduction in real wages. If it does not happen there may be a case for intervention in the labour market.

6. *Price Policies, Export of Foodgrains and the Poor*

Price policies are not the same as free market policies. Government policies can be used as an instrument for Government intervention in order to achieve public objectives. Tariffs, indirect taxes and subsidies permit prices to affect allocated resources cutting the links between buyers and sellers, that would prevail in their absence.

It is by now clear that the Government Plans to liberalise international trade in foodgrains allowing domestic prices to international levels. Currently, Indian wheat prices are roughly 10 per cent more than the international prices and rice prices 30 per cent less, and coarse grains and pulses prices 10 per cent more. However, the recently agreed GATT Agreement is likely to push up relatively the prices of wheat and coarse cereals by 5 per cent while bringing down the rice prices. In the net, therefore, liberalisation of agricultural trade in the Post-GATT scenário may involve a rise in the domestic relative prices of foodgrains by about 15 to 20 per cent. The effect of such a price rise (as measured by calculation of price elasticities) would be the squeeze of the consumption of the poor while leaving that of such relatively affluent unaffected. In this case export surpluses of about 10 to 15 million tonnes may be possible in 2000 AD, but at the cost of the poor consuming significantly less than even the inadequate amounts they consume today. It should be noted that while the effect of exporting foodgrains upon domestic prices and availability is direct and therefore more obvious, similar results would occur even if other non-food cash crop exports were encouraged, in so far are these imply acreage shifts away from foodgrains rather than substantially increasing total supply (Food Exports and Food Requirements by J.M. Economic and Political Weekly, August 27, 1994, P.2261).

7. *Structural Adjustments and Labour Markets*

Detailed studies of labour market in 12 countries during the adjustment period (ILO, Vol. 30, 1991, p.531) show that labour market rigidities are only one of the three reasons for emergence of unemployment. The evidence on real wage casts considerable doubt on theoretical concerns about the aggregate real wage rigidity and labour market inflexibility as obstacles to adjustment. Real wage declines have been far more dramatic than the fall in GDP. Secondly, sectoral employment shifts have been generally in the desired direction, that is towards tradeables, although for the low income countries, this has meant that agricultural employment has increased relatively to manufacturing employment. Shifts of employment into services and commerce are indicative of weak GDP growth and hence weak growth of labour demand. As regards labour market institutions, they were not perceptible obstacles to adjustment. In some countries, such as Bolivia, the functioning of the capital market seems to be partly responsible for poor growth. The shift of labour back into agriculture has been one aspect of adjustment in some countries following liberalisation. Growth of casual labour, decreased worker benefits and decline in wage differential for skills and possibly for education are other aspects. Developing countries have long resisted being relegated to the role of primary producers in the international economic order, and it is unlikely that structural adjustment which relies on a shift of labour into agriculture is going to be sustainable for long.

8. Structural Adjustments V/s. Distortions in Policies

Srinivasan, T.N.(1988) argued forcefully against any special concession for the poor households during adjustment period on the plea that there are no particular features in adjustment policies that make the incidence of the cost more skewed compared to any other set of policies and secondly he makes a distinction between the choice of specific adjustment policy which hurts the poor from the effects of adjustment policy perse.

For a number of reasons, Srinivasan's arguments are debatable. The outcomes of any particular adjustment policy depend upon a number of factors, viz., (i) the exporters of a product whether they are self-employed small peasants or capitalists (ii) the commodity exported whether staple food of the poor or not, (iii) proportion of the poor in different sectors, (iv) weight accorded to the poor in overall policies, and (v) contractionary effects of adjustment. If the exporters are poor and small peasants, adjustment through devaluation will benefit the poor. When the commodity exported is staple food of the poor, prices will rise and poor will be hurt. The contractionary effects of adjustment will hurt the poor as a consequence of contraction of public investment associated with further contraction of private investment. When the axe falls on social expenditure, the poor are the victims of a decline in health and education services.

Whether the so called structural rigidities are largely synonymous with policy distortions is essentially an empirical issue and therefore Srinivasan's assertions are unwarranted. It is illustrated empirically in the WIDER sample that a cut back in public investment or in interest rate hike results in sharp output contraction. The Indian experts also corroborates the findings of wider sample.

9. Newly Poor V/s. Chronically Poor and Structural Adjustment

The effects of structural adjustment could be on all types of following poor: (i) the newly poor, these are direct victims of structural adjustments such as employees of rural health and school teachers in village retrenched as a consequence of cut back in public expenditure in the areas of health and education; (ii) border line poor pushed into poverty: these comprise of individuals and families whose incomes are so low that price increases by structural adjustments pushed them below the border line; and (iii) the chronically poor : these are people who are extremely poor even before the adjustment programmes were undertaken. The concern here is with all the categories of rural poor not just the newly poor or the border line poor pushed into the poverty. (Chapter-III, Analytical Issues in Structural Adjustment and Household Welfare, by ILO).

10. Domestic Structural Adjustment as complimentary to International Adjustment in International Trade

Domestic structural adjustment is necessary to compliment structural adjustment in international trade area. While devaluation provides an incentive to exports and disincentives to imports, its success depends upon (a) the extent to which domestic inflation is contained, (b) growth of output which enables more to be exported. Structural adjustments such as privatisation and wage freeze are done at the behest of World Bank and IMF. After nearly 10 years of application, some of these measures proved to be less efficient and, indeed, more harmful than was expected.

11. Structural Adjustment and the Role of the State in Agriculture

As far as agriculture is concerned, there is recently a new development resulting from what could be termed "the project quarrel". At the end of colonial period and during the beginning period of the independence, agricultural policy issues were mainly in terms of institutional choices. Since 1960, there was a tendency for administrators to limit the roles to a management of variety of projects proposed by various organisations. As a consequence, Plans had a tendency to become mere lists of projects not necessarily coherent. Such an approach had the merit of recognising ground realities. But with the discussion mainly focused upon micro economic issues, its drawback was that macro economic choice were often neglected. (FAO, Impact of Structural Adjustment on Small Holders, P.31). The emphasis put on structural adjustment corrects this to some extent. It is now necessary to think about an agricultural policy, in terms of equilibria, balance of payment and rate of exchange. In such context, there is a temptation of leave out the projects approach and be content with a macro economic policy. There is a need to combine the two approaches. However the logic of two types of action is so different that they would be perfectly antagonistic without an effort to state the conditions under which they would be complimentary (FAO, P.32).

A main advantage of successful structural adjustment is the disappearance of economic schizophrenia involved in the distinction between current and shadow prices. By imposing real exchange rates, major cause of difference between social utility values and current prices is removed. The removal of distortive tax and subsidies as well as imposition of modern tax system such as the value-added to tax obey the same logic. Privatisation of activity undertaken by the State Trading Organisations removes some price distortions though it can also have side effects such as depriving farmers of free access to technical information. If such side-effects are undesirable they may be corrected by relevant projects. In addition there are situations where public intervention is obviously necessary independent of any structural adjustment programme.

It is important to identify carefully the means and purposes of state intervention in agriculture. Clearly structural adjustment measures such as purely economic interventions have some influence over the others such as providing non-marketable facilities, marketable facilities, price distortions and regulations to subsidies and levies. If the adjustment results in true price system i.e., a price system that correctly reflects the scarcities in the economy, the necessity of providing market facilities and removing price distortions or regulations is far less evident than otherwise. Even capitalist model shows a very mixed record and seldom any where rural capitalists generated a pattern of self-sustaining growth. Even in developed countries while a vital role is played by private sector in production and of marketing agricultural products, the role of the State is also essential in determining floor and ceiling prices for agricultural commodities, stock piling of excess quantities and providing a legal framework for all transactions, especially relating to land ownership. In these countries, a sort of division of labour between State and private enterprise has been put into operation. Developing countries should draw lessons from this particular division of labour.

12. Freeing the Land Market : Capital Flows into Land V/s Landlessness

Freeing the land market from the restriction now in force on acquisition beyond ceiling level and on leasing out will attract flows of urban investment into land besides encouraging retention of rural surpluses for investment of land. This has certainly happened on a large scale in Coastal Andhra where urban investments have flown into acquisition of Government and private lands all over the sea coast for purposes of prawn culture ; but simultaneously this had the effect of dispossesion of small farmers of their small bits of land, besides having adverse effects on the eco-system of the area. Immediately this has not generated adverse effects on employment. But after the phase of construction of ponds is completed, continuing conversion of paddy lands to pisciculture will result in less employment within agriculture. If growth needs to be combined with poverty alleviation, the small farmer in the coastal belt should be enabled to have access to economies of scale through group farming or alternatively the division of labour must be encouraged between the large and the small, the former concentrating on marketing, extension and technology activity while the small farmers concentrates on production with assistance from the large in improving their productivity. In effect the ancillary concept which is widely known in industry needs to be applied to agriculture also.

13. Structural Adjustment and Labour Market

Some of the important issues in the area of labour market are considered by T.S. Papola (1994). They include issues such as compatibility of policies of structural adjustment with existing labour market institutions, direction of reform of labour market institutions and the short-term, long-term and medium-term implications of structural adjustment for employment.

There are two aspects of the functioning of the labour markets in developing countries which are targets of frontal attack in the process of structural adjustments. Specific targets of attack are legal provisions protecting job tenure and fixation of minimum wages. Labour market reforms advocated as a part of the structural reform package, call for flexibility in the labour market. In concrete form, it would mean relatively complete freedom to enterprises in hiring and firing of workers and determination of wages through the unfiltered play of market forces.

There are, however, several questions that need to be examined in putting this market-led logic into practice. First, there is the moral and social question: whether labour should be treated as a commodity like any other. Removing a worker from employment without reasonable notice and without reasonable compensation to survive is not socially acceptable. Even on an economic basis, there are at least two questions that need to be asked: first, whether job security and low and uncertain wages lead to higher efficiency and productivity than employment with a minimum job security and minimum assured wages, and second, whether job security provisions and minimum wage legislation tend to discourage employment growth, as is argued by the proponents of labour market flexibility.

The cornerstone of the theory of labour market flexibility is the concept of labour market clearing. But labour markets do not necessarily clear; persistence of unemployment is not an uncommon phenomenon. Also labour markets everywhere are segmented; and, wage differentials unrelated to efficiency, productivity and relative demand supply situation in the occupational labour markets, are the rule rather than exceptions. The fact, however, remains that since information is not a free good, and labour supply and mobility is not a function solely of the wage rate, the concept of labour market clearing remains a myth.

The attack on the provision of statutory minimum wages is also controversial. In many countries, including India, the statutory minimum wage is a floor level wage aimed at providing a subsistence income and is mostly relevant to the unorganised sector, characterised by miserably low levels of earnings. In these situations, the statutorily fixed minimum wage is generally lower than the average wage level and its revision also follows the general trends in the labour market. Some recent studies of World Bank and I.L.O. have shown that there is no adverse impact on employment, while in some other cases, the findings are mixed.

Some studies from India confirm the adverse effects of job security provision on employment levels in Indian industry. In addition to job security provisions, some of these and other studies have also brought out the sharp rise in real wages as a reason for employment growth in the manufacturing sector. However, the hypothesis that real wage increases during the 1980s prompted employers to opt for capital-intensive technologies which led to stagnation in employment in the Indian manufacturing industries stands suspect in the light of the evidence that productivity growth in the registered manufacturing sector has been much faster than the increase in real wages in practically every industry group at 2-digit level.

The Industrial Disputes Act, which makes it necessary for enterprises employing 300 or more workers to seek government permission to effect lay-offs, retrenchments and closures is seen to be the major culprit. It is, however, doubtful that the increase in capital-labour ratios were mainly induced by inflexibility in labour adjustment caused by job security legislation; they may have as well been dictated by changes in product structure induced by market conditions rather than by relative prices and conditions in the factor markets. Further, it should be noted that the stagnation in employment in 1980s was mainly due to two major industry groups, namely, cotton textiles and food products. Decline in these two industries was caused mainly by the closure of a large number of mills due to sickness.

The existing legal provisions relating to notice and compensation required to be given to workers for lay-off and retrenchment in India, seem to have been generally accepted as reasonable.

As regards employment implications, it is extremely difficult to access the magnitude of job losses involved in industrial restructuring with a more flexible exit policy, particularly, because adjustment is a continuing process. Even if the magnitude of such loss is small in relation to the aggregate employment, one cannot, however, afford to lose sight of hardship caused to individual workers rendered jobless. The benefits provided under the existing legal framework as compensation for lay-off and retrenchment are highly inadequate, particularly in the given situation of scarcity of jobs and rather limited possibility of quickly finding alternative jobs. The case for raising them, probably doubling, is eminently justified. Also, the need to pay the separation benefits promptly is obvious.

In the ultimate analysis, the success and speed of labour adjustment and therefore, to a certain extent, of industrial restructuring and structural adjustment, would depend on the aggregate labour market situation. A faster growth of employment opportunities would reduce the resistance to labour adjustment and make restructuring easier. On the other hand, slow growth of employment leading to an accentuation of unemployment situation, would render labour adjustment difficult even if legal provision for hiring and firing are made more flexible. It is, therefore, pertinent to examine the prospects of employment generation in aggregate in the context of the structural adjustment programme. The most crucial question, therefore, is how quickly the structural reforms programme succeeds in leading the economy on to a higher growth path.

14. Structural Adjustment and Aggregate Demand

The importance of aggregate demand in the context of structural adjustment is emphasised by Amit Bahduri (1993) in a paper prepared for ILO. He writes "Unless the restructuring of Indian industries is attempted in conditions of non-recessionary aggregated demand, there is little hope that these policies will succeed in bringing about the required structural adjustments in the Indian economy.

15. Structural Adjustment and the Informal Sector

Amitabh Kundu (1993) examines how structural adjustment policies are likely to affect the employment in the informal sector. Macro policies are likely to have their major effect on the informal sector since both organised sector and agricultural sector are likely to be affected only marginally. Large industrial houses are likely to start the production of commodities, which are currently reserved for small and tiny sectors. Further, in a liberalised regime it is no longer necessary to sub-contract to ancillaries. For these reasons, informal sector is likely to be affected more.

16. Structural Adjustments : Theoretical Constraints and Experience

Deepak Nayyar in his evaluation of Economic Reforms (1993) suggests evaluation at two levels: (1) in terms of limitations in theoretical constraints and the problems associated with transition, and (2) in terms of experience regarding the possible impact of structural reform.

As regards theoretical constraints, the excessive concern with resource allocation, in terms of static allocative efficiency criteria, and resource utilisation, in terms of competition through de-regulation and openness, is considered misplaced. The optimistic scenario implicit in programmes of economic liberalisation is that structural reform would impart both efficiency and dynamism to the growth process in the medium-term. The transition from stabilisation to growth, however, is by no means assured. The trade policy reform may stimulate output by creating economic efficiency gains, but it can also move an economy from a situation of too much protection to a situation of too little protection, and if the manufacturing sector is unable to cope with such a rapid transition the outcome may be forced de-industrialisation. Industrial deregulation which removes barriers to entry and limits on growth may increase competition among firms and improve resource utilisation, but it often leads to retrenchment or closures and cannot wish away barriers to exit. Deregulation in the financial sector diverts scarce resources from productive uses into speculative activities. Public sector reform may not resolve the real problems of efficiency and productivity but can end up socialising the costs and privatising the benefits.

As regards the experience on the impact of structural reform. The Indian experience so far is just two years. We do not as yet have any concrete evidence to validate or to refute the hypothesis that structural reform would impart efficiency and dynamism to the process of economic growth.

As regards industrial policy reform, some recent developments in India suggest that acquisitions, mergers or take-overs by firms in the industrial sector have enabled the enlarged corporate entity to capture a preponderant market share.

As regards trade policy reform, the rapid liberalisation of the import regime, which has dismantled import licensing and slashed customs duties across the board except in the sphere of consumer goods, may force a de-industrialisation in some sectors, particularly capital goods.

As regards the policy for foreign investment, the recent Indian experience suggests that direct investment by international firms is on the increase. The sectoral composition of this investment, concentrated mostly in consumer goods and destined for the home market, is not likely to promote exports much. Moreover, the increase in direct investment is likely to be modest rather than phenomenal. The reforms in the public sector have been shallow and superficial. The approach to public sector reform which emphasised the assets, sales and closures represents the most rudimentary forms of privatisation and restructuring.

Financial sector reforms implemented so far in India, have sought to reduce interventions practised by the government and controls exercised by the central bank. As a result, it would now be difficult to use interest rate for resource allocation in the private sector. Further, the rise in the interest rates on government securities would definitely increase the burden of public debt on the exchequer.

17. Assessment of Indian Experience of Structural Adjustment and Poverty :

It is difficult to provide an assessment of the Indian

experience with stabilisation and reform in terms of their impact on growth, employment and poverty. The reason is that the process began just over two years ago and even for this relatively short period complete evidence is not yet available. The short term impact of macro economic adjustment on output and growth is almost always adverse. The stabilisation experience in India so far is no exception. It is reasonable to presume that growth in employment in the agricultural sector was not affected much, in so far as the increase in output was sustained, entirely because of the sequence of good monsoons and possibly despite the stabilisation policies. The allocations for the social sectors - education, health, family welfare, water supply, sanitation, housing, urban development, social welfare of the under privileged, nutrition and labour welfare- stagnated in real terms and declined a little as a proportion of GDP. Budget support for poverty alleviation programmes declined in nominal terms and as a proportion of total expenditure in 1991-92, although it recovered somewhat in 1992-93. But, at constant prices or as a proportion of GDP, expenditure on poverty programmes in both 1991-92 and 1992-93 was lower than it was in 1989-90 and 1990-91. The number of families assisted under the Integrated Rural Development Programme, which seeks to promote self-employment among the rural poor by providing productive assets or inputs through a mix of subsidies and bank credit, declined steadily from 3.4 million in 1989-90 to 2 million in 1992-93. The employment generated under the Jawahar Rozgar Yojana, which seeks to create employment for the rural poor on works that are meant to create productive assets in the rural sector, also declined from 864 million mandays in 1989-90 to 778 million mandays in 1992-93. In both, the decline was pronounced during the period of adjustment, whether 1991-92 or 1992-93.

It would be reasonable to ask whether this stabilisation

promises a transition to growth for that could ease some of these problems. As a proportion GDP, both gross domestic savings and gross domestic investment registered a decline during the period of stabilisation. The decline in domestic saving and net domestic investment, as a proportion of NDP, was even more pronounced. It would appear that the process of macro-economic adjustment is based on the investment squeeze and in so far as investment still exceeds saving at a macro-level, the corresponding excess of imports over exports is being financed by borrowing abroad. This must have adverse implications for economic growth in the medium-term.

As regards the wide context, it is important to emphasise institutional reforms in the agrarian sector, the spread of education in society and, above all, the strategic role of State intervention have been in a sense, necessary conditions for capitalist development among late industrialisers. The reform process in India must recognise the significance of these lessons.

18. Structural Adjustment in Agriculture : A View Point on the Needed Reform

Srinivasan and Bhagavati in a Report submitted to the Finance Minister on the Structural Adjustments (1993) consider among others the reforms in agriculture. They urge the Government to address the following areas in concrete policy reforms :

1. Foreign trade in agricultural output and input.
2. Public Distribution System (PDS) with respect of foodgrains, edible oils and sugarcane.
3. Subsidisation (explicit and implicit) of agricultural inputs, fertilisers, irrigation water, electricity, etc.
4. Agricultural credit.

They find the effect of traditional trade policy in regard to agricultural goods was to contribute to a big gap between border prices and domestic prices, the domestic prices of agricultural goods being lower than border prices for most agricultural commodities. At the same time, inputs in agriculture are subsidised. Considering the overall effects of subsidised prices and taxes, they find that the effect has been to bias the Government provided incentives against agriculture. Rice and cotton within agriculture are deprotected while oil seeds and sugarcane receive high protection. They see no reason for reliance on quantitative restrictions and plead for abolition of them. They want a conversion of restriction into equivalent import and export tariffs. As seen earlier this is a controversial suggestion.

As regards the Public Distribution System, they recommended a better targeting and abolition of FCI in view of the high overheads and storage cost of that organisation. Besides better targeting of the poor, commodity based targeting, introduction of food stamps and direct purchases from the market instead of compulsory procurement from the millers/farmers by the PDS are recommended. Despite the inadequacies of FCI, FCI has played a notable role in procurement and public distribution. Its abolition could not be without adverse consequences.

As regards subsidies for agricultural inputs, they see a case for removing existing subsidies on three major agricultural inputs, namely, fertilizer, irrigation water and electricity. In view of the gap between domestic and import parity price, they plead for total removal of fertilizer subsidies. They have made several recommendations for improved management of irrigation systems besides removal of irrigation subsidies. As regards power generating and its price they plead for a thorough review of all aspects associated with the generation.

As regards agricultural credit, they note that the farmers cultivating above five acres receive an interest rate subsidies on term loans of above one billion rupees per annum and since this is inequitable they plead for removal of interest subsidies. The suggestions of Srinivasan and Bhagavathi on subsidies as well as on credit need to be considered in relation to their impact on poverty.

References

1. Paul Streeten, "Structural Adjustment : A Survey of the Issues and Options", World Development Report, Vol. 15, No. 12, P.1470. 1987.
2. R.M. Bird and S. Horton, Government Policy and the Poor in Developing Countries, University of Toronto Press, 1989.
3. ILO Report, Susan Horton, Ravi Kanbur & Dipak Mazumdar, "Labour Markets in an Era of Adjustment", International Labour Review, Vol. 130, P.531, 1991.
4. Srinivasan, T.N. (1988) cited in references Susan Horton and Others, "Labour Markets in an Era of Adjustment", International Labour Review, Vol. 130, No. 56, 1991.
5. FAO, "Structural Adjustment and Household Welfare in Rural Areas : A Micro-Economic Perspective", Economic and Social Development Paper (100), United Nations, Rome, 1991.
6. FAO, "Impact of Structural Adjustment on Smallholders", Economic and Social Development Paper (103), United Nations, Rome, P.31, 1992.
7. ILO-ARTEP, "Social Dimensions of Structural Adjustment in India", 1972.
8. Amit Bhaduri, "Structural Adjustment, Labour and Employment in India", Working Paper of ILO-ARTEP, New Delhi, Dec. 1993.
9. Amitabh Kundu, "Employment Growth, Changing Workforce Structure and Poverty Employment Linkages in Urban Areas - An Analysis with Special Reference to Informal Economy", Working Paper of ILO-ARTEP, New Delhi, Dec. 1993.
10. Deepak Nayyar, "Economic Reforms in India : A Critical Assessment", ILO-ARTEP Working Paper, New Delhi, 1993.
11. Srinivasan and Bhagavathi, "Structural Adjustments", Report submitted to the Ministry of Finance, Govt. of India, 1993.
12. T.S. Papola, "Structural Adjustment, Labour Market Flexibility and Employment", Presidential Address at 35th Annual Conference of the Indian Society of Labour Economics, Gandhi Labour Institute, Ahmedabad, 1994.
13. J.M. Economic and Political Weekly, P. 2261, August 27, 1994.

2

*Social Security And Structural Adjustment**

Introduction

THE term 'social security' was first officially used in the United States when it was enacted in 1935 (B.N.Som, 1994). This term thereafter spread widely throughout the world and was included in the Atlantic Charter. Subsequently, International Labour Organisation adopted the term and eventually passed a convention, Convention No. 102, describing various forms of social security that each citizen should be entitled to. The two major forms are 1) social insurance and 2) social assistance.

In social insurance scheme, as distinguished from social assistance scheme, the contribution is shared by employer and the workers. The state may or may not participate in supplementing the scheme. Such a scheme is generally compulsory in nature. Social assistance scheme is such that the total cost of programme is met by the state or local bodies of government and the benefits are paid as legal right and is basically a means-tested programme. It is akin to social welfare activity also. In the unorganised sector of developing countries, most of the schemes under social security are social assistance schemes.

* The author acknowledges with thanks the assistance of Kalyani, Dr. and Mrs. Sambamurthy in the preparation of this paper.

In our country social security has so far benefited by and large only the organised sector. Workers in rural areas and self employed in agriculture do not have any worthwhile social security schemes to depend upon (Som, 1994).

The most important social security need of the poor is food security. But, food security cannot be ensured without access to adequate purchasing power for the wage earners. Since the means of obtaining purchases is employment at a minimum wage, employment security is essential for achieving food security. In the case of self-employed social assistance for obtaining productive assets and for improving productivity becomes a necessity. Sukhatme (1993) forcibly brings out the need for health security for making food intervention effective. Thus, there are strong linkages among the three types of securities, namely, food, employment and health[1].

2. Food Security

Food security is defined by World Bank as access by all people at all times to enough food and to active healthy life. An essential element is availability of food and ability to acquire it (World Bank 1986 cited by Krishna Rao, 1993).

Food insecurity could be of two forms : transitory insecurity resulting from decline in household's access to enough food, the worst form being famine; and .chronic food insecurity resulting in continuously inadequate diet caused by inability to acquire food. Food subsidy schemes generally aim at the second form of insecurity. While India has achieved moderate success in combating transitory food insecurity caused by crop failure due to droughts and flood it has failed to make a dent on chronic food insecurity (Radha Krishna and Hanumantha Rao, 1994).

The dimensions of food insecurity could be obtained from NSS data. The NSS 38th Round, 1983 sought data on the perceptions of households on adequacy of food. The percentage distribution of households by type of response on the question "whether all members of households get two square meals a day" is given in Table-1. At the All-India level, 16.19 per cent of households as in 1983 reported that they got two square meals a day only during some months of the year. Another 2.35 per cent reported "no" to the question. Thus, 19 per cent of rural households reported hunger[2]. There are large variations across the states. In states like Bihar, Orissa and West Bengal, the hungry households exceeded 1/3rd of total households.

TABLE – 1

Percentage Distribution of Households by Type of Response on the Question - Whether all Members of the Household get Two Square Meals a Day. : 1983.

State	Only some months in the year		No	
	Rural	Urban	Rural	Urban
Andhra Pradesh	14.69	6.93	0.82	0.04
Assam	12.49	7.23	3.58	1.79
Bihar	31.81	9.14	5.42	2.89
Gujarat	2.78	1.05	0.07	0.09
Haryana	0.73	0.53	0.12	-
Himachal Pradesh	3.08	0.74	0.24	-
Jammu & Kashmir	1.51	0.88	0.30	0.12
Karnataka	17.81	10.37	0.93	0.58
Kerala	15.29	11.67	3.68	1.85
Madhya Pradesh	13.35	4.86	1.72	0.37
Maharashtra	9.31	5.00	0.68	0.42
Orissa	31.80	11.33	5.02	0.84
Punjab	1.33	1.80	0.24	0.82
Rajasthan	3.11	1.18	0.69	0.27
Sikkim	-	0.60	0.69	-
Tamilnadu	16.06	7.15	1.36	1.05
Uttar Pradesh	10.39	3.86	0.62	0.71
West Bengal	31.01	6.14	8.60	1.35
All-India	16.19	5.56	2.35	0.77

Source : Sarvekshana, Vol.XIII, No.2, Issue No. 41, Oct-Dec. 1989, pp.36.

The extent of reported food insecurity in urban areas was less as compared to rural areas but not insignificant as in some states like Orissa, Kerala and Karnataka. The data on percentage of households with less than the calorie norm of 2,700 calories per consumption unit in 1983 further substantiates extent of hunger (Table-2). As many as 16.9 per cent of persons in rural areas and 21 per cent in urban areas consume less than 70 per cent of the required norm of 2,700 calories per consumption unit. The distribution of households by monthly per capita expenditure for calorie intake level (Table - 3) throws light on the poverty level of the persons with less than 70 per cent of calorie intake level. As per the expert group on poverty (1993), the poverty line for 1983 was Rs. 89.45 for rural and Rs. 117.64 for urban. Using these cut-off points, we could see from Table-3 that the calorie intake levels for poor as compared to non-poor, both in urban and rural areas are much lower suggesting the relation between food insecurity and poverty of households. Table-4 shows trends in cereal consumption from NSS Rounds. In 1972-73, 27th Round, the cereal consumption in rural areas percapita was 15.26 kg/month per person. As in 1988-89, the consumption was only 14.56 kgs/month in rural areas. Similar decline could be seen in urban areas also. The decline was associated with shift from coarse cereal to rice and wheat both in rural and urban areas.

The data for 1983 and subsequent fall in trends in cereal consumption shows beyond doubt that chronic food insecurity problem has not been resolved.

We should however examine the point of view that the norm of 2,700 calorie is too high and calorie consumption below the norm does not reflect hunger since calorie needs are not rigidly given but depend upon a number of characteristics associated with the individual. Further, food intervention programmes are not helpful to the poor who suffer

TABLE – 2

Per 1000 Distribution of Persons/Households with less than the Calorie norm of 2,700 calories per consumption unit : All India, 1983.

	<70	70-80	80-90	90-100	100-110	110-120	120-150	150 & above	All
RURAL									
Persons	169	109	131	129	113	93	158	98	1000
Households	155	99	122	124	111	93	170	126	1000
URBAN									
Persons	210	147	163	144	107	74	104	51	1000
Households	174	121	144	143	114	83	135	86	1000

Source : Sarvekshana, 58th Issue, Jan-Mar 1994, Vol. XVII, No.3

from ill-health. Health intervention should be considered more important than food intervention particularly in the case of poor children from backward castes who are found to suffer from diarrhoea. Sukhatme (1993) also finds no relation between food intake and productivity. Sukhatme is right in pointing out the importance of health, but he ignores the fact that ill health could be caused by low food intake. We may also examine another contention that as income rises calories are derived from high value calorie substitutes and therefore a lower cereal consumption need not reflect hunger. But, if this is so, we should find a negative relation between income and cereal consumption. But the data do not show negative relation between percapita cereal consumption and percapita expenditure of the household. Quantity of total cereals as per 43rd Round 1987-88 is seen to increase from 9.78 kg/month in rural areas for less than Rs. 65 expenditure group to 14.19 kgs/month around the poverty line in rural areas and goes up to 28.37 kgs at the highest income level. Even in urban areas, those below the poverty line consume less cereals and consumption increases as we approach the poverty line.

TABLE – 3

Per 1000 Distribution of Households by Monthly Percapita Expenditure for Calorie Intake Level : 1983

Monthly Percapita Expenditure Class	*Calorie Intake Level (% of norm)*				
(Rs.)	*<70*	*70-80*	*80-90*	*90-100*	*All class*
			RURAL		
POOR					
0 - 30	110	3	1	1	10
30 - 40	109	29	13	4	23
40 - 50	166	89	49	27	47
50 - 60	175	142	111	69	72
60 - 70	141	182	137	114	90
70 - 85	134	220	228	206	114
NON-POOR					
85 - 100	67	143	168	184	130
100 - 125	53	116	165	198	166
125 - 150	22	38	65	92	102
150 - 200	13	24	44	70	106
200 - 250	5	8	11	20	46
250 - 300	2	3	4	8	22
300 & above	3	3	4	7	34
All Households	11375	7606	9517	9660	77331
			URBAN		
POOR					
0 - 30	27	-	-	-	5
30 - 40	26	1	-	-	5
40 - 50	53	10	4	-	11
50 - 60	100	29	13	6	25
60 - 70	115	69	38	18	38
70 - 85	183	144	87	49	76
85 - 100	144	151	132	79	87
100 - 125	154	246	213	190	151
NON-POOR					
125 - 150	75	136	161	163	119
150 - 200	71	124	183	211	167
200 - 250	25	46	83	121	103
250 - 300	9	20	39	63	67
300 & above	18	24	48	99	147
Sample Households	6507	4716	5824	5875	4092

Source: Sarvekshana, 58th Issue, Vol.XVII No.3, Jan-Mar 1994, pp.S-7 & S-20.

TABLE – 4

Quantity of Consumption of Rice, Wheat & Total Cereals Per Person for a Period of 30 Days by NSS Rounds : All-India Rural & Urban

NSS Survey Round (Year)	*Rice*		*Wheat*		*Total Cereals*	
	Rural	*Urban*	*Rural*	*Urban*	*Rural*	*Urban*
27th (1972-73) *	6.59	4.94	3.88	4.82	15.26	11.24
28th (1973-74) **	6.90	5.38	3.52	4.32	15.09	11.32
32nd (1977-78) *	7.12	5.48	4.05	4.87	15.25	11.62
38th (1983) *	6.63	5.32	4.46	4.82	14.80	11.30
42nd (1986-87) **	7.11	5.33	4.77	4.83	14.28	10.94
43rd (1987-88) *	7.04	5.35	4.94	4.48	14.47	11.19
44th (1988-89) *	7.07	5.35	4.73	4.81	14.56	11.06

* - Results of Quinquennial surveys.

** - Results of annual surveys.

Source : Sarvekshana, 43rd Round, Vol.XV, No.1, July-Sept 1991, pp.34.

The continuous increase of cereal consumption with rise in income suggests that hunger is due to lack of purchasing power.

While low purchasing capacity results in low entitlements to poor given the money income, a higher rate of increase in the price of wage goods results in erosion of purchasing power and causes food insecurity. We examined data on percapita cereal consumption and consumer price index number for middle rural population as provided by Expert Group for select years. It is clear from the data that the 80s are marked by higher inflation rate as compared to the 70s, the inflation rate in the 80s being more than double what was observed for the 70s. The lower percapita cereal consumption in the 80s should be partly attributed to erosion of purchasing power of the poor.

3. *Public Intervention and Food Security*

A number of studies (Mahendra Dev and Suryanarayana, 1991, Steplhen Howes & Shikha Jha, 1992, Geeta & Suryanarayana, 1993, Jose Mooij, 1994, Kirit. S. Parikh, 1994) examined the functioning of PDS and found it to be a blunt instrument for providing income support to the poor. It continues to have a bias towards urban areas and non-poor. The impact of PDS on open market prices, except in Kerala, as a safety net for the weaker section is minimal. In some states like Karnataka, financial viability of fair price shops is also very poor. Kirit Parikh (1993) examined the cost effectiveness of public distribution system and found that for every rupee spent on PDS the amount reaching the poor was less than 0.22 paise in all the states.

Arjun Sengupta in R.A. Narayan Reddy Memorial lecture (September 7th 1995), recently suggested redesigning of PDS so as to cover the entire requirements of the poor for consumption of cereals at substantially subsidised prices. He visualised that by this procedure, the open market prices of cereals will also fall since the quantity the poor were purchasing before from the open market will be released. According to Arjun Sengupta's calculation, as in 1993 around 30 per cent of the population were estimated to be below poverty line. These constitute about 51 million families. Total offtake of wheat and rice in 1993 was 13m tonnes of which 4.2m tonnes were consumed by the poor and 9.1m tonnes by relatively better-off section. If we had a scheme in 1993 to enable 51m families of the poor to receive ration of 20 kg. of rice and wheat per month at 50 per cent of market price, the offtake of poor from PDS will increase from 4.2m tonnes to 12.1m tonnes. This also, according to him will reduce the maintenance loss of stocks by FCI.

The problem of identification of poor so that the scheme

could be targeted only to them is recognised to be not easy. The task of identification should be left to the jurisdiction of local panchayats by making them supervise and guide the working of fair-price shops. The local panchayat with the responsibility of identification of poor and with further responsibility for supervision of fair-price shops ultimately could become the kingpin of the whole system. Sengupta estimated the total cost of additional subsidy to be less than Rs. 2,200 crores. This is less than a quarter of 1 per cent of GDP. A small surcharge on taxes of central government budget could take care of this expenditure without increasing the fiscal deficit.

4. Structural Adjustment & Food Security

Structural adjustment is expected to have effects on food security via a) changes in the rate of growth and consequently employment, b) prices of wage goods and the general rate of inflation and c) government policies affecting prices of foodgrains and food subsidy. The period of structural adjustment was preceded by a stabilisation programme marked by lower growth rate. The first year of economic reform witnessed a decline in the growth rate of GDP at factor cost to 0.6 per cent. There was however a recovery in the succeeding years. Yet the growth rate of GDP continues to be less than 5 per cent. In the context of jobless growth which is the characteristic feature of this period, this must have affected the employment prospects in the country. Added to this the year 1991-92 was marked by a fall in agricultural production. The percapita net availability of total foodgrains fell down from 510 grams per day in 1990-91 to 468 grams per day in 1991-92 and further to 464 grams per day in 1992-93. The procurement price policy of the government also added to the problems of food security as market prices followed closely the procurement prices. Index number of wholesale prices of rice, wheat and pulses showed the fastest rise in 1990-91 and 1991-92, the consumer price index of agricultural labourers rose by around 20 per cent between 1990-91 and 1991-92. In addition, capital formation in agriculture has come down affecting employment prospects for agricultural labour. Thus, agricultural labour faced double squeeze - lower employment coupled with higher prices for wage goods. This must have certainly affected the food security by affecting the real wage position which continued to show a decline through 1992.

TABLE – 5

Income Groups and Total Cereals Consumption for Poor & Non-poor Total Cereals in Kg percapita per month (43rd R 87 - 88)

Rural	*Cereal Consumption*	*Urban*	*Cereal Consumption*
	POOR		
<65	9.78	<90	9.16
65 - 80	11.82	90 - 110	10.63
80 - 95	12.85	110 - 135	10.95
95 - 110	13.64	135 - 160	11.30
110 - 125	14.19		
	NON - POOR		
125 - 140	14.64	160 - 185	11.47
140 - 160	15.10	185 - 215	11.20
160 - 180	15.40	215 - 255	11.50
180 - 250	15.90	255 - 310	11.64
250 - 280	16.30	310 - 385	11.58
280 - 385	16.91	385 - 520	11.33
> 385	20.32	520 - 700	11.36
		> 700	12.26
All Groups	14.47	All Groups	11.19

Source: Sarvekshaṇa, July-Sept 1991, pp.S-127 & S-158.

Poverty line as per 1987-88 is 152.1 for urban & 131.8 for rural areas.

The government responded to this position by revamping the public distribution system with more focus on backward and tribal areas. Further, there was also an increase in the allocations to rural development in 1993-94 and in subsequent budgets. The effects of these are yet to be seen. Guhan (1993) shows that only 0.15 paise out of every rupee spent on employment programmes goes to the beneficiaries. If this is the order of the leakages, one should infer that structural adjustment period was marked by adverse effects on the food security of the poor.

5. Employment Security

Security of employment is essential for obtaining food security. A number of trends have been affecting security of employment. Of these, the major trend is the shift to agricultural and casual labour. The shift to agricultural labour affects the ability of these groups to obtain self provision of food. Besides, the trends in the labour market such as shift from kind to money wages subject the labour to food insecurity.

Though the daily status unemployment rate shows a declining trend over time, it is still 6.09 per cent for All-India as in 1987-88. Some states such as Kerala, Tamilnadu, West Bengal, Haryana and Andhra Pradesh show much higher rise. The states with low rates of unemployment are found to be those with high self-employed agricultural population. Time criterion is not adequate to capture the unemployment of self-employed population (Parthasarathy, 1995).

6. Employment Security & Structural Adjustment

Structural adjustment affect the poor in several ways. New power projects set up by private and public sector displace people. In several states there is no proper rehabilitation or resettlement policy for displaced people. This creates a new class of poor people affected by government policies. Most of the mining areas are located in tribal areas and mining enterprises displace tribals from their habitations. Structural adjustment by encouraging multinational business using sophisticated technology in agricultural sector could displace people engaged in traditional sectors. Workers occupied in the traditional processing sector lose in competition in the input and product markets. Those displaced are not absorbed because of lack of skills and training in new occupations generated. Structural adjustment again creates a class of new poor. The entry of big business into agriculture has affected marketing and market patterns. Vertical integration between the farm and the factory and direct transport of farm produce to factory will result in displacement of women fruit vendors who buy the produce from the farm and sell in the markets. They may be occupied in new occupations that emerge, i.e., packaging, storing, etc. But, this takes time and large number of people particularly, women are bound to suffer from unemployment.

Displacement is seen particularly among artisanal fishermen. Artisanal fishermen cannot compete with mechanised boat owners. Both may survive for some time without conflict as long as total resources to be exploited are in plenty. Once the marine resources get exhausted social conflicts are generated as artisanal fishermen lose out in competition to mechanised boat owners. Rate of growth may be a solution since there is percolation effect. But, there is bound to be frictional unemployment and also unemployment due to lack of skills in new occupations generated.

7. The Period of Economic Reform & Employment

The years following economic reform since 1990-91 were marked by reduced financial allocation for Jawahar Rozgar Yojana and IRDP (Gupta. S.P, 1994). Central government outlay for poverty alleviation at constant 1980-81 prices also showed a reduction during the economic reform phase as compared to 1989-90 (Gupta 1994, pp. 4.5). Thus, the period of economic reform was characterised by less employment, less income to the poor and a higher incidence of poverty. Gupta's figures (1994) on poverty ratios (Table-6) shows that rural poverty which declined upto 1989-90 (45thR NSS) showed a reversal since the 45th round. Similarly, urban poverty also showed an increase since 1990-91. In absolute numbers, there was an addition of 12m to rural poor between 1989-90 and 1990-91 and 37m between 1990-91 and 1991-92 and 14m between 1991-92 and 1992-93. Thus rural poverty in absolute numbers increased by 62m within three years at an average per annum increase of 20m. Urban poverty increased in the same period by 10m.

TABLE – 6

Poverty : NSS Case

Year	*Poverty Ratio %*			*No. of Poor (million)*		
	Rural	*Urban*	*Total*	*Rural*	*Urban*	*Total*
1987-88 43R	39.10	40.10	39.30	231.40	78.70	310.10
1988-89 44R	39.20	38.40	39.00	236.20	77.70	313.90
1989-90 45R	33.70	36.00	34.30	206.70	75.10	281.80
1990-91 46R	35.00	37.00	35.50	218.40	79.50	297.90
1991-92 47R (July-Dec 1991)	40.00	37.60	39.40	255.60	81.60	337.20
1992-93 48R (Jan-Dec)	41.72	37.75	40.69	268.97	85.81	354.78

Source: 'Structural Adjustment & Poverty in India : Policy & Research Issues' November 1994, pp.31, 4.4.

The experience of economic reform and its impact during the short period has not been happy. What the medium-term has in store for Indian poor is anybody's guess. It is essentially dependent upon rate of growth and the composition of growth and its effects on employment. With past experience as a guide, we may achieve a high growth rate, the benefits of which may flow to the affluent and middle class. The poor may not gain because jobs are not found to grow with incomes. This type of scenario could call for effective safety nets for unorganised sectors in the form of right to work at a minimum subsidised wage and guarantee against unemployment through unemployment insurance.

8. Health Security

Dimensions of hunger were shown earlier state-wise. Hunger is the main cause for malnutrition and ill-health. It was also shown earlier that hunger was mainly due to poverty. Even though poor people are affected more by ill-health they do not and cannot afford to spend as much on medicines and health problems as the better-off sections. The 43rd round of NSS provides data on expenditure on medicines, doctors, nurses, midwives and hospital charges by monthly percapita expenditure class. It is seen from the data that poor people spend less both in the absolute as well as per cent terms as compared to non-poor. This is true of rural as well as urban areas (Table-7). Of total expenditure on health, taking all classes, 85 per cent of expenditure is on medicines. The cost of medicines is likely to increase if patent rights are given to drugs under the new economic reforms. The new economic reforms policy is likely to increase cost of maintaining health of the poor.

TABLE – 7

Expenditure on Medicines, Doctors, Nurses, Midwife & Hospital Charges by Monthly Percapita Expenditure Class: All-India

Monthly percapita Expenditure classes (Rs.)	*Expenditure on medicines, doctors, nurse, midwife and hospital charges (Rs.)*	*Total Expenditure (%)*
RURAL		
Less than 65	0.85	1.58
65 - 80	1.48	2.02
80 - 95	1.92	2.19
95 - 110	2.60	2.53
110 - 125	3.46	2.95
125 - 140	4.46	3.36
140 - 160	5.46	3.36
160 - 180	6.79	4.00
180 - 215	8.96	4.56
215 - 280	12.93	6.08
280 - 385	18.35	5.71
more than 385	41.58	6.61
All Classes	6.66	4.21
URBAN		
Less than 90	1.65	2.20
90 - 110	2.31	2.29
110 - 125	2.86	2.34
125 - 160	4.12	2.80
160 - 185	5.23	3.03
185 - 215	5.90	2.95
215 - 255	7.54	3.22
255 - 310	9.26	3.31
310 - 385	13.51	3.93
385 - 520	15.51	3.53
520 - 700	20.24	3.41
More than 700	42.84	3.59
All Classes	8.14	0.86

Source : Sarvekshana Vol.No.1, July-Sep 1991, pp.S-469 & 470.

Privatisation of health services is also likely to affect the maintenance cost of health for the poor. The average amount of payment made to hospital by the government and private hospitals category is provided in NSS 42nd round.

For rural areas, the average payment for private hospital was noted to be Rs. 735.38 as compared to Rs. 304.34 per government hospital, i.e., more than double the amount that is charged by government. In the urban areas, the position is still worse. Private hospitals charge more than three times what the government hospitals charge, Rs. 1206.01 as against Rs. 385.02 by the government (Table-8). Considering the hospitalised cases the difference between government and private hospital is also large in rural areas. But, in urban areas, private hospitals do not charge more than what the government hospitals charge in paying general ward. But for special wards, though private hospitals charge higher fees the difference is not so great (Table-9a). When the average total per hospitalised case is considered, the difference between government and private hospitals is quite abnormal in rural areas (Table-9b). Privatisation is bound to affect the poor adversely since the poor use the facilities of public hospitals much more than the non-poor. In urban areas, while among the top 10 per cent, only a little more than 1/3rd of the children are registered for paediatric care in public hospitals in the bottom 10 per cent, around 60 per cent are registered in public hospitals. In the rural areas, the average registrations at public hospitals is much less, only 20 per cent as against 50 per cent in urban areas. But, taking the primary health centres and the public hospitals together the per cent of poor children registered with the public hospitals is more than the corresponding per cent of the non-poor (Table-10a). The number of mothers registered with public hospitals among the poor are also more than the corresponding number for the non-poor (Table-10b).

TABLE – 8

Average Amount of Payment Made to Hospital in Rupees by Fractile Groups & Type of Hospital : All-India - NSS 42nd Round

Fractile Group	*Average Payment (Rs.0.00) by Hospital Type*			*Ratio of private to govt.*
	Govt.	*Private*	*All*	
		RURAL		
0 - 10	191.11	515.31	393.51	2.70
10 - 20	240.08	560.80	427.34	2.34
20 - 30	277.64	556.38	455.03	2.00
30 - 40	495.11	782.75	665.91	1.58
40 - 50	237.55	649.08	537.01	2.73
50 - 60	427.82	582.19	603.34	1.36
60 - 70	355.55	727.07	600.08	2.04
70 - 80	317.40	708.38	598.32	2.23
80 - 90	284.47	893.24	717.31	3.14
90 - 100	318.55	1089.95	882.25	3.42
All	320.34	735.38	597.06	2.30
		URBAN		
0 - 10	309.64	602.33	506.39	1.95
10 - 20	136.50	661.58	475.58	4.85
20 - 30	295.99	753.05	600.94	2.54
30 - 40	695.69	864.78	801.51	1.24
40 - 50	217.55	1177.10	759.30	5.41
50 - 60	360.30	1207.39	942.57	3.35
60 - 70	211.72	1020.23	771.99	4.82
70 - 80	486.03	1499.08	1203.61	3.08
80 - 90	444.49	18000.46	1427.53	40.50
90 - 100	945.05	2564.13	2049.14	2.71
All	385.02	1206.01	933.33	3.13

Source : Sarvekshana. 51st Issue, Vol.XV, No.4, April-June 1992, pp.S-418.

TABLE – 9(A)

Average Total Expenditure Per Hospitalised Case - 1987 : All - India - NSS 42nd Round

Fractile Group	*Government Hospital*			*Private Hospital*		
	Free ward	*Paying general ward*	*Paying special ward*	*Free ward*	*Paying general ward*	*Paying special ward*
			RURAL			
0 - 10	493.06	794.38	1385.68	1995.79	757.51	1489.14
10 - 20	812.93	2234.61	3146.54	626.87	677.81	1650.40
20 - 40	527.68	1607.77	540.93	655.71	1093.44	1682.57
40 - 60	480.62	873.94	516.10	611.94	1461.28	3444.03
60 - 80	482.15	1445.73	1085.3	752.84	1453.06	2980.15
80 - 90	1262.57	822.06	1978.68	1670.12	2540.72	2564.45
90 - 100	629.20	2463.89	2415.65	1628.10	3335.04	4389.72
All	582.12	1421.11	1268.08	975.21	1393.26	2862.86
			URBAN			
0 - 10	604.73	1161.5	1494.45	458.28	819.88	1072.3
10 - 20	461.74	1019.89	265.94	601.61	770.27	1917.87
20 - 40	583.23	1153.66	1265.48	547.65	986.87	1361.56
40 - 60	578.62	781.08	1052.04	745.70	936.53	1372.85
60 - 80	659.93	1035.23	2314.31	818.13	1133.57	1373.23
80 - 90	722.16	1100.29	1340.56	553.51	1163.94	2101.13
90 - 100	1043.34	1180.04	1523.95	588.11	1333.07	2104.15
All	630.40	1040.21	1482.62	665.65	1031.15	1637.85

Source: Sarvekshana, 51st Issue, Vol.XV, No. 4, April-June, 1992 pp. S-437.

TABLE – 9(B)

Ratio of Private to Government Average Total Expenditure Per Hospitalised Case - 1987 : All - India - NSS 42nd Round

Fractile Group	*Rural*			*Urban*		
	Free ward	*Paying general ward*	*Paying special ward*	*Free ward*	*Paying general ward*	*Paying special ward*
0 - 10	4.05	0.95	1.07	0.76	0.71	0.72
10 - 20	0.77	0.30	0.52	1.30	0.76	7.21
20 - 40	1.24	0.68	3.11	0.94	0.86	1.08
40 - 60	1.27	1.67	6.67	1.29	1.20	1.30
60 - 80	1.56	1.01	2.75	1.24	1.09	0.59
80 -90	1.32	3.09	1.30	0.77	1.06	1.57
90 - 100	2.59	1.35	1.82	0.56	1.13	1.38
All	1.68	0.98	2.26	1.06	0.99	1.10

What the medium-term has in store for the poor as a consequence of privatisation is anybody's guess. It is said that competition in private hospitals will result in better service to the poor. But, this is still an open question. The primary health centres need to be strengthened both in rural and urban areas to help the poor in short and medium-terms. The support that is now being provided by the joint family for the aged is likely to be lost by shift from joint to nuclear families. This is not the impact of economic reforms as such but economic reforms may accelerate process of adverse impact on households. In the medium-term with fast rate of economic growth with accelerated transfer of joint to nuclear family we could expect the number of aged with chronic diseases to increase. The most adversely affected will be casual labour in the unorganised sector. Many state governments are beginning to recognise this fact. But, implementation of social assistance programmes for the aged will require active voluntary associations for identification of the aged and for implementation of programmes.

9. Expenditure Compression in the Health Sector

Tulasidhar (1993) in an insightful article has shown the effects of expenditure compression on health sector. The cuts in transfers from central to state governments, especially the grants associated with structural adjustment, reduced the ability of state governments, especially of the poorer states to spend on social sector. The cut in spending was more in case of public health whereas the cut on facility based curative type expenditure is only marginal. This type of cut in expenditure on health causes allocative inefficiency and affects the poor more adversely.

More recently the share of social expenditure in total plan and non-plan expenditure of the central government has shown an increase. Yet, the share continues to be low at 6.1 per cent. The share of health and family welfare expenditure also has shown an increase in recent budgets. This amounts to 1.05 per cent of total plan and non-plan expenditure. What is much more important is the expenditure of the state governments. Even here the share has either remained constant or shown slight increase in recent years. But, considering the magnitude of the problem which is reflected in the human development index (UNDP,1995), the percentage share of expenditure on social services, health in particular could be said to be low. Further, all the basic indicators of health developed by the WHO suggest a dismal picture. For the early 1990s India, in comparison with China, a country which started with the same position in the 1950s showed a poor rating (Table-10). India's human development rank was 134 among the countries of the world suggesting the need for attention to human development strategy through social security measures among others.

TABLE – 10(A)

Percentage Distribution of Children (0-4) years Registered for Paediatric Care over Fractile Groups by Type of Medical Institution/Personnel Registered With (Persons)

Type of Institution/ Personnel Registered With	*0-10*	*10-20*	*20-40*	*40-60*	*60-80*	*80-90*	*90-100*	*All*
				RURAL				
Public hospital	22.34	27.13	30.55	30.62	30.66	40.88	33.52	30.35
Primary Health Centre	13.87	8.63	6.93	7.41	7.37	7.24	7.02	8.17
Public dispensary	1.16	0.17	1.21	0.65	0.54	0.93	0.60	0.78
Nursing home	2.72	0.67	0.47	0.86	1.15	1.09	2.67	1.17
Charitable Instt.	-	0.50	0.50	0.10	1.42	1.69	0.48	0.62
Private doctor	5.05	8.52	5.60	7.97	8.38	5.75	10.73	7.22
Others	14.86	11.82	17.46	21.54	24.06	16.40	29.13	19.16
Lady health visitor	33.10	32.51	32.06	22.39	21.42	21.49	12.60	26.11
Not reported	6.90	10.05	5.22	8.46	5.00	4.53	3.25	6.42
Total	100.00	100.00	100.00	100.00	100.00	100.00	100.00	100.00
				URBAN				
Public hospital	55.65	57.27	24.47	46.36	44.41	29.35	26.46	48.21
Primary Health Centre	10.75	1.94	2.59	1.92	2.60	0.40	4.62	3.48
Public dispensary	0.24	2.01	1.97	1.46	0.19	0.14	0.24	1.08
Nursing home	1.07	2.53	4.25	5.42	8.43	11.70	8.33	5.34
Charitable Instt.	1.98	0.43	0.71	0.59	1.00	1.93	1.51	1.00
Private doctor	1.76	5.81	6.15	6.98	9.31	11.65	15.90	7.13
Others	13.38	20.62	21.23	27.96	23.15	37.56	39.26	23.90
Lady health visitor	8.39	8.52	5.74	3.55	4.59	3.55	2.18	5.41
Not reported	6.78	0.87	2.89	5.76	6.32	3.72	1.50	4.45
Total	100.00	100.00	100.00	100.00	100.00	100.00	100.00	100.00

Source : Sarvekshana, 42nd Round, April-June 1991, pp.S-30 & S-49.

TABLE – 10 (B)

Percentage of Mothers Registered for Pre-natal Care & Their Percentage Distribution over Types of Institution/Personnel Registered with by Fractile Groups.

Fractile Group	% Regd.	Public Hospital	Primary Health Centre	Public Dispensary	Private Hospital	Nursing Home	Charitable Instt.	Private Doctor	Auxiliary nurse/ LHV	Others	Not	All
RURAL												
0 - 5	8.73	13.24	9.88	3.10	12.69	2.77	-	5.37	29.87	2.43	20.63	100.00
5 - 10	11.97	17.62	25.99	-	9.26	-	-	1.78	35.15	-	10.20	100.00
10 - 20	12.02	15.86	6.13	-	8.58	-	-	10.41	22.23	1.28	35.51	100.00
20 - 30	11.07	22.31	9.75	1.15	12.08	-	-	8.43	28.91	1.90	15.47	100.00
30 - 40	14.69	18.67	14.17	2.05	14.04	1.17	-	7.45	23.73	2.29	16.43	100.00
40 - 50	9.85	26.08	3.86	-	24.06	-	-	2.35	23.58	-	20.06	100.00
50 - 60	12.98	17.44	4.41	1.71	22.08	1.53	1.09	12.56	27.72	2.32	9.13	100.00
60 - 70	10.51	33.27	6.97	2.32	17.92	0.04	-	14.41	10.81	1.36	12.90	100.00
70 - 80	14.46	25.63	8.76	-	16.23	-	2.88	18.46	9.92	6.25	12.88	100.00
80 - 90	18.60	23.59	15.10	-	17.37	4.37	-	13.83	13.56	-	12.18	100.00
90 - 95	22.76	12.68	15.62	6.40	38.52	-	-	12.67	7.73	2.89	3.48	100.00
95 - 100	17.96	17.58	7.46	-	45.16	-	-	12.84	7.93	-	9.03	100.00
not reporting	-	-	-	-	-	-	-	-	-	-	-	-
All	12.60	20.51	10.44	1.16	16.44	0.92	0.34	9.97	21.85	1.71	16.67	100.00

(Contd...)

...Contd...

Fractile Group	% Regd.	Public Hospital	Primary Health Centre	Public Dispensary	Private Hospital	Nursing Home	Charitable Instt.	Private Doctor	Auxiliary nurse/ LHV	Others	Not	All
URBAN												
0 - 5	44.91	47.85	8.43	0.69	17.91	0.46	2.57	11.50	8.54	-	2.05	100.00
5 - 10	33.17	71.45	3.20	-	11.96	2.70	-	1.60	9.10	-	-	100.00
10 - 20	35.43	51.68	0.88	0.71	19.09	2.69	1.66	16.40	6.89	-	-	100.00
20 - 30	33.22	66.92	8.23	1.21	8.43	3.76	1.98	2.87	3.96	-	2.63	100.00
30 - 40	41.88	58.98	4.99	-	17.75	4.42	0.26	8.30	3.43	1.88	-	100.00
40 - 50	50.41	54.74	1.55	0.30	25.22	6.39	0.59	5.04	1.43	1.92	2.82	100.00
50 - 60	59.21	38.23	3.30	2.13	37.59	5.11	0.89	5.88	3.34	0.71	2.83	100.00
60 - 70	52.85	48.42	1.52	1.54	24.00	7.40	-	10.01	7.11	-	-	100.00
70 - 80	69.01	49.65	3.52	-	16.62	19.45	1.70	2.89	0.50	2.84	1.83	100.00
80 - 90	80.08	27.14	5.55	-	43.56	14.23	1.50	7.49	-	-	0.53	100.00
90 - 95	88.11	32.70	1.25	-	22.53	39.99	-	3.19	0.34	-	-	100.00
95 - 100	100.00	36.65	-	-	36.49	18.15	-	8.72	-	-	-	100.00
not reporting	12.41	39.68	-	-	-	60.32	-	-	-	-	-	100.00
All	46.83	50.33	3.92	0.68	22.81	7.45	1.10	7.52	4.09	0.79	1.29	100.00

Source : Sarvekshana Vol.XIV, No.4 Issue No. 47, April-June 1991, pp.S-105 & S-124

TABLE – 11

Basic Indicators of Health in Select Developing Countries

Basic Indicators of Health	*India*	*China*	*Rep. of Korea*	*Democratic Rep. of Korea*	*Srilanka*	*Thailand.*	*Indonesia*
Pre-natal care % of live births in 1990	40.59	80-89	82-89	>90	60-79	60-79	60-79
Deliveries attended % of live births in 1990	32	95	89	99	94	66	40
Maternal mortality per 100-1000 live births in 1993	252-499	100-249	25-99	25-99	25-99	100-249	252-499
% of live births in low birth weight, 1990	33	9	9	-	25	13	14
Age & Sex standardised per 100-1000 live births, 1990-95	1145	699	747	706	659	753	1009
Life expectancy at birth, 1993	61	71	71	71	72	69	63
Infant mortality per 1000, 1993	86	27	21	25	24	27	65
Under 5 mortality rate per 1000, 1992	124	43	9	33	19	33	111
Total fertility rate per 1000, 1990-95	3.9	2.2	1.8	2.4	2.5	2.2	3.1
Health expenditure percapita US dollars, 1990	21	11	365	-	18	72	12

Source : The World Health Report, 1995 (Bridging the Gap)

Ref : World Health Organisation, Geneva pp. 101-111.

10. Summary & Conclusions

Three major forms of social assistance to the unorganised sector namely food security, employment security and health security, are discussed in this paper. There were strong inter-linkages among these three types of security.

Food insecurity has two forms – Chronic and Transitory. In the Indian situation, chronic insecurity persists though we have achieved moderate success in combating transitory insecurity. The chronic food insecurity is found to be strongly related to poverty. Predominantly poor states like Bihar, Orissa and West Bengal are found to have a large proportion of households suffering from hunger. At the household level low cereal consumption is associated with low incomes.

Structural adjustments have affected food security adversely. This is attributed to rise in food prices and lower level of employment due to lower rate of growth and also reduced capital formation in agriculture. The period of economic reforms and structural adjustment is also associated with less allocation of resources for rural development and employment, less income to the poor and higher incidence of poverty. Since 1990-91 there has been an increase in the percentage of the poor as well as in their absolute number. Health security is affected by privatisation as the poor depend more on public hospitals. The expenditure compression on health sector in the early period of economic reform has affected allocative efficiency and affected the poorer states more adversely. In recent years there has been a revival of the share of social service sector expenditure and health expenditure. But, considering the dismal picture of human development as seen from UNDP and WHO reports there is need for attention to human development strategy through social security measures among others.

TABLE – 12

Some Basic Characteristics of Aged Persons for Rural & Urban Sectors - All - India NSS 42nd Round 1986-87 (60 years & above)

Description of Characteristics	*Rural*	*Urban*
Estimate of aged persons (lakhs)	394.51	87.35
P.C. of aged persons who are economically independent	234.02	28.94
P.C of aged persons living alone	7.99	5.94
P.C. of aged persons willing to move home for aged persons among aged persons living alone	19.10	17.60
P.C. of aged persons having chronic diseases	45.0	44.8
P.C. of physically immobile aged persons	5.4	5.5
P.C. of aged persons who are gainfully employed	40.55	26.76

Source : Sarvekshana, Oct-Dec. 1991, pp.105.

Notes

1. Study Group of National Commission on Labour Welfare. Recently several state governments have initiated several measures of social assistance which include old age pensions for agricultural labour, maternity benefits etc., the details of these which are covered by us.
2. A similar question repeated in 1990-91 (46th Round NSS) showed a decline in the percentage of hungry. But, what needs to be recognised is that these results were based on a small sample and comparison will not be valid.

References

Dev Mahendra. S & Suryanarayana. M.H (1991), "Is PDS Urban Biased and Pro-Rich? An Evaluation", Economic and Political Weekly, October 12, pp.2357-2366.

Geetha.S & Suryanarayana. M.H. (1993), "Revamping PDS : Some Issues and Implications", Economic and Political Weekly, October 9, pp.2207-2213.

Govt. of India (1993) "Supplementary Note from Prof. P.V. Sukhatme" in Report of the Expert Group and Estimation of Proportion and Number of Poor, Perspective Planning Division, Planning Commission.

Govt. of India, Ministry of Labour (1991), Report of the National Commission on Rural Labour, Study Group report on Economic and Social Security, pp.1-76.

Govt. of Andhra Pradesh, (1984), "Panchayat Raj and Rural Development, Rural Employment Guarantee Scheme", Andhra Pradesh.

Govt. of India, Ministry of Planning, Department of Statistics (1992), Sarvekshana, Journal of the National Sample Survey Organisation, April-June.

Govt. of India, Ministry of Planning, Department of Statistics (1991), Sarvekshana, Journal of the National Sample Survey Organisation, July-September.

Govt. of India, Ministry of Planning, Department of Statistics, (1994), Sarvekshana, Journal of the National Sample Survey Organisation, Jan-Mar.

Govt. of India, Ministry of Planning, Department of Statistics (1989), Sarvekshana, Journal of the National Sample Survey Organisation, Oct-Dec, pp.36.

Govt. of India, Ministry of Planning, Department of Statistics, (1991), Sarvekshana, Journal of the National Sample Survey Organisation, April-June.

Guhan.S (1995), "Social Expenditure in the Union Budget : 1991-96", Economic and Political Weekly, May 6, pp. 1095-1101.

Gupta Sen Arjun, (1995), "The Economic Reforms in Poverty", Ravi Narayana Reddy Memorial Lecture, September 7.

Gupta.S.P. (1995), "Economic Reforms and its Impact on the Poor", Economic and Political Weekly, June 3, pp.1188-1994.

Howes, Stephan & Jha Shikha (1992), "Urban Bias in Indian Public Distribution System", Economic and Political Weekly, May 9, pp.1022-1030.

Jose Mooj (1994), "Public Distribution System as Safety Net : Who is Saved", Economic and Political Weekly, January 15, pp. 119-126.

Krishna Rao, I.Y.R. (1993), "Andhra Pradesh : An Experiment in Food Security", Economic and Political Weekly, September 11, pp. 1911-1914.

Ministry of Foreign Affairs, Netherlands, (1994), "Structural Adjustments and Poverty in India : Policy and Research Issues : Papers and Proceedings", IDPAD Seminar, November.

Parikh Kirit (1993), "Who Gets How Much From PDS" How Effectively Does It Reach The Poor", Indira Gandhi Institute of Development research, Bombay.

Parthasarathy.G and Anand Jayshree (1995), "Employment and Unemployment in Andhra Pradesh : Trends and Dimensions", Economic and Political Weekly, April 15.

Som. B.M. (1994), "Towards Developing a Social Security System for the Agricultural Sector", New Delhi, 1994.

Tulasidhar.V.B (1993), "Maternal Education, Female Labour Force Participation and Child Mortality : Evidence from the Indian Census", Health Transition Review, Vol. 3, No2, pp.177-190.

UNDP, Human Development Report, 1995.

World Health Organisation, Geneva, The World Health Report, 1995 : Bridging the Gaps, pp.101-111.

3

Safety Nets For Vulnerable Sections

INTRODUCTION

Structural Adjustment Explained

Structural adjustment programmes within the New Economic Policy are aimed to restore external and internal balances and promote the efficient allocation of resources through reduction or elimination of distortions in product and factor markets. In general, they seek to reduce public expenditure, enhance public revenue, stimulate an increase in foreign exchange earnings reduce foreign exchange expenditure, contain inflationary pressures and improve efficiency of public bodies. Often a distinction is drawn between stabilisation and structural adjustment. The former refers to short-term policies designed to correct imbalances between domestic absorption and domestic supply. The latter consists of policies designed to influence the equilibrium configuration itself through structural reallocations (between tradables and non-tradables) and through changes in ground rules of production and exchange (FAO, 1991, p.2).

The World Bank World Development Report, 1990 recognises that not will benefit from NEP. Of these, the first group are old and disabled. These can be helped through income transfers. The second group remain acutely vulnerable to adverse events. They require 'Safetynets' by which the World Bank means some form of income insurance to help people through short term stress and calamities. This is considered particularly important when food security is threatened.

There is a growing concern on the likely impact of the adjustment in India on the vulnerable sections, especially within the unorganised sector, both in the rural and urban areas. The concern is reflected in the last minute increased allocation for rural development in the Eighth Plan. This certainly suggests a retreat from the facile notion that faster economic growth by itself can take care of the poverty question.

The Controversy over Structural Adjustment and its Impact on Poor

Srinivasan in a working paper prepared for the World Bank argues forcefully against any special concern for the poor/ low income households during adjustment on the following grounds;

- There are no particular features of adjustment policies that make the incidence of the cost more skewed compared with any other set of policies;
- The possibility that the poor may be hurt (relatively) more in a period of adjustment, because adjustment policies are inherently skewed against, needs to be distinguished from the choice by the regime in power of a particular adjustment policy that hurts the poor more, compared with another feasible adjustment policy with similar total costs which would have hurt the poor less; and
- Aggregate demand management during a period of structural adjustment hurt the poor not because of structural adjustments but because of distortionary domestic policies which restrict resource movement.

The arguments of Srinivasan are, however, not acceptable for the following reasons (FAO, 1991, pp.7-11) :

1. It is not true to say that adjustment policies are no more skewed against the poor than any other set of policies;
2. Very little is known about the income-distributional effects of some adjustment policies, such as devaluation;
3. It is arguable – and illustrated empirically in the WIDER sample – that even under fairly diverse conditions attempts to curtail aggregate demand e.g., through a cut back in public investment (or interest hikers) result in sharp output contraction;
4. Given demand, public and private investments complement each other in varying degrees, but also public investment may be crucial for attracting private investment in a backward region; and
5. A hike in interest rates is justified on the ground that it will stimulate savings and rule out projects with relative low profitability. There is limited evidence, favouring the positive effect of higher interest rate on savings in the WIDER sample.

Taylor (1987) in a paper prepared for WIDER argues, given the high share of nominal costs made up of interest demand, interest rate hikes typically reduce aggregate demand in the short term and also tend to be inflationary. As a result there is often stagnation. This is confirmed in several WIDER country studies, e.g. Tanzania and Brazil. He emphasises, "only employing contractionary policies scarcely makes economic sense. If as a consequence poverty and unemployment spread, productive firms go bankrupt and financial system turn fragile, recovery from such problems is immensely difficult, as demonstrated by the experience in Mexico, and other countries in which orthodox remedies have been applied to the extreme".

Since the contractionary effects of demand are much sharper than anticipated, the hardships borne by low-income households during a period of adjustment warrant special concern : What reinforces this concern is the possibility that the contractionary effects may be so strong that a recovery may become immensely difficult. The argument, that, in the absence of adjustment policies the condition of the poor could be even worse, should not be used to evade the adverse impact of adjustment policies on the poor and on the choice of alternative adjustments that will minimise the current as well as the future cost on the poor.

Stabilisation Policies and Inflation

The New Economic Policy in India involved emergency action towards stabilisation in the short-term and structural reforms in the economy to cope with medium and long-term situations. Stabilisation policies were intended to reduce the level of fiscal deficit and also reduce the balance of payment gap. The new Government which assumed office in 1991 moved urgently to implement a programme of economic stabilisation through fiscal correction. A key element in the stabilisation effort was to restore fiscal discipline. Both the balance of payment problems which were building up over the past few years and the persistent inflationary pressure were the result of large budgetary fiscal deficits which characterized the economy year after year. A reversal of the trend of fiscal expansionism was considered necessary to restore macro economic balance in the economy. The signal was given in the budget for 1991-92 which was presented on 24th July. The measure covered included :

1. A sharp decline in the budget deficit and fiscal deficit; and
2. A hike in the bank rate from 10 to 11 per cent and

subsequently since July from 11 to 12 per cent. All other rates linked to the bank rate also underwent similar upward revisions. Upward revisions were made also in the lending rate of scheduled commercial banks.

The above two measures should be said to be counter inflationary.

But, there are aspects of NEP which contribute to higher prices for the commodities purchased by vulnerable sections in particular. First, subsidies on fertilizers have been reduced as part of the measures towards reduction in fiscal deficit. To compensate the farmers for increased cost as a result of reduction in subsidies, procurement prices have been increased. The procurement price of paddy common variety, which was Rs. 185/- per quintal in 1989-90 was raised to Rs. 205/- in 1990-91. In 1991-92, there was again a further rise to Rs. 230/- by 12.20 per cent. Similar rise in prices was noticeable for wheat and coarse grams (see Table-1).

A rise in procurement price is found to induce a rise in open market prices also. Further, the expectations of discontinuance of all sorts of social controls over trade, by themselves, trigger speculative trends in prices both on the part of big farmers as well as traders.

The rise in procurement price involved a rise in issue prices to ensure that there was no increase in the subsidy adding to the fiscal deficit. The issue price for common rice which was Rs. 289/- on the 1st June, 1990 rose to Rs. 377/- i.e. by 30.45 per cent.

TABLE – 1

Procurement/Minimum Support Prices of Foodgrains

(Rs. Per quintal)

Commodities	*1987-88*	*1988-89*	*1989-90*	*1990-91*	*1991-92*
Paddy					
Common variety	150	160	185	205	230
Fine variety	154	170	195	215	240
Superfine variety	158	180	205	225	250
Wheat	166	173	183	215	225
Coarse Grains					
(i.e. Jowar, Bajra & Ragi)	135	145	165	180	205
Maize	135	145	165	180	210
Barley	135	135	145	180	200
Pulses					
Gram	280	290	325	421	450
Moong	325	360	425	480	545
Urad	325	360	425	480	545

Source : RBI, Bulletin, Vol.XLVI, No. 8, August 1992, P.1225.

For wheat also, there was a similar order of rise. Between 1-5-1990 and 28-12-1991, the price of wheat under the public distribution system rose from Rs. 234/- per quintal to Rs. 280/- per quintal i.e., by 19.66 per cent (see Table-2). The trends in wholesale price index show that subsequent to the introduction of NEP, there is not only a overall higher rate of inflation but also the prices of commodities consumed by the most vulnerable sections have increased at a faster rate. While the wholesale price index rose by 12.1 per cent during the financial year 1990-91, the rate of inflation for primary articles was 17.1 per cent.

TABLE – 2

Issue Prices of Foodgrains

(Rs. Per Quintal)

Commodity	*With effect from*					
	1-10-86	*1-10-87*	*25-1-89*	*1-6-90*	*28-12-91*	
Rice						
Common	239	239	244	289	377	
Fine	251	264	304	349	437	
Superfine	266	277	325	370	458	
	1-4-86	17-7-86	1-5-87	22-3-88	1-5-90	28-12-91
Wheat						
Public Distribution System	190	190	195	204	234	280
Roller Floor Mills	220	205	210	N.A.	N.A.	N.A.
Open Market Sale	205	205	210	240	N.A.	N.A.

Source: Reserve Bank of India Bulletin, Vol. XLVI, August, 1992, P.1226.

On a point-to-point-basis while the rate of inflation was 13.5 per cent during 1990-91 for all commodities, for primary articles it was 18.9 per cent. Similar variations are noted in consumer price index for industrial workers. While the general index in 1990-91 rose by 13.7 per cent, the food index rose by 16.9 per cent (see Table-3). Thus food articles which have a higher weight in the budget of the vulnerable sections show a higher rate of inflation than other articles in the period associated with NEP. There was a slight slowing down of inflation between 1991 and 1992, but the rate of inflation for food articles continued to be higher than for all the commodities.

TABLE – 3

Trends in WPI and CPI

Items/Crops	Changes during financial year				Annual rate of inflation (Point to Point)			
	1988-89	1989-90	1990-91	1991-92	1988-89	1989-90	1990-91	1991-92
A) Wholesale price index (1981-82=100)								
All Commodities	5.7	9.1	12.1	11.7	6.3	8.1	13.5	12.1
1) Primary articles	-0.2	6.4	17.1	16.6	2.2	3.6	18.9	16.3
2) Fuel, Power, Light and Lubricants	5.1	6.3	14.4	10.6	4.2	2.3	19.2	11.2
3) Manufactured products	9.2	11.1	8.9	9.0	7.9	11.8	9.6	9.7*
B) Consumer Price Index (1982=100)								
(For industrial workers)								
General Index	8.5	6.6	13.6	11.9	8.5	5.4	13.7	13.1
1) Food Index	8.3	5.3	16.3	15.5	9.5	2.3	16.9	15.5
2) Pan, Supari, Tobacco & intoxicants	9.8	15.3	10.3	10.1	7.9	16.7	8.5	16.5
3) Fuel and light	8.5	4.8	14.4	2.0	8.8	6.8	12.2	5.2
4) Housing	5.8	7.9	7.9	3.1	6.7	7.5	8.2	7.0
5) Clothing, bedding and footwear	8.9	11.2	7.4	7.5	8.3	10.7	7.6	10.3
6) Miscellaneous	8.7	9.2	10.1	9.2	8.2	7.5	10.5	13.2

• WPI upto February 1, 1992 (Provisional)

$ CPI upto November, 1991.

@ CPI upto December, 1991.

Source: Government of India, Ministry of Finance, Economic Survey, 1991-92, Part II, P.44.

Within the food articles, cereals show the highest rate of rise since End-September 1990. The rate of rise of cereals was 15.10 per cent between End-September 1990 and February

2, 1991. For the same period in 1991-92, it was 16.67 per cent (see Table-4).

TABLE – 4

Variations of Prices : 1990-91 and 1991-92

Items/Crops	*Percentage change (Point to Point) (Base: 1981-82=100)* 1990-91 End-March End-Sept.	1991-92 End-March End-Sept.	1990-91 End-Sept.- 1st Feb.	1991-92 End-Sept.- 1st Feb.*
1. Food Articles	12.97	16.98	6.44	1.99
a) Foodgrains	9.64	9.99	13.58	13.82
1) Cereals	9.87	9.93	15.10	16.67
i) Rice	8.28	17.33	4.80	9.32
ii) Wheat	17.59	-4.05	30.84	26.25
b) Fruits & Vegetables	26.00	32.78	-2.66	16.10
i) Fruits	15.03	17.79	4.46	1.34
ii) Vegetables	50.09	67.60	-14.58	44.54
c) Milk	4.60	3.86	0.66	5.47
d) Eggs, Fish & Meat	8.38	9.63	2.49	9.38
e) Condiments & Spices	12.25	41.49	16.90	-2.57
f) Other food articles	14.23	8.39	1.49	-10.60

* Provisional

Source : Government of India, Ministry of Finance, Economic Survey, 1991-92, Part II, P.47.

In conclusion, there is an association between stabilisation policies and higher rate of inflation for commodities consumed which have a greater weight in the budgets of vulnerable sections.

The Consumer Price Index Numbers for Agricultural Labourers (CPIAL), which are generally used for measuring the impact of prices on the most vulnerable sections of the rural community, i.e., agricultural labour, show that the index number rose from 853 in April 1991 to 1046 in March 1992, i.e. by 22.63 per cent (see Table-5). This suggests that the poorest sections of the community have been forced to bear the heaviest burdens of price rise following the NEP.

TABLE – 5

Consumer Price Index Numbers for Agricultural Labourers All-India (Base: July 1960-June 1961=100)

Year	*General Index*	*Food IWRCY*
1970-71	192	
1989-90	752	
1990-91	831	
April, 1991.	853	
November, 1991.	999	
December, 1991.	1008	
January, 1992.	1015	
February, 1992.	1038	
March, 1992.	1046	
April, 1992.	1046	
June, 1992.	1068	1175
July, 1992.	1090	1200

Source : RBI Bulletin, August 1992, P.S-889 and Govt. of India, Ministry of Labour

Impact of Inflation on Vulnerable Sections

The impact of inflation on vulnerable sections depends upon:

1. The share of expenditure on commodities subject to high inflationary rate;
2. The income elasticity of demand; and
3. The price elasticity of demand.

We may draw upon the results of consumer expenditure survey. NSS 4th Round, July 1988-89 to indicate the weights of different commodities in the budgets of poorer sections. The share of cereal in the total expenditure on cereals and food for the six bottom income groups of NSS, accounting for 43 per cent of the total rural population, and five bottom urban income groups accounting for 33 per cent of total urban households is given in Table-6.

TABLE – 6

Percentage Share of Cereals, Total Food and Non-Food in Total Expenditure by Monthly Per Capita Expenditure Classes : 1988-89

Monthly per capita expenditure class	*Percentage share of households in each expenditure group*	*Percentage share of cereals in total expenditure*	*Percentage share of food in total expenditure*
RURAL			
1. 00-65	2.5	44.71	73.70
2. 65-80	4.0	42.21	75.00
3. 80-95	7.0	40.41	68.98
4. 95-110	9.4	38.65	74.23
5. 110-125	10.1	35.83	73.29
6. 125-140	10.1	34.13	72.36
All classes including higher income.	100.00	26.01	63.85
URBAN			
1. 00-90	3.0	35.45	75.24
2. 90-110	4.2	32.77	71.93
3. 110-135	7.7	29.05	71.55
4. 135-160	9.1	26.02	70.39
5. 160-185	9.3	23.24	67.93
All classes including higher income			

Source : Sarvekshana, Vol. XIV, No. 3, Issue No. 46, January-March, 1991, pp. S-6, S-8, S-9, S-11.

For the bottom income groups the share of expenditure on cereals alone in the rural areas is around 40 per cent i.e., one and half times the overall share. In the urban areas also the share of bottom expenditure groups on cereals is around 30 per cent roughly double the overall share. The quantity of cereal consumption of lower income groups, both in rural in urban areas is lower than the average (Table-7).

TABLE – 7

Quantity of Consumption of Cereals Per Person for a Period of 30 Days Per Each Monthly Per Capita Expenditure Class : All-India 1988-89

Rural		*Urban*	
Monthly per capita expenditure class (Rs.)	*Quantity of cereal consumption (in Kgs.)*	*Monthly per capita expenditure class (Rs.)*	*Quantity of cereal consumption (in Kgs.)*
00-65	9.60	00-90	8.71
65-80	11.24	90-110	10.30
80-95	12.37	110-135	10.57
95-110	13.10	135-160	11.01
110-125	13.83	160-185	11.22
All classes	14.56	All classes	11.06

Source : Sarvekshana, Vol.XIV, No.3, Issue No. 46, January-May 1991, pp.S-7,S-10.

This needs to be considered against further evidence generated by the NSS for 1983. More than 80 per cent of the calories of the low income groups are got from cereals and the minimum norms of calories are not met for these groups. Among them, the per capita calorie intake is less than 2000, and reduced intake cereals is found to be associated with reduced calorie intake. Among the low income groups around 40 per cent of the persons reported that they had two square meals a day in only some months of the year, while for the overall the corresponding percentage was only 16 per cent in rural areas. Even in urban areas around 20 per cent of the poor reported that they had two square meals a day only in some months of the year, while for the overall the corresponding percentage was 5.56 per cent. Thus there is strong evidence to suggest that among the poorer households, there are significant proportions of hungry people, and incidence of hunger is inversely related to income level. It is against this background we have to view with concern the erosion of real income of the vulnerable sections and its impact on cereal consumption.

TABLE – 8

Expenditure Elasticities for Food at 1986-87 Prices

	Real Expenditure Group			*Urban Expenditure Group*		
Class	*Cereals*	*Food*	*Calorie*	*Cereals*	*Food*	*Calorie*
1. Very poor	0.886	0.994	0.926	0.839	0.983	0.897
2. Moderately poor	0.608	0.863	0.703	0.363	0.816	0.566
3. Lower Non-poor	0.318	0.745	0.496	0.194	0.796	0.471
4. Higher Non-poor	0.151	0.401	0.282	0.059	0.475	0.288

Source : Radhakrishna, R. : "Food and Nutrition : Challenges for Policy", (1991), Indian Society of Agricultural Statistics, New Delhi.

Radhakrishna's data on expenditure elasticities (Table-8) show that, notwithstanding the observed time trend decline in cereal consumption, cross-sectional data show a high expenditure elasticities for cereal and food consumption particularly for the ultra poor and poor. Considering rural areas for the ultra poor, the expenditure elasticities are as high as 0.9 per cent. Given 40 per cent share of cereal expenditure in the budget of the ultra poor in rural areas, a 20 per cent rise in cereal prices will mean a reduction of around 18 per cent in cereal consumption, and 7 per cent decline in the real income. Similarly for the moderately poor in rural areas, a 20 per cent rise in cereal prices will result in a reduction of cereal consumption of 12 per cent and erosion of real income of 5 per cent.

There are similar adverse impact on the poor in urban areas. Thus the heaviest burdens of adjustments are placed on the poorest : their food security is severely threatened. It was seen earlier that between April 1991 and March 1992, the CPIAL increased by 22.6 per cent. Agricultural labourers form more than one half of the vulnerable sections. For this group, money wages respond to price rise only with a considerable lag. As a consequence, the real incomes of the agricultural labourers dropped by around one-fifth adding to the numbers of the poor and also threatening their food security.

The higher price elasticities for cereals (Table-9) and food for the poor households also suggest that the burdens of adjustments are more on the poor.

TABLE – 9

Calorie Price Elasticities

Class	*Rural expenditure groups*		*Urban expenditure groups*	
	Cereals	*All food prices*	*Cereals*	*All food prices*
1. Very poor	-0.716	-0.889	-0.527	-0.804
2. Moderately poor	-0.506	-0.710	-0.268	-0.537
3. Lower Non-poor	-0.272	-0.494	-0.173	-0.466
4. Higher Non-poor	-0.162	-0.405	-0.036	-0.308
5. Aggregate	-0.366	-0.581	-0.166	-0.490

Source : Radhakrishna R. : Dr. Rajendra Prasad Memorial Lecture, 1991 : "Food and Nutrition : Challenges for Policy", Indian Society of Agricultural Statistics, New Delhi.

OTHER MACRO-ECONOMIC SHOCKS

If inflation eroded the real incomes of the vulnerable sections, the contraction in the economy as a result of New Economic Policy in the short run contributed to decline in employment. The growth of economy slowed down substantially in 1991-92. Agricultural output in 1991-92 could be maintained only at the level of 1990-91. Industrial growth which was buoyant in earlier years slowed down considerably in the second half of 1990-91, and tuned into a decline by the beginning of 1991-92. Industrial production as a whole for 1991-92 showed a negative growth of 0.8 per cent. The decline in the rate of growth of industrial production was not unrelated to the stabilisation policies undertaken by the Government. Firstly import compression methods initiated in 1990-91 and continued during the current year have affected the availability of imported raw material, spares and components and capital goods to import dependent industries. Secondly, imports were made costlier as a result of the downward adjustment of the exchange value of the rupee in July 1990-91 while export industries were yet to pick up in response to devaluation. Thirdly credit controls along with the hike in interest rates have affected the availability and cost of finance particularly working capital to the industry and pushed up the cost of production. Fourthly, the escalation in the prices of manufactured goods might have led to the build up of some consumer resistance and a slump in effective demand. Fifthly reduction in public expenditure and other fiscal adjustment measures have also resulted in a perceptible fall in the effective demand for the products of many manufacturing industries. The stagnation of agricultural and industrial production worsened the employment position which continued to be bad since the late eighties. Employment in the organised sector, particularly in the private sector rose from 73.74 lakhs in 1986 to 74.70 lakhs in 1989, i.e, hardly by 0.4 per cent per annum. The public sector employment showed a less unfavourable position. During the period 1986 to 1989 it rose from 176.84 lakhs to 185.15 i.e. by an annual rate of 1.54 per cent. But as a consequence of the NEP and measures towards reduction in public expenditure, the rate of growth of employment in the public sector also should have slowed down. In 1991-92, the inadequate absorption in the organised sector coupled with stagnation in agricultural sector should have worsened the unemployment position both in rural and urban areas.

Other Macro-Economic Shocks

The Case of Handloom Weavers

The NEP had also an adverse impact on handloom weavers. Export euphoria without regard for the livelihood and poor within the unorganised sector was a major factor leading to the crisis of handloom weavers, particularly in the State of Andhra Pradesh. In the later half of 1991, the State witnessed several starvation and suicide deaths of handloom weavers. These were not unrelated to the NEP. Export of yarn rose from 40 million kgs in 1987-88 to 52 million in 1988-89 and to 90 million in 1989-90 resulting in scarcity of yarn. The scarcity of yarn affected the handloom sector much more than the others as hank yarn production was only 50 per cent of total production and even out of this nearly half of it was directed towards the powerloom sector. Scarcity of yarn resulted in increase of its price. Yarn of 40 count (4.5 kgs) which was priced at Rs. 100/- in 1983 rose to Rs. 120/- in 1986 and to Rs. 215/- in 1987 and to Rs. 295/- in August 1991. The weaver, who could not shift the rising cost to the consumer, had to bear the burden of rising price. A rise in input price was associated with a decline in demand under the influence of new economic policy. There has also been a withdrawal of active support to the handloom weaving sector by the State Government. Special concession shown to the handloom weaving sector in the State through purchase of handloom cloths by the Government Departments was stopped. The Andhra Pradesh government also suspended the purchase of Janata cloth and even suspended its payments of arrears to the APCO. The APCO in its turn suspended payment of arrears to primary cooperatives. The primary coöperatives could not pay their wages to member weavers for months together. The weaver had to resort to loans from money lenders at high rates of interest. When even this was not possible he starved or in some cases committed suicide. Certainly, the origin's of economic crisis have much deeper roots, but, the New Economic Policy which showed no concern for the plight of the workers in the unorganised sector, was ruthless and condemned them to joblessness, starvation and suicides.

Structural Reforms, in the Medium-Term & Long Term and Employment in the Unorganised Sector

The effects of the structural reforms in the medium and long-term is likely to be a greater in road of big business into the domain of unorganised sector. Households in the unorganised sector are likely to face much severe competition in the input markets and lose in competition with big business in obtaining the raw materials. Basket makers will lose in competition with paper mills in obtaining bamboo just as handloom weavers lose in competition with powerlooms and textile mills in obtaining yarn. Economies of scale, technology, and consumer preference are likely to favour big business as against the household sector. As big business enters into agro-processing, there are likely to be changes in both the technology of processing as well as marketing. The shift in processing from household enterprises to factories on an increasing scale, with adoption of more capital intensive technology is likely to reduce the elasticity of employment to output. Similarly, changes in the structures of marketing with the entry of big business will imply reduced elasticity of employment to marketed output as trucks entering straight to the production centres replace the fruit and vegetable vendors who play a key role in shifting the primary produce to the assembling centres. Thus the entry of big business can be expected to displace both the petty producers and petty traders. These displacing effects in specific enterprises could however be compensated with increased momentum of growth and shift to higher rate of growth. In the medium term however, the displacing effects are likely to be more pronounced than the absorbing effects as shifts to far higher growth rates are likely to be slow. Safety nets for those who are likely to be thrown out of jobs within the unorganised sector are likely to be even more important than safety nets for the organised sector.

In the medium and long-term, issues of food security are likely to become more prominent. The faster integration of the agricultural sector with wider economy including international economy is likely to shift land use away from foodgrains to commercial and export crops. Paddy fields are likely to be brought under pisciculture. Area under coarse grains will give place to horticultural crops and also to casuarina and other tree crops with the rise in the price of fuel. Acceleration of such trends is likely to be associated with displacement of marginal farmers by those who convert agriculture into a business notwithstanding the ceiling laws. In the long-term, these such trends are not undesirable. But in the medium term, unless yield levels of foodgrains rise to compensate for the loss in area, there is likely to be a reduced rate of growth of available food supplies threatening the food security of the poor. The prospects of the poor being caught up in a double squeeze, employment and income loss, coupled with price rise are real in the medium term, and protection for the poor needs to be built into the structural reform if there needs to be an adjustment with human face.

Further cuts in public spending especially in the social sector can affect the current welfare and the human capital of the poor. In the economic process initiated over the last one year heavy cut have been observed on many social expenditure heads, targeted towards the poor including health, education, housing and sanitation. Fiscal adjustment at the level of the states, very often result in cut in subsidies for the poor. For instance in Andhra Pradesh the post-NEP period witnessed the withdrawal of Rs.2/- a Kg. Rice and reduction in the quantum of subsidised rice issued to the poor. At the All-India level the estimates for poverty in 1991-92 show that the number of poor went up by 10.7 million as compared to annual trend decline of 15.5 million between 1987-88 and 1990-91 (Gupta and Padmasini, 1992). It is against this background that there is a need for adjustment policies which do not increase the cost on the poor (Table-10).

TABLE – 10

Estimates of Poverty Ratio : 1990-91 & 1991-92

Year	*Rural*	*Urban*	*Total*
1987-88	51.00 (302.6)	33.38 (65.1)	46.44 (367.7)
1990-91	42.42 (264.7)	26.38 (56.3)	38.33 (321.00)
1991-92	43.02 (272.8)	26.81 (58.9)	38.85 (331.7)
Decline in poverty between 1987-88 and 1990-91	8.58 (37.9)	7.00 (8.8)	8.11 (46.7)
Increase in poverty between 1990-91 and 1991-92	0.60 (6.1)	0.43 (2.6)	0.52 (10.7)

Notes: 1) Figures in parenthesis indicate the number of poor in million.
2) The estimates are based on NSS Consumer Expenditure Distribution of 1987-88 (43rd Round).

Source: Gupta, S.P. and Raman S. Padmasini : "Poverty/Social Cost Painful Contraction", Economic Times, 31st Aug, 1992, P.9.

PUBLIC DISTRIBUTION AS A SAFETY NET

A Review

The term safety nets is popularised by the World Bank. It is used to convey protection through income insurance against short term stress and calamities to those who remain acutely vulnerable to adverse events. It is recognised that some of the poor including the working poor and those in remote region cannot fully participate in the development process and the old or disabled may never be able to do so. For this group income transfers are recommended as distinct from income insurance recommended for the working poor subjected to short-term stress. However, the distinction between 'income transfers' and 'income insurance' is likely to get blurred in situations except in the case of old or disabled poor when the adjustments are likely to be prolonged. In cases where protection to the poor needs to be built into the medium-term and long-term structural reforms, the appropriateness of the term 'safety nets' may be questioned.

Protection to the working poor is needed against erosion of real incomes due to inflation : loss of employment and incomes due to stagflation : and reduced access to and higher cost or public services such as health and education as these services are privatised under the influence of NEP.

We examine a range of policies in which both income insurance and income transfers are blended under the following headings :

1. Public distribution
2. Public employment, and other programmes.

Public Distribution

Public Distribution is given an important role in protecting the vulnerable sections against price rise and for stabilisation of prices in Indian Food Policy over a period. Since 1961 public distribution of foodgrains has shown an increase from around 5.3 per cent of total net availability to 14.3 per cent in 1987-88 (Table-11). Public distribution which was fed mainly from imports throughout the fifties shifted mainly to internal procurement. In addition to the general public distribution system in some state special distribution programmes have been in operation. These included the two rupees-per-kg-rice scheme in Andhra Pradesh which has been implemented from 1983 to 1992 and is modified only recently for the targeted poorer groups with incomes below Rs. 6,000/- per household per annum : a similar scheme in Tamil Nadu for targeted low income groups with income below Rs. 12,000/- the 'food for all' programmes, in Gujarat under which households with annual income less than Rs. 5,000/- are supplied rice and wheat at much lower price : the programme of subsidised wheat in Himachal Pradesh targeted for interior and remote areas; the subsidised rice scheme in Karnataka for target groups of household with an annual income of Rs.3,600 and less; the subsidised rice scheme in Tripura

TABLE – 11

Net Availability, Procurement and Public Distribution of Foodgrains : All-India

Year	*Net availability of foodgrains (Million tons)*	*Public Distribution*	*Net Procurement*	*Public Distribution as percentage of net availability*
1961	75.69	3.98	0.54	5.3
1971	94.31	7.82	8.86	8.3
1981	114.29	13.01	12.98	11.4
1988	128.37	18.31	14.06	14.03

Source : FCI, Statistical Panorama, 1990, New Delhi, 1990. P.72.

targeted only to households who own less than 10 acres of paddy land. In all these special distribution programmes partial requirements, often less than one-third, are met and the household had to meet its other requirements from the open market. Besides special distribution programmes, a sizeable quantity of foodgrains now gets distributed through various employment generation/guarantee programmes. In these programmes foodgrains are made available at further subsidised rates (i.e. prices are lower than those charged at the fair price shops) as part of wage payment. Since 1985, there has also been a scheme for tribal areas under which foodgrains are distributed at specially subsidised rates to people living in the area covered by the Integrated Tribal Development Projects. However, the total distributed under employment and other programmes accounted for less than 1/10 of the total under public distribution (Table-12).

Quite a few writers examined the issue whether public distribution, as it is now being operated, is successful in providing protection to (i) the vulnerable sections; (ii) vulnerable sectors; (iii) vulnerable regions, and (iv) vulnerable seasons and years.

Tyagi (1990) sought to answer the following questions in his examination of public distribution in relation to vulnerable sections.

1. Has the distribution in different states been proportionate to the number of poor people in each state?
2. Have the quantities distributed in different states gone to the really poor?
3. Have the share of supplies through the fair price shops and the difference between the issue prices and prices that would have prevailed in the absence of government

TABLE – 12

All-India Off-Take of Foodgrains From Central Pool Under All Schemes : 1984-85 To 1988-89

(in million tonnes)

	Rice			Wheat						
Year	PDS	NREP/ Others	Total	PDS	NREP/ Others	Roller Floor Mills	Open sales	Total	Coarse grams	Grams
1985	5.99	0.11	6.10	3.18	0.25	5.01	0.64	9.08	10	15.19
1986	7.39	0.28	7.67	4.27	1.78	2.37	2.54	10.96	1	18.63
1987	8.16	0.59	8.75	5.70	2.94	-	3.88	12.52	-	21.27
1988	8.60	0.28	8.88	7.37	1.06	-	1.67	10.10	-	18.98

Source : FCI Statistical Panorama, 1990, P.147.

Others include Food for Work, RLEGP, Nutrition Programme, Relief Works, Floor Relief, etc.

> intervention been large enough to compensate for the increase in open market prices as a consequence of procurement. By three measures viz., (i) the relationship between incidence of poverty state-wise and per capita quantity distributed; (ii) per capita income and per capita distribution ; and (iii) per capita distribution of foodgrains, he concludes the distribution of foodgrains through the fair price shops has been not, in favour of poor.

Tyagi's study also points out urban bias in public distribution. During the period June to December 1988 more than 60 per cent of total rice distributed in the state of Maharashtra was in urban areas while the share of urban population was only 35 per cent in Maharashtra. In West Bengal the statutory rationing areas, i.e. metropolitan Calcutta accounted for 37 per cent of total foodgrains. The volume distributed in the Union Territories of Delhi was also substantial Kerala and Jammu and Kashmir were the two states where the off-take for rural areas was about 85 per cent of the total off-take from the public distribution system. Again the results available from 35th Round of NSS regarding social consumption based on the State Sample Report also confirm the view that the public distribution system has tended to benefit mostly the urban areas. Tyagi also cites evidence to show that a significant proportion of purchases from the public distribution system in the states of Gujarat and Tamil Nadu were by the non-poor. His critical examination of PEO study on public distribution system suggests that less than one-third of the beneficiaries really belonged to the group which was intended to be the beneficiaries of the public distribution system.

Evidence from NSS 42nd Round, July 1986-87, shows improvement in the share of the poorer groups in the public distribution as compared to the findings of Tyagi based on 35th Round. Even so, the non-poor, both in rural and urban areas appropriate more than 50 per cent of the quantities issued under public distribution as in 1986-87 (Table-13).

TABLE – 13

The Share of Top 60 Per Cent of The Expenditure : Classes in Total Persons Served by PDS : All-India : 1986-87 By Item

Item	*Rural*	*Urban*
Rice	50.0	44.6
Wheat	55.2	52.2
Bajra	50.0	38.3
Jowar	43.4	34.8
Other Cereals	54.0	42.5
Pulses	75.0	62.3
Edible Oils	54.8	49.7
Sugar	58.3	52.2
Coal	78.1	67.9
Kerosene	52.7	50.0
Standard Cloth	43.8	34.2

Source : Sarvekshana, April-June, 1990.

Dev and Suryanarayana infer quite wrongly, by looking at the percentage of PDS purchase by fragile groups that the PDS is not favouring the middle over rich groups (Dev & Suryanarayana 1991, p. 2365). The issue is not whether the non-target groups are obtaining less proportion of purchases from PDS, but whether the benefits intended for the poor are being appropriated by the non-poor or not.

Percentage of persons served by PDS within the urban sector is uniformly higher for all commodities, though the incidence of poverty is more in rural areas. Even when the percentage of market dependents is considered the urban percentages are distinctly higher as compared to rural except in the case of rice (Table-14). The share of rural areas in PDS distribution is less than their share in population and poverty in respect of total cereals, pulses, edible oils. Only in respect of standard cloth, it is distinctly higher (Table-15).

TABLE – 14

Percentage of Persons Served by PDS in Rural and Urban Areas : 1986-87

Item	*As percentage of all persons*		*As percentage of market dependants only*	
	*Rural**	*Urban**	*Rural**	*Urban**
Rice	22.73	32.21 (16.76)	39.74 (19.08)	39.11
Wheat	9.44	21.18 (12.64)	31.29 (19.33)	36.70
Edible Oil	14.45	24.95 (25.86)	16.68 (59.27)	26.63
Sugar	57.24	79.28 (61.20)	73.60 (46.78)	85.63
Kerosene	45.32	53.67 (11.04)	51.02 (14.51)	64.45

* Derived from Data presented in Table - 1 and Table - 2 .

** Sarvekshana, April-June, 1989, Table S-2, Page 12.

Figures in parenthesis are percentages of quantity purchased from PDS in total purchases.

TABLE – 15

Share of Rural Areas In Total Quantity Purchased Per Person Serviced From the PDS : All-India : 1986-87

Item	*Percentage share in quantity*	*Percentage share in values*	*Share in total persons serviced*
Rice	73.5	71.2	70.5
Wheat	66.5	64.6	60.2
Bajra	88.9	89.0	84.2
Jowar	82.9	80.7	93.1
Other Cereals	84.6	82.4	80.5
Total Cereals	73.1	71.0	N.A.
Pulses	68.6	66.3	70.7
Edible Oil	64.0	53.0	66.4
Kerosene	76.6	65.0	74.0
Sugar	74.6	74.1	71.6
Coal	27.0	32.2	20.9
ST Cloth	81.7	78.1	86.6
All	-	70.5	-

Source : Sarvekshana, Vol. XIV, No.4, Issue No. 43, April-June.

The per capita consumption of foodgrains from PDS in rural areas is only 70 per cent of the corresponding per capita use of PDS in urban areas, at all-India level. The estimated per capita subsidy from PDS as a ratio of corresponding subsidy in urban areas was only 79 per cent (Howes and Jha, 1992, see also Table-16). The urban man continues to gain more from the PDS on the average than the rural person though the rural person on the average is poorer.

TABLE – 16

Ratio of Rural to Urban Per Capita Foodgrain Consumption from PDS and Ratio of Per Capita Rural to Urban Subsidy on All Goods

State	*Rural to urban ratio of per capita consumption of foodgrain from PDS 1986-87*	*Rural-Urban ratio of subsidy from PDS 1986-87*
Andhra Pradesh	1.349	1.68
Assam	0.585	0.93
Bihar	0.220	0.65
Gujarat	1.622	1.20
Haryana	0.276	1.15
Himachal Pradesh	2.731	0.98
Jammu & Kashmir	0.377	0.39
Karnataka	0.637	1.41
Kerala	1.199	1.04
Madhya Pradesh	0.588	0.80
Maharashtra	0.877	0.64
Orissa	0.237	0.36
Punjab	0.330	0.55
Rajasthan	1.080	1.67
Tamil Nadu	1.057	0.64
Uttar Pradesh	0.518	0.24
West Bengal	0.320	0.43
All-India	0.697	0.79

Source : Howes and Jha, Op.cit., Economic and Political Weekly, May 9, 1992, pp. 1023 & 1026.

At the all-India level, it should be concluded, there is a persistence of urban bias. If Dev and Suryanarayana find rural bias at all-India level, instead of urban bias, in respect of rice, coarse cereals, sugar and cloth, it is because they use an inappropriate criterion, i.e., PDS market quantity per market dependant (Dev & Suryanarayana, 1991, EPW, P.2365). What could be said in fairness to the trends in public distribution system is compared to the past, there is evidence of rural bias in states like Andhra Pradesh, Gujarat, Himachal Pradesh and Kerala (See Table-17).

TABLE – 17

Off-Take of Foodgrains Through the PDS : State-wise

State	*Per capita off-take quinquennium ending 1988 per annum*
High Poverty States	
(45% or above)	
Bihar	9.954
Madhya Pradesh	9.192
Uttar Pradesh	7.175
Orissa	13.340
Medium Poverty States	
(Between 20 & 45%)	
Tamil Nadu	31.075
West Bengal	32.749
Maharashtra	22.701
Andhra Pradesh	23.286
Karnataka	23.167
Rajasthan	18.587
Gujarat	21.802
Kerala	61.893
Low Poverty States	
(Below 20%)	
Haryana	10.040
Punjab	9.490
All - India	**21.738**

Source : Tyagi, Op.cit., P.89.

The high concentration of PDS benefits to only a few states is seen much more sharply in the household data of 1986-87. In respect of rice, three states, viz., Andhra Pradesh, Kerala and Tamil Nadu account for more than two-third of PDS utilisation by the rural households. The states of Uttar Pradesh,

Bihar, Orissa and Madhya Pradesh account for less than 5 per cent of PDS utilisation of rice in rural areas. By all the other criteria, viz., percentage of purchasing persons served by PDS, PDS quantity as percentage of total quantity purchased, quantity per market dependant, poorer states are the poorest gainers (Table-18).

TABLE – 18

Participation in PDS State-wise : 1986-87 Rural Areas : Rice

State	*Percentage of purchasing persons served*	*PDS Quantity as % of total quantity purchased*	*Quantity per market dependant (Kgs.)*	*Percent share in total All-India PDS*
Andhra Pradesh	73.30	32.54	3.173	31.78
Assam	48.77	14.41	1.362	2.79
Bihar	1.02	0.42	0.032	Neg.
Gujarat	61.42	46.53	0.746	3.23
Haryana	9.50	7.29	0.045	Neg.
Himachal Pradesh	44.69	35.80	1.636	1.12
Jammu & Kashmir	37.45	37.91	2.856	2.19
Karnataka	68.64	22.22	0.861	5.75
Kerala	91.23	51.36	4.256	22.75
Madhya Pradesh	67.87	6.14	0.346	1.67
Maharashtra	59.88	27.45	0.57	4.65
Orissa	1.53	0.40	0.049	Neg.
Punjab	NIL	7.47	-	NIL
Rajasthan	4.87	18.66	0.043	Neg.
Tamil Nadu	63.70	4.45	1.448	11.01
Uttar Pradesh	4.73	6.59	0.203	2.12
West Bengal	27.81	16.76	0.726	6.05
All India	39.74	16.76	1.107	100.00

Source : Sarvekshana, Op.cit.

As regards wheat, three states, viz., Maharashtra, Rajasthan, and West Bengal account for around three-fifth of the total benefits from PDS in rural areas. Again the states with the highest incidence of poverty, viz., Bihar, Madhya Pradesh, Orissa and Uttar Pradesh show a poor record (Table-19). Even in urban areas, the PDS benefits are distributed unequally across the states. Urban areas in the states with the highest incidence of poverty are served as poorly as the rural parts of these states both in respect of rice and wheat (Table-20 and 21).

TABLE – 19

Participation in PDS State-wise : 1986-87 ; Rural Areas : Wheat

State	*Percentage of purchasing persons served*	*PDS Quantity as % of total quantity purchased*	*Quantity per market dependant (Kgs.)*	*Percent share in total All-India PDS*
Andhra Pradesh	42.13	20.39	0.246	0.4
Assam	12.35	17.79	0.210	0.4
Bihar	1.23	1.51	0.087	2.12
Gujarat	49.94	37.02	1.960	2.93
Haryana	NIL	-	-	NIL
Himachal Pradesh	16.47	17.01	1.490	0.10
Jammu & Kashmir	25.28	19.35	2.527	1.05
Karnataka	74.61	49.86	0.540	4.72
Kerala	99.19	92.04	1.420	6.02
Madhya Pradesh	16.05	7.17	0.587	5.74
Maharashtra	57.42	43.13	1.150	21.81
Orissa	17.88	18.11	0.565	0.53
Punjab	0.95	0.63	0.011	0.10
Rajasthan	22.42	16.21	2.475	20.55
Tamil Nadu	82.47	77.46	1.008	2.70
Uttar Pradesh	4.03	2.43	0.228	5.96
West Bengal	58.75	49.03	1.342	15.03
All-India	31.30	19.33		

TABLE – 20

Participants in PDS State-wise : Urban Areas : 1986-87 : Rice

(in percentage)

State	*Percentage of purchasing persons served*	*PDS Quantity as % of total quantity purchased*	*Quantity per market dependant (Kgs.)*	*PDS Percent in total All-India PDS%*
Andhra Pradesh	50.24	21.47	2.125	18.28
Assam	45.86	14.83	1.469	1.59
Bihar	0.86	0.29	0.021	0.12
Gujarat	47.09	26.21	0.465	0.15
Haryana	13.33	8.89	0.510	0.15
Himachal Pradesh	34.61	20.48	0.825	1.87
Jammu & Kashmir	79.81	63.87	5.723	4.28
Karnataka	62.72	25.69	1.442	11.80
Madhya Pradesh	21.91	10.47	0.438	2.38
Maharashtra	44.92	27.77	0.760	9.93
Orissa	0.88	0.41	0.046	0.08
Punjab	8.19	5.15	0.068	0.14
Rajasthan	5.12	15.94	0.168	0.47
Tamil Nadu	50.58	12.17	1.031	11.52
Uttar Pradesh	9.12	8.03	0.278	2.36
West Bengal	43.71	19.48	1.610	14.82
All-India	39.10	19.02	1.063	100.00

TABLE – 21

Participants in PDS State-wise : Urban Areas : 1986-87 : Wheat

(in percentage)

State	*Percentage of purchasing persons served*	*PDS Quantity as % of total quantity purchased*	*Quantity per market dependant (Kgs.)*	*PDS Percent in total All-India PDS%*
Andhra Pradesh	51.21	47.98	0.845	31.1
Assam	5.26	1.65	0.024	-
Bihar	9.37	7.05	0.405	2.82
Gujarat	30.33	19.63	1.239	5.91
Haryana	NIL	-	-	NIL
Himachal Pradesh	0.25	8.81	0.441	-
Jammu & Kashmir	0.75	58.54	3.661	1.01
Karnataka	60.74	43.78	0.645	5.13
Kerala	94.82	91.48	1.307	2.25
Madhya Pradesh	11.17	5.65	0.487	3.31
Maharashtra	33.84	21.45	0.947	17.30
Orissa	22.91	25.02	0.814	0.93
Punjab	0.68	0.05	0.006	NIL
Rajasthan	6.61	3.61	0.501	1.93
Tamil Nadu	67.25	63.48	0.733	4.51
Uttar Pradesh	5.11	3.32	0.296	4.23
West Bengal	74.68	69.87	3.097	24.34
All-India	36.69	19.33	1.051	100.00

Weather shocks threaten the food security of the vulnerable sections as they result in sharp reductions in the net production. Public distribution could soften the risks if it is found to vary inversely with the movements in net production. We examine the data on the direction of change on net production and public distribution at all-India level for the period 1970-1988. In 15 out of the 18 observations public distribution increases in quantity when net production falls and declines when net production rises. Procurement however does not show a firm positive relationship with production (Table-22).

TABLE – 22

Net Production of Foodgrains and PDS : All-India : Procurement

(in million tonnes)

Year	*Net Production of foodgrains*	*Change (+) or (-)*	*Public Distribution*	*Change (+) or (-)*	*Net procurement*	*Change (+) or (-)*
1970	87.06		8.84		6.71	
1971	94.87	+	7.82	-	8.86	+
1972	92.02	-	10.49	+	7.76	-
1973	84.90	-	11.41	+	8.42	+
1974	91.58	+	10.79	-	5.65	-
1975	87.35	-	11.25	+	9.56	+
1976	105.91	+	9.17	-	12.85	+
1977	97.27	-	11.73	+	9.97	-
1978	110.61	+	10.98	-	11.10	+
1979	115.41	+	11.66	+	13.85	+
1980	95.99	-	14.99	+	11.18	-
1981	113.39	+	13.01	-	12.98	+
1982	116.63	+	14.76	+	15.42	+
1983	113.33	-	16.21	+	15.67	+
1984	133.33	+	13.33	-	18.72	+
1985	127.35	-	15.80	+	20.12	+
1986	131.64	+	17.60	+	19.69	-
1987	125.41	-	18.37	+	15.72	-
1988	121.11	-	18.31	-	14.06	-

Though public distribution has been attempted to even out supplies over years, its share in per capita consumption of cereals was less than 7 per cent in rural areas and around 14 per cent in urban areas (Table-23).

TABLE – 23

Per capita of Purchased Quantity From PDS and Per Capita Consumption of Cereals : 1986-87 : All-India.

Item	*Rural*		*Urban*		*PDS purchased per capita as percentage of total consumption*	
	Purchased per capita per month (Kgs.)	*Consumption per capita per month (Kgs.)*	*Purchased per capita (Kgs.)*	*Consumption per capita (Kgs.)*	*Rural*	*Urban*
Rice	0.63	7.11	0.86	5.33	8.86	16.14
Wheat	0.23	4.77	0.61	4.83	4.82	12.66
Bajra	0.002	0.53	0.002	0.17	0.04	1.10
Jowar	0.01	1.02	0.006	0.46	1.00	1.38
Other cereals	N.A.	N.A.	-	-	N.A.	N.A.
Total cereals	0.88	14.28	1.498	10.94	6.76	13.69

Source : Sarvekshana, Vol XII, No. 4, April-June, 1989, Issue No. 39.

Its share in coarse cereals which have a higher weightage in the consumption of the poor is the lowest. As seen earlier the low per capita supplies under the PDS, the substantial proportion of the benefits by the non-poor, and total neglect of PDS in the states with the highest incidence of poverty result in little impact of the public distribution on the overall consumption of cereals. An examination of state-wise data on the quantum of public distribution per capita and per capita consumption of cereals does not show the impact of public distribution on the level of per capita consumption. All the states grouped under 'high incidence of poverty' viz, Bihar, Madhya Pradesh, Orissa and Uttar Pradesh show higher than all-India average per capita cereal consumption, despite low levels of public distribution. It is worth noting that all these are surplus states except Bihar. On the other hand all the South Indian States and Maharashtra which record higher levels of

PDS show less than all-India average per capita cereal consumption. Thus it appears that PDS has little effect in influencing the variations in the levels of per capita consumption across the states. (Table-24).

The more critical variable in influencing the level of per capita cereal consumption is found to be per capita production. The level of per capita production, influences the position of entitlements both via employment and via reduced prices. The absence of any perceptible impact of PDS on cereal consumption is also seen in the time series data. While the quantity of public distribution of cereals rose in the 1980s as compared to late 1970s, (as compared to late 1970s) both in rural and urban area (Table-25).

Though this attributed to the shifts in consumption to non-cereals, yet, in view of the high and persisting correlation between cereal change, and calorie change, the absence of perceptible impact of public distribution on the level of cereals consumption should be a cause for concern. The gains of real incomes through PDS at subsidised prices are not possibly utilised for improving cereal consumption but are diverted to other uses.

A closer examination of the trends in cereal consumption by fragile groups between 1977-78 and 1986-87, brings out that while the cereal consumption per capita declined between two points, no such decline is observable for the bottom 10 per cent and bottom 30 per cent of the population. On the other hand, there is a slight improvement of the cereal consumption level of the poorest 30 per cent, possibly because of higher level of income in the latter year, both in rural and urban areas (Table-26). This shows that thc observed secular decline in cereal consumption is restricted to non-poor groups, and the poorer sections, who are starved of adequate calorie intake, get them through increased cereal consumption.

TABLE – 24

Per Capita Production, Per Capita Consumption of Cereals and Off-take from PDS : In late 80s : State-wise

State	*Per capita production per annum (quinquennial ending, 1988-89) (Kgs.)*	*Per capita consumption average for 1986-87 to 1988-89 (Kgs Per month)[2] (rural)*	*PDS average for 1986 to 1988 (Kgs. Per annum)[3]*	*Off-take as percentage of production*	*Off-take percentage of consumption*
Andhra Pradesh	166	14.16	26	15.66	15.30
Assam	120	13.92	36	30.00	21.55
Bihar	127	15.54	14	11.02	7.51
Gujarat	91	11.76	30	15.71	21.26
Haryana	493	14.93	11	2.23	6.14
Himachal Pradesh	225	15.19	30	13.33	16.46
Jammu & Kashmir	191	17.54	53	27.75	25.18
Karnataka	147	13.42	29	19.73	18.01
Kerala	40	10.13	66	165.00	54.29
Madhya Pradesh	203	15.46	13	6.40	7.01
Maharashtra	113	12.45	30	26.55	20.08
Orissa	177	16.19	17	9.60	8.75
Punjab	887	12.24	24	18.32	16.16
Rajasthan	162	16.56	28	17.28	14.09
Tamil Nadu	131	12.38	24	18.32	16.16
Uttar Pradesh	230	15.39	10	4.35	5.41
West Bengal	158	15.35	32	20.25	17.37
All-India	182	14.44	25	13.74	14.43

1. Computed by using estimated population figures and production figures from FCI, Statistical Panorama.
2. Computed from Sarvekshana, January-March, 1991 and July-September, 1991
3. Computed from FCI, Statistical Panorama.

TABLE – 25

Per Capita Consumption of Cereals (in Kgs.) Per Month and Per Capita off-take of Public Distribution : All-India

Round	*Year*	*Rural*			*Urban*			*Off-take of PDS percapita (in Kgs.)*
		Rice	*Wheat*	*All Cereals*	*Rice*	*Wheat*	*All Cereals*	
27th	1972-73	6.59	3.88	15.26	4.94	4.82	11.24	21
28th	1973-74	6.90	3.52	15.09	5.38	4.32	11.32	18
32nd	1977-78	7.12	4.05	15.25	5.48	4.32	11.32	16
38th	1983	6.63	4.46	14.80	5.32	4.82	11.20	23
42nd	1986-87	7.11	4.77	14.28	5.33	4.83	10.94	20
43rd	1987-88	7.04	4.94	14.47	5.35	4.48	11.19	23
44th	1988-89	7.07	4.73	14.56	5.35	4.81	11.06	-

Source : Sarvekshana, July-September, 1991. P.34.

TABLE – 26

Consumption of Cereals (Quantity in Kgs.) Per Capita Per Month, 1977-78 and 1986-87 by Fractile Expenditure Group

	Rural		*Urban*	
	1977-78	*1986-87*	*1977-78*	*1986-87*
Bottom 10%	9.64	9.75	8.36	9.32
Bottom 30%	11.21	11.49	10.15	10.23
All	15.25	14.28	11.62	10.94

Note: Estimated from the relevant Rounds of NSS.

This shows that the observed secular decline in cereal consumption is restricted to non-poor groups, and the poorer sections, who are starved of adequate calorie intake, get them through increased cereal consumption.

Reason for No Purchase/Part Purchase from PDS

The NSS Round on Utilisation of public distribution system elicited from all the households no purchase/part purchase from public distribution system. The percentage of households not possessing ration cards does not seem to be higher in states with poor public distribution system as compared to those with better public distribution system. For instance in rural areas, the percentage of households reporting no purchase/part purchase for rice for Bihar, Orissa and Uttar Pradesh, the states with low quantity under public distribution system, are less than the all-India average. The more substantial reason for low quantity under public distribution system in these states is the non-availability of rice in ration shops. Similarly for wheat also the percentage reporting no purchase/part purchase is lower both in Bihar and Orissa as compared to the all-India average. The more substantial reason for no purchase in the case of wheat is 'not required". This is so in many of the states. A considerable percentage in Bihar, Rajasthan and Uttar Pradesh report non-availability in ration shops as the reason for no purchase/part purchase.

In the urban areas both for rice and wheat, surprisingly the percentage of households reporting no purchase/part purchase due to the non-possession of ration cards is much higher as compared to rural areas. As against 4.32 per cent reporting non-possession of the ration cards in rural areas, in urban areas as many as 13.27 per cent reported non-possession as the reason for no/part purchase of wheat. Similarly in the case of rice, the percentage of households reporting non-possession as the reason for urban areas is roughly double the corresponding percentage for rural areas. In states with low benefits from public distribution system as Bihar, Orissa and Uttar Pradesh, the substantial reason for no purchase even in urban areas is non-availability in ration shops.

Non-possibility of credit purchase is not reported as a reason for no purchase/part purchase by significant proportions either in rural or in urban areas. As between rural and urban areas non-possibility of credit purchase as a reason is cited by a little higher percentage in urban areas as compared to rural areas. In brief, it is the unsatisfactory function of the ration shops and non-availability of rations in the shops that account for the poor benefits from public distribution system (see appendices I to IV). It is the indifference of the state governments to the needs of the vulnerable sections, particularly in the surplus states with high incidence of poverty, such as Orissa, Madhya Pradesh and Uttar Pradesh and the callousness of state administration to the food security needs in a deficit but very poor state such as Bihar that account for the low impact of the public distribution in relation to food security.

ISSUES IN REVAMPING PUBLIC DISTRIBUTION SYSTEM

There is less of urban bias and less of class bias in the benefits of public distribution than in the past. Yet our review in the preceding section has shown that it suffers from several deficiencies. Around one-half of the quantum of cereals distributed under public distribution system are appropriated by the non-poor. The state with high concentration of rural poverty gain very little from public distribution. Further public distribution accounts only for a small proportion of the total consumption and it has little impact on the cereal consumption even in states in which it is relatively more significant. As a result, its impact on food security and nutrition of the poor has been uncertain for these reasons. A sharper targeting of public distribution system along with a higher ration for the poor are considered necessary for protecting the poor. The difficulties in the targeting based on income level are well known from the experience of Andhra Pradesh. While the poor formed 40 per cent by all accounts in Andhra Pradesh, the green card holders accounted for 80 per cent. Bogus cards are found to multiply as the difference between the open market price and a fixed issue price rise. Due to enormous and rising burdens of subsidy on the state, expenditure on power and irrigation, two vital requirements of the state, had to be cut down. For meeting the procurement needs of a growing public distribution system through a levy on millers, the state had to compensate the millers by permitting exports outside the state. This resulted in a steep rise in open market prices nullifying the benefits from the public distribution system to the poor. (Radhakrishna, 1991).

A sharply targeted distribution system, which guarantees the food security of the vulnerable sections, but does not act as a disincentive to long-term growth of agriculture in the process of procurement, and simultaneously does not impose serious burden of food subsidies on the state exchequer, is necessary. A public distribution system linked with employment in public works is considered to have the potential to serve these objectives. An estimate of the requirements of public distribution linked to employment is shown in Tables 27-28. Employment requirements of the usual status employed by principal status and the requirements of the underemployed are separately estimated on the assumption of 300 days of work for fully unemployed and 100 days for underemployed and available for work. The employment requirements of the rural areas are more than 2.5 times the corresponding requirements of urban areas. On the assumption of 2 Kgs. of foodgrains per worker from the PDS, the total requirements work out to 16.4 million tonnes. The requirements are slightly less than the quantity distributed under the PDS and exceed the procurement by only slight margins. But the employment requirement is several times the employment generated under the Jawahar Rozgar Yojana. It appears doubtful, whether the state could launch an employment programme of this dimension, without adding to inflation further. The state-wise estimates of requirements on similar lines are shown in Table-28. Total requirements of usual status unemployed and underemployed for both males and females in rural and urban areas are shown. As in the case of all-India, mandays required per usual status unemployed is assumed to be 300 and for under employed 100. On the basis of these assumptions and using the data provided by NSS 43rd Round, we provide the state-wise requirements in several states the off-take of 1987-88 was not adequate even to meet the requirements of an employment linked to PDS, though overall position of off-take was adequate to meet the requirements, contribution to procurement was limited only to a few states, such as Andhra Pradesh, Punjab and Haryana. States such as Orissa, some of the surplus states contribute very little to the central pool and

TABLE – 27

Estimates of Unemployed : Rural-Urban : 1987-88 (NSS 47th Round) and Requirements of A Public Distribution System Linked to An Employment Programme.

Particulars	*Rural*			*Urban*			*Grand Total*
	Males	*Females*	*Total*	*Males*	*Females*	*Total*	*(Rural+Urban)*
1. Usual Status unemployed excluding the subsidiary status unemployed (In millions)	3.0	2.3	5.3	3.0	1.0	4.0	9.30
2. Under employed (Employed but available for additional Work (In millions)	34.2	8.9	43.1	8.4	2.3	10.7	53.8
3. Employment requirement (in million mandays)							
i) Usual status unemployed at 300 days per worker	900	690	1590	900	300	1200	2790
ii) Under employed at the rate of 100 days per worker	3420	890	4310	840	230	1070	5380
Total (Million Days)	4320	1580	5900	1740	530	2270	8170
4. Requirements of PDS at 2 Kgs. Per manday (in million tonnes)	8.640	3.160	11.800	3.840	1.060	4.540	16.340
5. Estimated requirements as percentage of actual under PDS in 1987-88	-	-	-	-	-	-	89.2
6. Estimated requirements as percentage of actual procurement in 1987-88.	-	-	-	-	-	-	103.9
7. Estimated employment required as ratio of actual generated under JRY	-	-	-	-	-	-	0.10 (Approximate)

All data on employment from Sarvekshana, September, 1990.

TABLE – 28

Requirements of an Employment linked PDS : 1987-88 : State-wise

State	Total mandays of employment required (millions)	PDS at 2 Kgs. per manday (million tonnes)	Off-take in PDS 1988 (million tonnes)	% Off-take requirement	Procurement in 1988 (million mandays)	Procurement as % of PDS	Mandays employed in million days generated under JRY 1989-90*
Andhra Pradesh	734	1.468	1.119	76.2	1.517	69.20	72.7
Assam	234	0.468	0.757	61.0	0.007	-	0.7
Bihar	832	1.664	0.960	578.69	-	-	92.7
Gujarat	416	0.842	1.319	63.84	-	-	20.2
Haryana	142	0.284	0.192	67.60	1.579	55.60	3.4
Himachal Pradesh	28	0.056	0.200	357.1	-	-	3.8
Jammu & Kashmir	239	0.558	0.406	72.7	0.012	-	5.2
Karnataka	414	0.828	1.051	123.31	0.066	-	40.7
Kerala	648	1.296	1.883	145.3	-	-	23.1
Madhya Pradesh	432	0.864	0.632	73.1	0.320	37.0	93.2
Maharashtra	645	1.290	2.064	160.1	0.167	12.9	79.6
Orissa	363	0.726	0.597	82.2	0.068	9.3	51.7
Punjab	175	0.350	0.033	9.4	8.110	23.10	3.4
Rajasthan	348	0.696	1.148	164.9	0.020	2.87	44.4
Tamil Nadu	990	1.980	1.273	65.3	0.564	28.4	91.1
Uttar Pradesh	667	1.334	1.294	97.0	1.128	84.6	162.5
West Bengal	748	1.496	1.989	132.9	0.063	42.1	55.9
All-India	8170	16.340	18.98	116.0	13.637	83.59	864.3

* Ministry of Rural Development

the off-take in these is not adequate to meet the requirements of vulnerable sections.

The employed linked PDS has several advantages. It contributes to self targeting. It does not impose burdens higher than what is currently undertaken, either by way of procurement or by way of public distribution. It has the potential to meet the nutritional needs of the poorest sections much better than the current public distribution system. It is superior to area targeting and in which large numbers of poor outside the area are likely to be excluded while significant numbers of non-poor within the area are likely to be included.

However, a number of well-meaning objections could be raised against an employment linked public distribution system. Past experience shows that foodgrains released under employment programme are not adequately utilised. For instance in 1989-90, out of the quantum of 0.67 million tonnes of foodgrains released under the programme only 0.44 million tonnes are utilised. The linking of the two will mean that the failure of food delivery system will affect the employment programme also. (Dreze, 1990, p.97). Further, since inflation affects adversely all the labour in the unorganised sector, who do not have compensatory support, it is not politically feasible to restrict the public distribution system, only to those who opt for public works.

Therefore, a more realistic target for purpose of protection against inflation should be households. (1) which derive their incomes from sale of labour power, (2) essentially market-dependent, (3) cannot transfer the burden of inflation to other groups in societies, (4) do not enjoy compensatory support benefits against price rise. The agricultural and other labour in rural areas and the casual labour in urban areas belong to such groups. We provide an estimate of PDS requirements state-wise, when labour households are taken as the target groups of PDS. (Table-29).

TABLE – 29

Estimates of PDS Requirement for Serving Rural and Urban Households : 1986-87

State	*Rural Labour (in millions)*	*Casual labour in urban areas (in millions)*	*Total (in millions) Rural+Urban*	*PDS Requirement of cereals at 100 Kgs. per capita per annum (in million tonnes)*	*Utilisation of PDS of cereals (in million tonnes)**	*Requirement as a ratio of utilisation*
Andhra Pradesh	18.98	1.18	20.16	2.016	1.73 (1.78)	1.17
Assam	2.02	0.07	2.09	0.209	0.16 (0.94)	1.31
Bihar	24.40	0.53	24.93	2.493	0.08 (1.29)	31.16
Gujarat	8.18	0.96	9.14	0.914	0.31 (1.29)	2.95
Haryana	2.10	0.26	2.36	0.236	- (0.14)	-
Himachal Pradesh	0.31	0.01	0.32	0.032	0.10 (0.14)	2.36
Jammu & Kashmir	0.95	0.14	1.09	0.109	0.20 (0.43)	0.16
Karnataka	11.14	0.16	11.30	1.130	0.36 (1.43)	0.30
Kerala	8.43	0.82	9.25	0.925	1.30 (1.90)	0.87
Madhya Pradesh	13.99	1.16	15.15	1.515	0.18 (0.89)	8.42
Maharashtra	15.41	1.84	17.25	1.725	0.92 (2.37)	1.88
Orissa	10.81	0.30	11.11	1.111	0.03 (0.54)	37.00
Punjab	4.33	0.44	4.17	0.477	- (0.23)	-
Rajasthan	5.49	0.73	6.22	0.622	0.36 (1.30)	1.73
Tamil Nadu	13.60	2.56	16.16	1.616	0.77 (1.28)	2.10
Uttar Pradesh	26.39	1.80	8.19	2.819	0.27 (1.41)	1.67
West Bengal	16.34	1.17	17.51	1.751	1.05 (2.05)	1.67
All-India	184.09	16.36	200.45	20.00	8.83 (21.27)	2.27 (0.94)

Labour Population from NSS 42nd Round.
Figures in parenthesis relate to off-take from central pool as reported in Statistical Panorama, FCI.
This does include coarse cereals which form insignificant proportions in most states. (Figures in brackets are the off-take for

Besides, there are destitutes, without earning members in the family. They need to be protected by income transfers through social security and their money incomes should be protected against erosion through inflation. Limiting the public distribution to labour households and to the physically disabled will imply that public distribution will not cover even all those designated as poor. In the rural areas, the bulk of the small and marginal farmers will not be covered. Similarly, the self-employed poor are not covered by public distribution within the urban areas. This may appear discriminatory but there are critical problems in widening the coverage of public distribution so as to include even all the poor, by income criterion. A widened coverage, with a reasonable quantum under PDS will imply much larger level of procurement than what is being currently undertaken. A larger procurement, at less than open market price will be resisted by farmers/millers, and will imply larger element of subsidy if issue price is kept low. Further, keeping the procurement of cereal prices low might conflict with long-term rate of growth of foodgrains. The hike in procurement prices to attract a larger quantum of procurement has the potential to trigger further increases in open market prices, resulting in vicious circle of hike in procurement prices, rise in open market prices and a further hikes in procurement prices to obtain more procurement. Further, a wider coverage will also imply less distribution per household with little impact on nutritional levels, and also little benefits, unless the issue price is kept very low. Besides a wider coverage of public distribution could be counter productive given the dual market system. Growing subsidies lead to larger fiscal deficits and could result in frustrating the macro-economic policies in checking inflation. The self-employed should be assisted basically through improvement of their output and productivity.

With sharper targeting, our estimates show that around 200

million population with labour households (1986-87) could be covered. This would cover more than 50 per cent of their total requirements and will have substantial impact on the nutritional level of the group. All this could be achieved, with political will even without significant increases in off-take. The choice of labour as the target group will also confer greater benefits on-states with higher incidence of poverty, and will correct the inequities associated with the current public distribution system. If the estimates of public utilisation at the household level are to be relied upon there is a wide and inexplicable gap between the off-take from central poor, as reported by FCI, and the utilisation as estimated in NSS 42nd Round. The estimates from the household data are lower than the off-take for all the states, but what is worth noting is that the gap between the two sets of figures is the widest in the states recording high incidence of poverty. As seen earlier, this is not due to the lower access to ration shops in the states, but because the delivery and supply systems in the poorer states are extremely poor. These need to be corrected.

It should be recognised that sharper targeting outlined earlier, could succeed only, if the steep rise in the open market prices are kept in check. A mix of policies which combine PDS with open market sale and in extreme cases imports will become necessary. But surest guarantee against hike in the prices of food articles is adequate rate of growth of foodgrain production in particular.

PUBLIC EMPLOYMENT AND OTHER SAFETY NETS

A well-targeted public distribution could help to ensure the most vulnerable section against erosion of real incomes but the structural adjustments also create loss of employment and incomes for the poor. The most visible aspect of this is the unemployment in the organised sector. As sick units get closed down under the pressure of competition, and as public sector units incurring losses also tend to get closed down. Within the organised sector, there are pressures for relief for the workers. There is suffering also in rural areas and in the unorganised sector which does not get noticed because there are no organised pressures for relief. As a result of NEP, the poor within the unorganised sector are likely to be affected in four ways:

1. Cuts in financial outlays on rural development schemes of the Ministry of Rural Development (Table-30);
2. Withdrawal of subsidies and of support to target oriented credit programmes ;
3. Reduced public investment in agriculture; and
4. Accelerated displacement effects. What needs to be recognised is that these developments have been taking place in the context of considerable unemployment and underemployment. Jawahar Rozgar Yojana as seen earlier covers only a tenth of the unemployed mandays.

The employment absorption effects however depend upon:

1. The rate of growth of investment due to increased investment and the extent to which the higher rate of growth compensates for the decline in elasticity of employment;
2. The degree to which training and skills are developed to benefit from the new occupations in manufacturing and services;
3. The extent to which small and marginal farmers are assisted to gain from the credit market and commodity markets to benefits from the new technology and change in consumer preferences.

TABLE – 30

Schemes of the Ministry of Rural Development and Financial Outlays Thereof

(rupees in crores)

Name of the Plan/Scheme	*Approved outlay for 1990-91*	*Approved outlay for 1991-92*	*Approved outlay for 1992-93*
1. Rural Water Supply Program	423.00	758.00	460.00
2. Rural Sanitation	20.00	37.59	20.00
3. I.R.D.P.	390.00	390.40	390.20
4. T.R.Y.S.E.M.	8.00	8.00	8.00
5. Drought Prone Area Program	51.26	56.00	51.26
6. Desert Development Program	50.00	55.00	50.00
7. Jawahar Rozgar Yojana	2100.00	2100.00	2046.00
8. Land Reforms	25.33	34.61	25.02
9. D.W.C.R.A.	11.49	13.00	13.00
10. Grants to N.I.R.D.	2.20	3.60	2.00
11. Assistance to CAPART	5.50	6.00	5.00
12. Organisation of Training Courses, Seminars & Workshops	0.35	0.50	0.25
13. Strengthening of Extension Training Centres	3.00	3.50	1.00
14. Strengthening of State Training Centres	5.00	6.00	1.50
15. Communication Cell	0.25	0.30	0.25
16. Promotion of Voluntary Scheme	2.00	5.00	5.00
17. Organisation of Beneficiaries	4.00	4.00	1.00
18. Panchayat Development and Training	2.00	2.00	1.00
19. Rural Godowns	4.00	5.00	0.01
20. Agricultural Marketing			
(a) Rural Marketing	5.00	6.00	0.01
(b) Centre for Agricultural Marketing	0.30	1.00	4.00
(c) Estimated Expenditure of DMI	1.70	2.00	3.00
21. Building for AARRO	0.30	0.50	0.50
22. Roads in special Problems Areas	14.40	10.00	2.00
23. Rural Housing (NEW)	-	-	10.00
Total	3129.08	3508.00	3100.00

Source : Government of India, Ministry of Rural Development, Annual Report, 1991-92, P.73.

A strengthened public employment programme, preferably with guaranteed employment, at a minimum wage, coupled with vigorous programmes of human development covering health, primary and vocational education and skill development are necessary. Such programmes need to be woven into sustainable local resource development within a decentralised policy. Also economic organisations of the petty producers are needed for protection against the aggressive onslaughts by big business, for improved access to credit, for upgradation of technology, and for obtaining economies of scale. Thus in the medium and long-term, the new economic policy needs to shift from the limited concept of safety nets to a wider strategy of human development. The strategy becomes compelling in the context of known trends of cumulative causation of poverty for backward regions and under privileged groups in society and the failure of markets to correct these trends.

SUMMARY AND CONCLUSION

Stabilisation policies initiated in 1991 are found to cause stagflation affecting the poor adversely. The inflation rate was the highest in respect of cereals and food articles which have a higher weightage in the budgets of the poor. While the general inflation rate rose to around 14 per cent in 1991-92, the CPIAL index rose by more than 20 per cent. Heaviest burdens of adjustment are placed on the weakest shoulders. This is morally indefensible, bad economics, and is politically wrong.

A detailed review of public distribution system shows that, as it is now being operated, it benefits the poor persons and poor regions very little and leaves little impact on the cereal consumption and calorie intake of the poor. A revamped public distribution system geared to the needs of the labour household is seen to achieve the goal of protection of the poorer people and poorer regions with the same level of procurement, given political will.

Public distribution could however help only those with employment and money incomes. In so far the structural adjustments result in unemployment and displacement of petty producers, there is a need to expand public employment programme. Such a programme should be geared to a sustainable local resources development within a decentralised polity. Petty producers should be enabled to protect themselves against the onslaughts of big business, and develop organisational strength for upgradation of technology and for obtaining economies of scale.

In the medium and long-term there is a need to move away from the limited concept of safety nets to a strategy of human development.

APPENDIX – I

Reason for No Purchase/Part Purchase From PDS : 1986-87 : Rice : Rural Areas

State	*Unsatisfactory Function*								
	(1)	*(2)*	*(3)*	*(4)*	*(5)*	*(6)*	*(7)*	*(8)*	*(9)*
Andhra Pradesh	7.76	35.69	25.46	5.30	14.84	0.34	1.46	8.40	100
Assam	8.72	42.00	13.01	4.89	15.06	0.57	0.42	12.00	100
Bihar	3.43	28.59	48.79	1.06	2.24	0.67	0.23	13.23	100
Gujarat	13.13	41.98	5.45	16.79	10.35	0.56	3.05	7.68	100
Haryana	2.52	65.11	27.83	1.43	0.65	-	0.31	2.02	100
Himachal Pradesh	2.78	43.02	24.31	6.16	7.62	0.22	5.00	9.75	100
Jammu & Kashmir	5.34	47.05	26.80	1.30	4.76	-	1.62	12.45	100
Karnataka	13.87	12.22	13.06	2.69	49.92	0.25	1.04	6.21	100
Kerala	8.12	2.72	0.22	10.73	75.14	0.01	0.59	1.49	100
Madhya Pradesh	12.09	48.17	19.07	3.73	2.00	0.26	3.75	0.78	100
Maharashtra	10.44	33.28	12.16	11.63	19.93	0.83	4.16	0.79	100
Orissa	1.92	28.25	46.79	0.86	1.30	0.15	0.20	18.59	100
Punjab	3.20	70.25	22.49	1.05	0.13	-	-	2.88	100
Rajasthan	1.09	51.17	46.28	0.14	0.05	-	0.05	1.04	100
Tamil Nadu	10.99	21.02	5.37	10.60	41.78	1.40	2.25	5.89	100
Uttar Pradesh	5.20	52.36	33.70	0.64	0.40	0.11	0.13	7.00	100
West Bengal	7.60	22.62	20.34	22.65	15.13	0.17	3.74	7.55	100
All-India	7.76	35.60	25.46	5.30	14.84	0.34	1.46	8.40	100

LEGEND

1. Not entitled to ration card/no ration card
2. Not required
3. Not available in ration shop
4. Quantities not significant
5. Not available in ration shop
6. Not available in sufficient quantity.
7. Credit purchase not possible.
8. Others
9. Total

APPENDIX – II

Reason for No Purchase/Part Purchase From PDS : 1986-87 : Wheat : Rural Areas

State	*(1)*	*(2)*	*(3)*	*(4)*	*(5)*	*(6)*	*(7)*	*(8)*	*(9)*
Andhra Pradesh	1.84	79.23	16.21	0.21	0.13	-	-	2.34	100
Assam	4.54	64.58	19.20	-	1.08	-	-	3.19	100
Bihar	2.12	35.09	43.01	1.05	2.10	0.25	0.32	12.95	100
Gujarat	7.81	65.63	4.19	10.03	1.72	0.04	1.74	7.37	100
Haryana	-	1.51	77.77	20.12	-	-	-	0.55	100
Himachal Pradesh	1.35	64.05	18.24	1.12	0.56	-	0.60	13.94	100
Jammu & Kashmir	1.72	72.89	15.59	-	0.45	-	0.50	9.45	100
Karnataka	10.02	57.99	13.85	2.19	8.54	0.05	1.32	4.20	100
Kerala	2.81	80.94	9.06	0.66	0.08	-	0.86	2.69	100
Madhya Pradesh	6.88	60.03	17.48	3.07	1.04	0.18	2.69	8.38	100
Maharashtra	8.63	45.30	10.11	12.28	12.21	0.25	3.38	6.54	100
Orissa	0.33	82.58	9.22	-	0.13	-	-	5.82	100
Punjab	2.44	74.18	19.47	0.30	0.29	-	0.19	3.11	100
Rajasthan	1.30	60.38	33.88	0.87	0.82	0.08	0.39	1.72	100
Tamil Nadu	5.58	79.73	9.00	0.97	0.33	-	8.70	3.04	100
Uttar Pradesh	5.15	55.51	31.41	0.39	0.17	0.11	0.13	7.00	100
West Bengal	3.92	61.66	19.75	7.05	2.11	0.06	1.94	3.05	100
All-India	4.32	60.91	22.38	2.35	1.79	0.10	0.87	6.18	100

LEGEND

1. Not entitled to ration card/no ration card
2. Not required
3. Not available in ration shop
4. Quantities not significant
5. Not available in ration shop
6. Not available in sufficient quantity.
7. Credit purchase not possible.
8. Others
9. Total

APPENDIX – III

Reason for No Purchase/Part Purchase From PDS : 1986-87 : Rice : Urban Areas

State	*Unsatisfactory Function*								
	(1)	*(2)*	*(3)*	*(4)*	*(5)*	*(6)*	*(7)*	*(8)*	*(9)*
Andhra Pradesh	42.69	3.90	2.74	5.07	40.79	0.33	0.19	4.08	100
Assam	20.41	9.19	16.43	14.17	30.14	-	0.68	7.91	100
Bihar	11.40	9.19	58.43	8.82	1.18	0.83	-	10.41	100
Gujarat	15.70	27.87	6.73	29.40	8.20	-	0.70	10.85	100
Haryana	9.52	47.25	29.70	9.88	1.40	-	0.09	1.69	100
Himachal Pradesh	18.00	15.50	14.72	26.61	11.95	1.46	1.35	8.53	100
Jammu & Kashmir	12.23	10.68	5.08	12.21	47.27	1.00	0.73	3.48	100
Karnataka	22.08	3.40	4.06	8.59	56.17	0.24	0.65	3.74	100
Kerala	6.11	2.48	1.75	11.76	74.06	-	0.55	2.20	100
Madhya Pradesh	16.32	23.05	20.90	25.22	7.06	0.57	1.82	4.76	100
Maharashtra	14.96	9.63	2.27	43.19	23.56	0.30	1.82	4.76	100
Orissa	11.62	6.54	54.93	5.90	2.76	-	0.39	17.60	100
Punjab	19.74	36.31	28.59	5.90	2.76	-	0.39	17.60	100
Rajasthan	3.33	38.71	53.36	2.28	0.23	-	1.49	3.89	100
Tamil Nadu	21.29	5.38	2.24	21.36	41.61	1.26	1.31	4.32	100
Uttar Pradesh	10.76	25.84	44.67	10.82	1.44	0.43	0.64	4.95	100
West Bengal	13.96	4.23	7.89	40.92	27.73	1.75	1.15	2.03	100
All-India	50.70	27.87	6.73	29.40	8.20	-	0.70	10.85	100

LEGEND

1. Not entitled to ration card/no ration card
2. Not required
3. Not available in ration shop
4. Quantities not significant
5. Not available in ration shop
6. Not available in sufficient quantity.
7. Credit purchase not possible.
8. Others
9. Total

APPENDIX – IV

Reason for No Purchase/Part Purchase From PDS : 1986-87 : Wheat : Urban Areas

State	*(1)*	*(2)*	*(3)*	*(4)*	*(5)*	*(6)*	*(7)*	*(8)*	*(9)*
Andhra Pradesh	7.08	69.91	17.50	2.15	0.56	-	0.30	2.34	100
Assam	20.41	55.77	22.00	2.03	1.10	-	0.24	2.30	100
Bihar	8.22	19.55	46.33	9.91	4.14	0.44	-	9.13	100
Gujarat	13.27	38.12	5.02	28.33	3.28	-	0.94	11.03	100
Haryana	6.52	64.63	27.35	0.84	-	-	-	0.45	100
Himachal Pradesh	4.02	61.28	14.87	4.75	0.85	-	0.46	13.10	100
Jammu & Kashmir	4.16	67.33	13.17	1.90	9.99	-	-	3.45	100
Karnataka	22.15	35.23	7.88	15.07	12.93	-	0.55	4.92	100
Kerala	4.72	70.42	9.54	1.89	1.06	-	0.45	10.25	100
Madhya Pradesh	13.97	26.36	22.06	25.26	5.63	0.31	1.34	4.91	100
Maharashtra	14.38	12.07	2.29	50.48	14.66	0.18	1.97	2.67	100
Orissa	6.28	61.18	18.51	3.15	0.72	-	-	9.65	100
Punjab	4.01	59.20	31.64	0.88	0.22	-	1.15	2.90	100
Rajasthan	2.97	38.63	51.10	4.05	0.38	-	0.09	2.12	100
Tamil Nadu	13.36	62.57	8.74	7.64	1.63	0.15	0.79	4.63	100
Uttar Pradesh	8.27	55.83	19.05	-	1.05	-	-	19.97	100
West Bengal	17.16	45.51	10.38	15.80	6.66	0.52	1.17	2.25	100
All-India	13.27	38.12	5.02	25.33	3.28	-	0.94	11.03	100

LEGEND

1. Not entitled to ration card/no ration card
2. Not required
3. Not available in ration shop
4. Quantities not significant
5. Not available in ration shop
6. Not available in sufficient quantity.
7. Credit purchase not possible.
8. Others
9. Total

References

1. Andhra Pradesh Paurahakkula Sangham (APCLC) (1992) : "Chirugupathala Baruvubathukulu, Cheneta Sankshobham Pi Oka Pariselana" (in Telugu), Guntur, March, 1992.
2. Bhattacharya, Nikelesh and others : Relative Prices of Food and the rural poor - The Case of India, (Mimeo).
3. Dev, Mahendra, S. and Suryanarayana, M.H. (1991) : "Is PDS Urban Biased and Pro-Rich? An Evaluation", Economic and Political Weekly, October 12.
4. Dreze, Jean (1980) : "Famine Prevention in India", The Political Economy of Hunger, Vol. 2, Jean Dreze and Amartya Sen (ed.)., Clarenden Press, Oxford.
5. FAO Economic & Social Development Paper, 100 (1991) : Structural Adjustment and Household Welfare in Rural Areas : A Micro-Perspective, Rome, P.2.
6. Food Corporation of India (1990) : Statistical Panorama, New Delhi.
7. Frontline (1991) : National Magazine from Madras, December 6.
8. Gupta and Padmasani (1992) : "Poverty/Social Cost : Painful Contraction", Economic Times, 31st August.
9. Howes, Stephan and Shikha Jha (1992) : "Urban Bias in Indian Public Distribution System", Economic and Political Weekly, May, 9.
10. Kannadurai (1992) : Digest Series No. 7, Critical Issues in the Public Distribution System in India : A Survey of Literature, MIDS, Madras, March.
11. Radhakrishna, R. (1991) : "Food and Nutrition : Challenges of Policy, Indian Society of Agricultural Statistics, New Delhi.
12. Radhakrishna, R. (1991) : "Political Economy of Grain Market Intervention in India", Economy, Society and Development, edited by C.T. Kurien, E.R. Prabhakar and S. Gopal, SAGE Publications, New Delhi.
13. R.B.I. Bulletin (1992) : Vol. XLVI, No. 8, August.
14. Sarvekshana (1990) : Vol. XIII, No. 4, Issue Nod. 43, April - June, 1988 : Special Number - Results of the Fourth Quinquennial Survey on Employment and Unemployment (All-India), NSS, 43rd Round, July 1987 - June 1988.
15. Srinivasan, T.N. (1988) : Structural Adjustment, Stabilisation and the Poor, EDI Working Paper, Washington, D.C., World Bank (Mimeo).
16. Taylor, L. (1987) : "Varieties of Stabilisation Experiences towards sensible macro-economics in the Third World, Prepared for WIDER, Helsinki, (Mimeo).
17. Tyagi, D.S. (1990) : Managing India's Food Economy, Sage Publications.
18. World Bank (1990) : World Development Report, Poverty.

Published in "New Economic Policy and Vulnerable Sections", IDPS, Jaipur, 1994.

4

New Economic Policy and Rural Employment

THE questions raised in this paper relate to : (1) impact of the New Economic Policy (NEP) on employment; (2) potential areas of labour absorption in the light of NEP; and (3) desired institutional changes for augmenting rural employment. The concern is essentially with those aspects of NEP which have a strong bearing on rural employment and unemployment. These are identified to be (a) withdrawal of subsidies on inputs in agriculture, especially fertiliser; (b) liberalisation of industrial policy in so far as it affects growth in agriculture and non-agriculture in rural areas, and labour absorption in industries from rural/agricultural sector; and (c) liberalisation of trade policy as it affects exports and imports, and consequently rural/agricultural employment.

1. Withdrawal of Subsidies and Rural Employment

It is well known that there are heavy subsidies for fertilisers, power and irrigation within agriculture (Mundle and Govinda Rao; EPW, May 1991). Of these, fertiliser subsidy is the most conspicuous, and has shown a phenomenal rise in recent years. Under the NEP it is proposed to withdraw the subsidies because they contributed to huge fiscal deficit. Further they distorted the allocation of resources and contributed to inter-personal and inter-regional inequity. Yet, their role in contributing to increased employment and output within agriculture can not be ignored. They reduce the cost of input to the farmer, and contribute to more intensive use of land. Such input use has contributed to the relaxation of severe constraints on land which have been operating in the Indian economy. There are direct and indirect employment benefits; direct benefits through employment generated in larger input use and indirect benefits through employment generated by additional output. We should therefore expect, other things being equal, withdrawal of subsidies for inputs in agriculture would reduce employment depending upon (a) price elasticity of input use, (b) elasticity of crop yield to input use; and (c) elasticity of employment to yield.

Taking fertiliser which is the most important input and in respect of which subsidies are most prominent, there is evidence to show that in many states of India (Sharma and Haque) elasticity of crop yield to fertiliser use is positive and the price elasticity of fertiliser use is negative. For instance, in A.P. a 10 per cent rise in fertiliser price was found to reduce fertiliser use by 4.0 per cent for rice, and in its turn 1.4 per cent fall in yield. For wheat in Punjab it was noted that price elasticity of fertiliser use was 0.9 and fertiliser elasticity of yield was 0.28. However in States like Orissa and West Bengal, where fertiliser use is not efficient, elasticity of fertiliser use on yield is either insignificant or negative. A more recent paper on "A Macro Analysis of Fertiliser Demand in India (Subramaniyan and Nirmala; IJAE, (January-March, 1991) further confirms the negative price elasticity of fertiliser use. In their static model the rise of fertiliser/product price by 10 per cent decreased fertiliser use by 4.16 per cent. Their dynamic model which uses less number of explanatory variables shows even higher price elasticity.

Estimates of employment elasticity of agricultural output vary largely. An earlier estimate by Tyagi for the period 1970-71 to 1978-79 showed that for all crops the elasticity was 0.769. In estimates covering the data upto 1983-84 the employment elasticity for all crops was noted to be less, i.e., 0.5945 (Sheila Bhalla; IJAE, October-December, 1987). Employment elasticities with respect to yield were noted to be lower. They were also found to vary largely as between the states and among different crops.

Across the states they varied from negative elasticities in the North-Western part of the country to high positive elasticities leading to high labour absorption growth in the States of Andhra Pradesh, Gujarat and Maharashtra. There are difficulties, however, in predicting future trends in labour absorption on the basis of past trends. Even so, estimates of past elasticities of employment to output, which range from 0.4 to 0.6 are helpful in judging the possible effects of withdrawal of subsidies for fertilisers on employment. With a 30.0 per cent rise in fertiliser prices, (with effect from August 1991, the average fertiliser price increase was 30 per cent, and small and marginal farmers were exempted from the price increase) assuming a fertiliser price elasticity of 0.4, fertiliser yield elasticity of 0.30 and employment elasticity of 0.4, the reduction in employment is of the order of 1.44 per cent. This may appear to be a small adverse employment effect, given a fertiliser price rise of 30.0 per cent. But it is not so. When related to unemployment rate, given a daily status unemployment rate of the order of 8.0 per cent, unemployment rate is likely to rise by 17 per cent.

There are a number of ways in which such adverse effects could be averted. A relative rise in the price of fertiliser price may induce substitution by organic manure. Such substitution is good from the point of view of sustainable agriculture development. But this is not automatic. It needs to be deliberately promoted. Secondly, a rise in product price along with a price rise of fertiliser price, as has been done in 1991-92, could arrest the increase in the relative price of fertiliser and work against disincentives to use. But rise in procurement prices, if followed by rise in issue price and also the open market price, will trigger inflation. If the rise in procurement price, if not accompanied by rise in issue price, will add to the budgetary deficit. Further, a rise in product price is not less inequitable than subsidy on fertilisers. Finally, non-price factors, such as better distribution of outlets, improved access to credit and improved fertiliser use practices could compensate for the rise in fertiliser prices. If the flow of benefits from subsidies and also questions of inter-personal equality are considered, there is certainly a case for reducing the subsidy and for the use of non-price factors for promoting fertiliser use. But the success of non-price factors has a gestation period. Lastly, higher investments in minor irrigation could be seen as an alternative at the margin. This is a better option from the view point of equity also. But even this has a gestation.

We should be prepared for some employment losses in the short run as a result of reduction of fertiliser subsidy and there is a need for a phased withdrawal of subsidies in agriculture.

2. *Liberalisation of Industrial and Trade Policies and Their Impact on Rural Employment*

Liberalisation of industrial policies has a bearing on rural employment in so far as they open up or close prospects of labour absorption from the rural/agricultural sector within the urban/industrial sector. It is expected to open up such prospects, as internal and international competition improves efficiency and foreign direct investment (FDI) adds to domestic gross capital formation. Both these are expected to step up growth rates and also employment, depending upon the changes in technology and their effects on elasticity of employment output. The most controversial aspect relates to the entry of transnationals. It is difficult to speculate on the extent to which gross domestic capital formation will rise as result of foreign direct investment. As it is, roughly, three quarters of foreign direct investment goes to industrialised countries. China, which has recently opened its doors to FDI is one of the largest recipients of FDI among the less developed countries and is a competitor to India (Ereye, Heinrich, and Erodel; ILO, 1988). The significance of transnationals is found to be even less in respect of employment in the less developed countries. The Multi-National Corporations (MNCs) account for only 1 per cent of the economically active population as against 10 per cent in developed countries (ILO : 1988). These facts suggest that the role of foreign direct investment in generating employment cannot be large. There is also a debate on the employment displacement effects of MNCs. The displacement controversy is built around two premises: (1) the probability that a local project would have emerged in the absence of direct foreign investment; and (2) the MNCs employ techniques which are more capital intensive than domestic enterprises. As regards the first premise, this is least likely in areas where local firms do not have access to knowledge. On the second premise, there appears to be adequate evidence that the techniques employed by MNCs are more capital intensive than those employed by local enterprises. Evidence from the U.K. shows that labour intensity is on average one-third higher in domestically owned enterprises than in foreign multi-nationals (ILO, 1988). The employment impact of inward direct investment depends on the mode of entry chosen by MNCs, and also the indirect positive effects from subcontracting vis-a-vis the negative external effects from replacement of host country supplies in foreign supplies.

A study of Exim Bank of India evaluating the foreign controlled enterprises with local enterprises (April, 1990) noticed no statistically significant difference between the export performance of Foreign Controlled Enterprises (FCEs) and Locally Controlled Enterprises (LCEs) in 43 Indian manufacturing industries. The mean scale of operation of the FCEs is greater than LCEs. The advertisement interests, profit margin, proportion of high income employees in total wage bill are higher. There is no direct evidence on the comparative impact on employment. But if a judgement is to be made in the light of preceding review, it should be concluded that the more capital-using techniques of MNCs will have some adverse effect on employment. The adverse effect of technology consequent on entry of MNCs could be compensated only by additions to investments and rates of growth far higher than what could be obtained without such investment. But in the short and medium term such compensatory benefits are unlikely to be realised. As a consequence we would expect the rate of labour absorption in the industrial sector to decline.

A likely impact of liberalisation is the entry of big business including MNCs into agro-processing, and liberalisation of trade policy may be expected to promote exports. The High Powered Committee on Agricultural Policies and Programmes under the Chairmanship of Bhanupratap Singh (July 1990, Ministry of Agriculture, Government of India) visualised a huge potential for export of agricultural products. Besides tea and coffee, our traditional export items, a number of other items such as fruits, vegetables, flowers are identified. Our location nearer to the importing countries is considered to give us a freight advantage. But one cannot expect growth of agricultural exports on a large scale in the short and medium term. Past trends in agricultural exports suggest the constraints to growth in the short and medium term. India's agricultural export performance between 1970 and 1986 has been noted to be unsatisfactory by any standard (Singh and Singh IJAE, July-September, 1989). Internal factors included sluggish growth of domestic agricultural production and rise in domestic consumption. Non-price factors such as quality also adversely affected the competitiveness of our exports. External factors having a bearing on our export performance are the protectionist policies pursued by the developed countries and non-tariff barriers. Besides, heavy subsidies provided by developed countries lead to over supplies in the world markets and contribute to declining terms of trade for agricultural products. The performance of cashew exports, exports of shrimps and exports of spices shows the problems not resolvable by liberalisation. The virtual monopoly of India in the export of cashew kernel exports came to an end on account of the fact that other producers of cashew in the world who did not have processing facilities started establishing cashew factories. Earlier they were exporting raw nuts to India. India's share of cashew kernel export which was almost one hundred per cent in 1950 declined sharply to 55 per cent in 1968. In 1955-56, U.S.A and U.S.S.R together accounted for more than 75 per cent of exports of kernels from India. In 1987-88 their share declined to 42 per cent (Rajasekharan and Radhakrishnan, IJAE, July-September, 1989). As regards cardamom, Guatemala, which was a marginal producer in the world cardamom scenario is now the major producer and supplier of cardamom. Better productivity and lower cost of production helped them to underquote Indian price in many instances and capture the world market (Thomas, Indiradevi, and Thomas : IJAE, July-September, 1989). Since 1984, tobacco exports have been experiencing negative growth. There is a need for long-term measures for efficient promotion of tobacco exports (Subba Rao : IJAE, July-September, 1989). As regards fruits, though production of oranges have increased, their exports had shown a declining trend after 1982 (Gadra and Bhole : IJAE,

July-September, 1989). The inadequacy of cold storage capacity and transport bottlenecks coupled with the non-availability of refrigerated shipping tonnage capacity are the main hurdles in the promotion of potato exports (Dahiya and Bhati, IJAE, July-September, 1989). Shrimp exports were found to have stagnated in quantitative terms in the eighties. Further, exports were found to be heavily dependent on Japan and U.S.A. changes in their import policies could affect our export earnings (Satyanarayana and Krishnan, IJAE, July-September, 1989). As regards exports of cotton yarn, cotton fabrics blended fabrics and polyester staple fibre, there is likely to be a conflict with rising domestic demand (Ghanekar, IJAE, July-September, 1989). It would be necessary to raise cotton production and reduce sharp fluctuation in cotton prices. Further, while export of cotton yarn might benefit the farming community and the textile industry, they have been found to affect the interests of the handloom weaver adversely by making the availability of yarn scarce and their prices exorbitantly high. Such developments have been found to affect the employment in the rural sector adversely.

In brief, liberalisation of trade per se is unlikely to expand agricultural and rural exports in the absence of the development of infrastructural facilities for export markets. Even if exports are stepped up through promotion of agro-processing, their short-term effects on employment are unlikely to be favourable since the employment intensity of modern processing is likely to be less than the corresponding intensity of traditional industry. There are only two conditions under which the shifts to modern agro-processing and exports contribute to improvement of rural employment. Firstly, such processing should result in the emergence of a whole range of new industries through backward and forward linkages resulting in addition to aggregate of employment even though employment in the specific processing industry gets reduced through modernisation. Secondly, modernisation of agro-processing should result in more efficient use of raw material and in addition contribute to utilisation of by-products which remain unutilised or wasted in the absence of shifts to modern-processing. Both these effects are likely to be seen only in the long-run and immediately one should expect a reduction in employment as traditional processing is replaced by modern processing.

3. *Potential Areas of Employment*

Past trends in employment and structure cannot be projected into the future. Yet they are helpful in providing insights into the possibility for future. One important fact that has been highlighted by several scholars is the declining percentage of labour force in agriculture since 1970. It is concluded from this that the ability of agriculture to absorb additional labour force has considerably declined. Further support for this conclusion is found from the rapidly declining per capita size of land holding, the increasing proportions of marginal and small farmers and the rising proportions seeking non-agricultural employment among them. The declining labour absorption within agriculture sector is attributed to the rapidly declining elasticity of employment within agriculture. A number of factors are identified for the reduced employment elasticities in agriculture. It appears that the most effective yield increasing and land augmenting technologies currently available in India also happen to be labour saving, at least in some regions and for some crop combinations. There are also two other effects leading to the same result, i.e., the late comer effect and Hayami labour-cost transaction effect (Sheila Bhalla, 1989). The first effect results in the use of technology developed in the advanced countries under labour scarce conditions. The second effect results in use of labour saving devices to reduce the supervisionary cost of labour. Further the concentration of production in regions with relative labour scarcity as in the North Western parts leads to the same results.

In the light of such developments we could examine the trends in employed labour force in rural areas (Table-I). The share of agriculture in employment declined both in rural areas and in all-India. The decline was sharper in all-India. Poor overall rate of growth of employment within agriculture, i.e. 0.75 per cent per annum as against 2.00 per cent for all sectors combined, contributed to this result. The declining importance of agriculture in labour absorption is also seen in its share in the total additions to employment. The share in the additions was less than 30 per cent in all-India, and in rural areas around 40 per cent.

Within the additions to non-agricultural employment in the rural labour, only one-fourth of the additions are accounted for by manufacturing. The rest are accounted for by construction and the tertiary sector. Construction accounts for the single largest in the additional absorption, accounting for around 30 per cent, in the additions to non-agriculture. Construction and transport could be identified as the fast growing sectors within non-agriculture in rural areas.

Past trends do suggest declining importance of agriculture in absorption of additional labour, and the need for promoting non-agricultural employment in rural areas. It needs to be recognised however that while the potential of crop production to generate employment is likely to be low, the potential of allied sectors, such as dairy, poultry, pisciculture, sericulture to generate rural employment is high. Income elasticity of demand for these products is high and is more than unity. From the view point of supply, land constraints operate less severely and their supply could be expanded even on small and marginal farms. Further a growth in agricultural production, and agricultural surplus are necessary to provide

TABLE – I

Share in Employment By Sectors : 1977-78 and 1987-88 : All-India

Sl.No.	Sectors	Percentage Share: Rural 1977-78	Rural 1987-88	Total 1977-78	Total 1987-88	Annual rate of growth per annum 1987-88 over 1977-78 (Total)	Percentage share in additions to labour force 1987-88 over 1977-78: Rural	Total
1.	Agriculture	83.33	78.21	72.56	64.15	0.75 (0.66)	41.70	27.13
2.	Mining & Quarrying	0.93	0.59	0.46	0.72	6.77 (5.64)	2.05	1.96
3.	Manufacturing	6.21	7.21	9.74	11.27	3.51 (2.85)	14.47	18.51
4.	Electricity, Gas & Water	0.21	0.19	0.28	0.36	5.54 (4.69)	0.20	0.75
5.	Construction	1.30	3.33	1.69	3.77	10.48 (11.31)	18.02	13.39
6.	Trade	3.26	4.00	5.77	7.26	4.36 (3.39)	9.38	14.19
7.	Transport	0.80	1.31	1.93	2.68	5.38 (6.49)	4.99	6.17
8.	Services	4.46	5.03	7.73	9.52	4.15 (2.54)	9.19	17.90
	Total	100.00	100.00	100.00	100.00	2.00 (1.31)	100.00	100.00

Notes : (1) The totals do not necessarily add upto 100 due to rounding off errors.
(2) Figures in parenthesis are the rates of growth of rural employment.

stimulus to employment in transport and trade even to support expanded manufacturing activity. What is important to recognise is that even while the share of manufacturing is high in additional employment, it is the service sector which has been generating much more employment, and this is due to growing rural-urban trade, consequent upon higher rates of flows of marketed surplus. These developments can not be sustained without a sustained growth in agricultural production and agricultural surplus.

Sustained growth of agriculture as a means of promoting employment becomes all the more important in the context of the observed and expected trends in employment in the organised manufacturing sector. The Indian industry has been undergoing a structural change over the past four decades, by and large, in a historically well-established pattern : from primary raw-material based industries to metal based industries, and from them to industries using processed intermediate inputs. This transition implied higher technology, increase in labour productivity and a decline in employment potential of output growth. Technological change in the individual groups as well as the shift in industrial structure have been contributing to reduce employment elasticities. Goldar's 1984 study indicated that the short run elasticity of employment with respect of industrial output is only 0.254 and industrial employment is extremely sensitive to variations in real labour costs. Goldar finds a one per cent increase in 'real labour costs reduced employment by 0.344 per cent within one year, and over long period, by more than one per cent. Papola's subsequent work suggests that employment elasticities with respect to industrial output may have declined subsequently in the late seventies and the early eighties (Sheila Bhalla, IJAE, 1987). These trends are likely to continue and in fact accelerate with liberalisation and opening of the economy as the compulsions of international competition are likely to further reduce the employment intensity partially because of the need for cost reduction and mostly for the reasons of improving the quality of the product (Papola : Monthly Commentary, May, 1991). Organised industrial sector is unlikely to contribute to employment generation in a significant way.

While the potential for labour absorption in the organised sector is limited past trends indicate better possibilities in the unorganised manufacturing sector. The unorganised manufacturing sector has grown at around 4 per cent during 1972-73 to 1987-88. A fact that is not well recognised is that about 53 per cent of employment in the manufacturing sector is located in rural areas and almost all of it is the unorganised sector. Papola identifies four significant aspects of recent trends of growth of manufacturing in the unorganised sector. These are :

1. Emergence of non-traditional and intermediate product based industries;
2. Demand based employment at reasonable levels of earning;
3. Emergence of a trend towards a relative shift of small manufacturing activity from the larger to smaller towns; and
4. Shift with not mere relocation but with additive component.

This potential needs to be recognised and positively encouraged by promoting adequate and suitable infrastructural support.

Such non-agricultural diversification in the rural areas needs to be rooted in sustained growth of agriculture, particularly the allied occupations.

4. Scope For Government Sponsored Employment Programmes and Modifications Required in Their Conceptual Framework

A conclusion of the earlier analysis is that the NEP is likely to result in less absorption of rural labour in the organised sector, more displacement of the traditional industries, and reduced rates of growth of rural employment with continuation of trends in declining employment elasticity in agriculture. All such consequences will mean that Rural Development Programmes, sponsored by public agencies will have to be on a much larger scale in the short and medium term of the operation of the NEP. There is also large scope for these programmes as considerations of sustainability and infrastructural requirements gain prominence. There will be also a need to enable the marginal and small farmers to take advantage of the shifts within agriculture from cereals to allied enterprises such as sericulture, pisciculture, horticulture, dairying and poultry. These allied enterprises are more employment intensive and add higher net values per hectare. But such enterprises are capital intensive and require improved markets. The marginal and small farmer need to be assisted to enable him to overcome these constraints.

There are four major directions in which the Rural Development Programmes need to be strengthened. Firstly, there is a need for a better integration of the programmes with the overall local development programmes. For this to be achieved the moves towards Panchayati Raj and decentralised development planning should be expedited. Secondly, there should be more effective integration of all the rural development programmes at the local level so that these programmes could reinforce each other so that the aggregate impact on poverty and employment could be larger. Thirdly, the leakages of the programme continue to be large and they need to be plugged. Capital subsidies have been a source of corruption. It is suggested that capital subsidies may be replaced by interest subsidies. Similarly, right to work at minimum wage of the slack season should be implemented and there is a need to encourage organisations of labour to undertake the construction work. Finally, it should be made obligatory on big business in agro-processing to provide their extension, processing and marketing facilities to small and marginal farmers through coordination of their activities with DRDA. While the shift of Rural Development Programmes in these directions is necessary their success depends upon; an improved rate of agricultural growth, especially allied occupations, an expanded and widely diffused non-agricultural employment in the rural areas, and an effective implementation of land reforms.

References

1. Bhalla, Shiela : "Trends in Employment in Indian Agriculture : Land and Asset Distribution", IJAE, October-December, 1987, pp. 537-560.
2. Dahiya, P.S., & Bhati, J.P. : "Trends and Potentiality of Potato Exports: Present Status and Future Strategy", IJAE, July-September, 1989.
3. Dantwala, M.L. & Others : "Search for Employment Oriented Growth Strategy : A Discussion", EPW, May 26, 1990, pp.1147-1162.
4. Gadre, N.A., & Bhole, B.D. : "Performance of Exports of Citrus Fruits in India", IJAE, July-September, 1989.
5. Ganekar, V.V. : "Export Trade of Cotton Yarn, Cotton Fabrics, Blended Fabrics, Polyster Staple Fibre", IJAE, July-September, 1989.
6. Government of India, Ministry of Agriculture :"Report of the High Powered Committee on Agricultural Policies and Programmes", July, 1990, New Delhi.
7. Hiraway, Indira : "Labour Absorption in Indian Economy : Some Issues", The Indian Journal of Labour Economics, Oct.-Dec., 1991.
8. Kreye Otto, Heinrichs Jurgen, and Frodel Folker :"Multinational Enterprises and Employment", ILO, Geneva, 1988.
9. Mundle, Sudipto & Govindarao, M. :"Volume and Composition of Government Subsidies in India - 1987-88", EPW, May 4, 1991, pp. 1157-1172.
10. Papola, T.S. : "Industry and Employment", Monthly Commentary, May 1991.

11. Planning Commission, Government of India :"Employment : Past Trends and Prospects for 1990s", Working Paper, May, 1990.

12. Rajasekharan, P. & Radhakrishnan, V. : "Performance of Cashew Exports", IJAE, July-Sept., 1989.

13. Satyanarayana, M. & Krishnan, M. : "Growth and Geographical Distribution and Import Penetration of Shrimp Exports from India", IJAE, July-Sept., 1989.

14. Sharma & Haque, T. : "Impact of Fertiliser subsidy on Growth and Equity", Highlights of Agricultural Research, IASRI, New Delhi, 1987.

15. Singh A.J. & Singh, R.P. : "Indian Agricultural Exports - Problem", IJAE, July-sept., 1989.

16. Subba Rao, N. : "Foreign Trade in Tobacco and Tobacco Products : Performance and Prospects", IJAE, July-Sept., 1989.

17. Subramaniyan, G. & Nirmala V. : "A Macro Analysis of Fertiliser Demand in India (1966-67 - 1985-86)", IJAE, Jan.-March, 1991, pp.12-18.

18. Thomas, E.K., Indira Devi, P., & Thomas K. Jesy : "Cardamom Export From India - Trends and Prospects", IJAE, July-Sept., 1989.

Published in the Bihar Journal of Agricultural Marketing, Vol.1, July-September 1993, No.3.

5

Agricultural Exports

(in the Context of Liberalisation and Globalisation of Agricultural Trade)

INTRODUCTION

Objectives

GULATI and Sharma (1991)[1] reviewed government intervention in external trade in agricultural products for the period earlier to 1990. In general, exports of commodities in short supply in India were prohibited and imports of such commodities were permitted. Thus exports of natural rubber, pulses and oilseeds were banned (except groundnuts for direct consumption). Import of edible oils has been a government monopoly, as are imports and exports of sugar. Imports of rice and wheat have also been effectively a government monopoly. Exports have been subject to quotas and in the case of the superfine Basmati grade of rice, to a minimum export price. Cotton imports were the domain of a state agency and cotton exports were subject to quotas and a minimum export price.

The effect of these policies was to make domestic prices and world prices differ. Gulati and Sharma provided estimate of nominal and effective protection coefficients (NPCs and EPCs) for several crops, considering each crop as an exportable and as an importable. On the importable hypothesis their study shows that wheat, rice and cotton were taxed; oil seeds and sugarcane were highly protected.

The year 1991 marks a watershed in the trade policy of the Government of India. In order to improve international competitiveness of our exports and restrain demand for imports, the Reserve Bank of India adjusted downwards by revaluating Rupee from 8.7 per cent to 9.7 per cent in relation to four major currencies on July 1, 1991 and further by 10 to 11 per cent in relation to five major currencies resulting in overall appreciation of these currencies in relation to Rupee by 21 to 23.1 per cent. The government also announced major structural reforms in the area of trade policy on July 4, 1991. These reforms meant far-reaching changes in the trade and exchange rate policies. As a consequence there was reduced protection to domestic industry resulting in reduced discrimination against agriculture.

The changes in the Exchange Rate System were expected to provide a powerful incentive for exports. The abolition of export subsidies following the adjustment of exchange rates which was earlier a source of frequent complaints regarding delays and corruption was also expected to help agriculture and agro-based exports. The removal of many restrictions on exports including restrictions on export of agricultural commodities should be said to help the promotion of agricultural exports.

In the light of the preceding review of liberalisation and its possible effects, this paper addresses itself to questions relating to : Differences between post-liberalisation period (1990-91 to 1991-93) and the immediate pre-liberalisation period (1988-89 and 1989-90). The Paper in addition, reviews the available empirical evidence on the impact of partial removal of trade barriers and subsidies under Uruguay Round

Negotiations. The analysis is preceded by a review of studies on past trends in Indian foreign trade in agricultural commodities.

PART – I

REVIEW OF EARLIER STUDIES ON TRENDS IN AGRICULTURAL TRADE

Ramesh Chand and Tewari[2] used the data of Food and Agriculture Organisation of the United Nations (FAO) to analyse the trends in agricultural exports for the period 1970-73 to 1985-88. Their study shows that agricultural exports as a proportion of the total exports declined from 38.0 per cent in 1970-73 to 25.6 per cent in 1985-88. During the same period imports declined from 33.9 per cent to 15.3 per cent. Taking individual commodities as in 1985-88 the highest share in total agricultural exports was recorded for Coffee, Tea, Cocoa i.e. 35.0 per cent followed by 14 per cent for fruits and vegetables. There was a trend of increase in the shares of both in 1980s. As regards imports, Vegetable oil accounted for the highest proportion in 1985-88 followed by Fruits and Vegetables. The share of both these commodities recorded an increase in 1980s.

Ratna Reddy and Badri Narayanan[3] examined the trade exports in Indian agriculture for the period 1962-85. They find a continuous decline in the share of agricultural exports from 44 per cent in 1960 to 28 per cent in 1985. Similarly, there was a decline in the share of agricultural imports from 29 per cent to 10 per cent. They also used the data from FAO Trade Year Books for different years. Taking individual commodities regarding the share in total agricultural exports, their results show a decline for Wheat and Wheat Flour, Rice, Cereals and Cereal Preparations, Sugar and Honey, Raw Cotton, Jute, Tobacco and Feeding Stuff. An increase was noted only in respect of Fruits and Vegetables, Coffee, Tea, Cocoa, Spices, Oil Seeds and Oils. As regards the share of individual agricultural commodities in total agricultural exports, Fruits and Vegetables, Sugarcane and Honey alone showed an increase.

Singh, Prasad and Dingar[4] studied trends in agricultural trade for the period 1970-71 to 1990-91. They find that the share of agricultural exports declined from 31.72 per cent in 1970-71 to 19.40 per cent in 1990-91. Similarly, the agricultural imports declined from 27.0 per cent to 2.61 per cent in the same period. They used the data from the reports of Economic Survey, Govt. of India, New Delhi. Taking individual commodities and considering only for the period 1980s Rice, Sugarcane, Tobacco, Raw Cotton, Fruits and Vegetables, Oil Cakes, Spices, Cashew Kernels and Fish and Fish preparations showed an increase. Considering 1990-91, the major commodities of exports are Tea and mate, Raw Cotton, Fish and Fish preparations. As regards imports, Oil seeds and oil accounted for a major proportion.

Though all the three studies throw some light on the trends, they do not focus on the differences in the post-liberalisation period as compared to pre-liberalisation period.

PART – II

VARIATIONS IN FOREIGN TRADE IN AGRICULTURAL COMMODITIES BETWEEN THE POST AND PRE LIBERALISATION PERIODS

Pre-liberalisation period, taken here, represents the average of 1988-89 and 1989-90. For the post-liberalisation period the average of 1990-91, 91-92 and 92-93 is considered. The database for the study is from the Reports of Economic Survey, Govt. of India, 1993-94. The changes studied relate to variations in :

1. Total agricultural exports and imports measured in quantity, measured in Rupee values and measured in US Dollars;
2. Pattern of agricultural exports and imports;
3. Growth rate of individual agricultural commodities
4. India's share in World Trade;
5. Share of exports in total production; and
6. Trends in Unit value Index of exports for individual commodities.

Variations in Total Agricultural Exports and Total Agricultural Imports

The annual average value of agricultural exports in Rupee terms is almost double in the post-liberalisation period as compared to pre-liberalisation period. Such an enormous rise in Rupee terms is mainly due to devaluation of Rupee in the post-liberalisation period. But the share of agricultural exports in total exports, when measured in Rupees rises only from 16.93 per cent to 18.27 per cent. Yet, it should be recognised that this is a reversal of trends of decline in the share observed in the past. In Dollar terms also there is a rise in the agricultural exports. But the rise is not spectacular. In Dollar terms, the rate of rise is around 21 per cent for a period of more than two years. (If mid points of the two periods are considered the difference between the periods is two and half years). Even when measured in Dollar terms, the share of agricultural exports in total exports rises from 18.29 per cent to 18.55 per cent.

When compared to the past trends, there is a reversal of declining trend in the share of agricultural exports in post-liberalisation period. But in comparison with long-term trend of growth rate measured in Dollars, which recorded an annual rate of 8.30 per cent between 1970-71 and 1989-90, there does not appear to be a rise in the post-liberalisation period.

Agricultural Imports

As in the earlier studies, agricultural imports show a declining trend. The decline is much more when measured in Dollar terms than when measured in Rupee terms. The share of agricultural imports also declined steeply both measured in Dollar terms and Rupee terms. The rate of decline of -47.67 per cent may be compared with the past trends between 1970-71 and 1985-86, when imports increased at the rate of 3.18 per cent. In brief the liberalisation period is marked by an increase in the growth rate of net exports of agricultural commodities.

Variations in Exports of Individual Agricultural Commodities

The individual commodities covered are those shown in Economic Survey 1993-94 and includes 13 commodities. The Economic Survey aggregate for the 13 commodities is more than the figures obtained when individual items are added. Apparently, there are some unspecified commodities included in the aggregate figures.

Post-liberalisation period shows a decline in the share of traditional items like Coffee, Tea and mate, and Spices. These accounted for 31.12 per cent in pre-liberalisation period. In post-liberalisation period, the corresponding figures was only 22.54 per cent. On the other hand, share of Fish and fish preparations. Rice, Cashew Kernels, Oil cake, Sugar and molasses and Raw cotton, showed an increase. The most spectacular increase was in respect of Raw cotton. In the post-liberalisation period, Fish and fish preparations emerged as the No. 1 export commodity in value terms (17 per cent in the total agricultural exports).

Rate of Growth : Post-Liberalisation Period compared to Pre-Liberalisation Period

Considering quantity, traditional items like Coffee, Tea and mate show a decline. Tea production has almost been stagnant for the last six years. Coffee production showed a sharp decline in 1990-91 and in 1991-92 as compared to the period 1989-90. It showed a rise again in 1992-93. But besides production, international developments have also affected trends in the export of Coffee and Tea. As in 1991, 56 per cent of the Tea exports and 57 per cent of the Coffee exports were accounted for by the erstwhile USSR[5]. The disintegration of USSR has resulted in a decline in demand for Tea and Coffee and in future this is likely to cause much more difficulty for Indian trade. There are however, differences in Coffee and Tea which need to be noted. The decline in exports of tea is both due to stagnation in production as well as increase in domestic demand, whereas decline in quantity of exports of Coffee is due to decline in international demand coupled with decline in production. Both these commodities show a decline in earnings in Rupee value also despite downward adjustment of the exchange rate of Rupee because of fall in international price in Dollar terms. World market for Coffee has been characterised by falling prices. With suspension of quotas since July 1989, market forces have shaped the fortunes of the world coffee market. In terms of Dollar value, the post-liberalisation period is marked by a fall of 20 per cent.

The other commodity showing a declining change in Dollar earnings is Spices. This is inspite of increase in productior by 18.54 per cent in the post-liberalisation period as compared to pre-liberalisation period.

Export of Spices has suffered because of fall in unit value realisation. Small Cardamom, which till recently was a major export item has dipped into low levels of export due to increase in home consumption and competition from other sources (Economic Survey, 1991, P.154).

Exports of Oil cakes showed a declining trend in percentage terms, from 1970-71 to 1985-86. Since then, they have shown on upward trend. The post-liberalisation period has been marked by an increase in the export of Oil cake. Oil cakes occupied the third rank in Million US $ in terms of value of exports : the first two being Fish and fish preparations and Tea. A sharp increase in the production of Oil seeds in the post-liberalisation period has been the contributing factor for increase in Oil cake exports.

Even in respect of Oil cake the decline in international prices resulted in a lesser percentage change in Dollar value as compared to the percentage change in quantity. A critical issue is whether India should export oil cake or use it domestically.

Tobacco exports in the post liberalisation period increased mainly because of high levels of production from 1990-91 to 1992-93 as compared to the earlier period. It must be noted that the percentage share of Tobacco in the exports to erstwhile USSR was around 42.0 per cent.[6] Tobacco is one of the few commodities for which the percentage change in Dollar terms exceeds the corresponding change in quantity terms. This is due to shift in trade to the general currency area in the post-liberalisation period. It is doubtful whether these favourable circumstances will continue in future.

Production of Cashew nuts expanded as a consequence of various development schemes. Increase in quantity of exports is mainly due to increase in production.

Sugar and Molasses show an enormous increase in exports in quantity, and also in value terms during the period because of low values earlier. This is due to favourable weather conditions, price incentives, increase in productivity of Sugar cane and developmental measures. It is one commodity for which the percentage change measured in Dollars is more than the percentage change measured in quantity since international prices showed a rise.

Raw cotton is another commodity which shows enormous increase in percentage change of exports. This is mainly because production during liberalisation period by far exceeded the domestic demand and exports were allowed freely. But in this case, unit value of index in terms of Dollar appears to have fallen and percentage change in Dollar value is less than the percentage change in quantity.

The change in exports of Rice is due to the policy of exports of Basmati Rice. In this case, the percentage change measured in US dollars is much less than the percentage change measured in quantity indicating a fall in the unit value index of exports.

Fish and Fish preparations have been rising continuously. The exports have responded to increase in production. But even here, percentage change in dollar earnings is less than percentage changes in quantity.

Though there is considerable scope for exports of Fruits and Vegetables, there are several obstacles in promoting exports. Measured in Dollar terms, the percentage change is the least. Miscellaneous processed fruits show even lower percentage increase measured in dollar terms reflecting the poor share of processed items in exports.

In brief, the liberalisation period witnessed an increase in the share of agricultural products both in quantity and in dollar terms. However, the rate of growth per annum in Dollar terms is not more than what was observed in the past. Further, for many export commodities, the percentage change in dollar earnings was less than the percentage change in quantity indicating declining unit value.

India's Share in World Exports

The total world agricultural exports measured in Dollar terms have grown at the rate of 7.79 per cent between 1985-1991 when measured in dollars. Indian exports in this period, measured in dollars increased only by 2.28 per cent. Considering individual commodities, the share of Indian exports in World Trade has declined except in the case of Cereals and Cereal preparation, Rice, Feeding Stock, and Oil Seeds. The share of India's traditional exports, in World trade, such as Tea and Mate and Spices show a sharp decline. India's share in World trade in Tea which was 26.00 per cent in 1985 was only 18.5 per cent in 1991. Spices declined much faster. The share was 19.3 per cent in 1985 and only 8.7 per cent in 1991. In brief domestic liberalisation has not helped India to gain a higher share in world trade as compared to the past.

Liberalisation - Production & Exports

The post-liberalisation period is marked by higher levels of production and also higher levels of export in respect of Rice. The share of rice exports in rice production rose from 0.68 per cent in 1990-91 to 1.50 per cent in 1992-93. Production of Cotton exports fluctuate largely from year to year. As against 8.73 per cent co-efficient of variation for the period 1985-86 to 1992-93 in respect of Rice, the corresponding co-efficient of variation is 43.63 per cent for Cotton. The exports show much larger instability than even production, the co-efficient of variation being 19.70 per cent. The share of exports in total production which was 22.37 per cent in 1990-91 fell down to 3.23 per cent in 1992-93. Adhocism in Cotton export policy as a result of pressures from different competing groups results in frequent and abrupt shifts in export policy of Cotton. Sugar production shows a consistent rise over the period. The exports also show a steep rise from 1990-91 to 1992-93 both in absolute terms and as a share of production. As a share of total production exports rise from 0.79 per cent to 2.10 per cent. But over a period instability in exports has been high, the co-efficient of variation being 97.51 per cent. Edible Oil imports have been responding to expanding oil production. With a rise in oil production in the post liberalisation period, the share of import of edible oils has fallen from 2.83 per cent to 0.51 per cent in 1992-93. Coffee production and Coffee exports have been stagnant in the post-liberalisation period. This is a mainly due to fall in international demand as suggested earlier. Tea exports have also been stagnant in the post-liberalisation period due to rise in domestic demand as well as stagnancy in production levels. The percentage share of Tobacco exports has shown a rise in the liberalisation period due to increase in levels of production as well as shift to general currency area. Fish exports have shown much more marked increase in the post-liberalisation period as compared to other commodities.

What is important to note is the marked instability in exports despite the observed trends of increase in post-liberalisation period.

Direction of India's Trade

The developed countries account for the bulk of exports and imports in India. Out of the developed countries, European Economic Community and USA has a major share. The post-liberalisation period shows a much more dependence on these two countries for exports of India. As compared to developed countries, the trade with LDCs formed only 15.4 per cent in

1989-90. Even after a rise in the post-liberalisation period, trade with less developed countries formed only one-fifth of the total exports of India. Even if further countries are added to the categories of LDCs the trade with LDCs is not more than 30 per cent in the post-liberalisation period. As regards imports, there was a decline in the trade with LDCs and increase in trade with OPEC countries because of a rise in the import of petroleum products. What needs to be noted is that the post-liberalisation period is marked by much more dependence of India on trade with developed countries of European Economic Community and USA.

Unit Value Index of Exports in India : Trends

The general index of Unit Value of Exports with base 1978-79=100 shows a rise since 1984-85 and upto 1988-89. Terms of trade which have been rising upto 1988-89 show a fall in the post-liberalisation period. Taking agricultural commodities, for which we have data only for the period 1984-85 to 1988-89, unit value index shows a fast rise for fish and fish preparations, Fruits and Vegetables, Crude animal and Vegetable material and Leather and leather manufacturing products. The least rate of rise is shown in respect of Coffee and Tea.

In brief the post-liberalisation period is marked by a decline in terms of trade of even agricultural commodities.

Trends in Exports in Post-Liberalisation Period and Critical Issues

1. Though it is seen that there is a relationship between exports and production, the regression studies suggest statistically significant relationship only in the case of sugarcane. In most commodities exports are found to be volatile fluctuating largely from year to year. The

prospects of steady growth of exports essentially depends upon sustained increase in production. The yield rates of production of most commodities have been growing at around 3.0 per cent. This is hardly adequate to meet the domestic demand given higher levels of incomes and higher nutrition levels.

2. Secondly, there is a conflict of interest between farmers and consumers in respect of exports. Marginal scarcities due to exports result in rise in domestic prices leading to an uproar from the consumers for stoppage of exports. Marginal increase in production of individual commodities are also likely to result in sharp drop in prices, resulting in plea for export from farmers. Thus, there is a need for reconciling the interests of the consumers for fair prices and producers for remunerative prices and for measures for stabilising domestic agricultural prices.

3. Border prices are some times seen as guides for designing an export policy. If border price exceeds the internal price, it is taken for a tax on agriculture and for promotion of exports to reduce the tax discrimination. If the border prices are seem to be less than internal prices, it is seen as subsidy for agriculture and there is a plea for removal of subsidies. Prof. Dantwala in a powerful article doubted the validity of border prices for guiding an export strategy, even when the comparative cost advantage principle is generally agreed to.

4. There is a conflict between the interests of several groups in society, for instance, the farmers are interested in export of Cotton to get a higher price. But the textile mills are interested in reduction of exports for getting cheap raw material and are

interested in export of yarn, the handloom weavers are interested in reasonable prices for yarn and are against indiscriminate exports of handloom yarn. Export policy is likely to be subjected to pressures from competing groups and to adhocism. Abrupt shifts in promotion and reduction of exports are likely to benefit only the traders and not the producers, consumers and handloom weavers. It needs to be considered whether market signals could be used to guide export policy. A maximum price of Raw Cotton may be fixed along with a minimum price for guiding export policy.

5. The conflict between short term interests of producers and long-term gains in terms of stabilisation of prices of agricultural products through the emergence of agro-industry, which under static conditions may be discounted, need to be recognised in formulating an export strategy.

PART – III

GLOBALISATION OF WORLD TRADE UNDER URUGUAY ROUND NEGOTIATIONS AND ITS IMPACT ON INDIAN AGRICULTURAL TRADE

The Uruguay round of negotiations of GATT created a lot of controversy. Opinions on the impact are sharply divided between the opposition party and the government. The farmers groups are also divided on the possible impact : while Sharad Joshi's group favours the Uruguay Round negotiations, Nanjunde Swamy's group is opposed to it. The empirical evidence however is meagre on the possible impact. In this section, we review the available empirical evidence and the likely impact of Uruguay Round of negotiations.

A successful conclusion of the Uruguay Round is expected

to lead to a partial trade reform which will be implemented throughout the remainder of the 1990s. Agricultural tariffs are expected to be reduced by 30 per cent for all agricultural commodities in all regions.

The reduction in tariff is assumed to occur entirely beginning with 1994. All the agricultural input subsidies are to be reduced by 30 per cent. Under partial agricultural liberalisation, the world prices are expected to rise for many of the major commodities; wheat, coarse grains, sugar, meat, vegetable oils and dairy products.

Simulation model conducted by OECD, shows that world agricultural prices with partial agricultural reforms rise : (percentage change in 2002 from base simulation 1984) for wheat 5.9 per cent, sugar 102 per cent, coarse cereals 3.6 per cent, beef, veal and sheep 4.7 per cent, other meats 1.0 per cent, vegetable oil 4.1 per cent, tea 3 per cent, dairy products 7.2 per cent, wool 2.0 per cent, cotton 3.7 per cent, other agricultural products 5.9 per cent, coffee -6.1 per cent, cocoa -4.0 per cent. Total agricultural trade reform is expected to result in much higher rise in prices.

In many regions, particularly OECD regions, production of agricultural commodities is significantly protected and the consumer price is high. A reduction in the rate of protection in these countries leads to a reduction in production and rise in world prices.

In terms of gains, partial agricultural trade liberalisation is expected to lead to a global gain of \$190 billion per annum. Of this amount, \$ 120 (billion) accrues to OECD countries and \$ 70 (billion) to the developing regions.

India's share in agriculture in world trade which had been declining is expected to rise as a result of the GATT negotiations. It is however, difficult to say how much India will gain since it depends not only on the price rise in the world market but on India ability to export. Much depends upon improvement in infrastructural facilities.

The consequence of the trade reforms in non-agricultural sectors, are likely to be also important in judging the impact. As import tariffs are reduced domestic demands for imports increase putting pressure on the trade balance. The countries have to resort to real exchange rate devaluation to increase the exports.

In brief, many trade reforms are likely to benefit developed countries and worsen the position of the developing countries in the short run, unless such reforms lead to a sufficient increase in flow of foreign capital, and opening of domestic markets make producers to innovate, develop new products, improve quality to match stringent standards.

Projections of the OECD from the effects of multilateral partial trade reforms are of interest. India is expected to get negative terms-of-trade shock, since it exports agricultural commodities which fall in price such as Tea and Coffee and is expected to import commodities such as vegetable oils which increase in price.

The scenario presented for rural sector by OECD Study is disturbing. Rural GDP decreases despite the increase in aggregate producer prices. First, there is a reduction in input subsidies raising the cost of production. Second, the increase in producer prices is not uniform. In particular, the world price of rice, tree crops and other foods decline. Third the domestic urban demand decreases because urban food prices increase and this leads to a substitution out of food into other commodities. The substitution effect into non-agricultural goods is strengthened by 30 per cent drop in manufacturing tariffs. Simultaneously, urban incomes decrease due to a rise in unemployment and a decline in the price in urban factors as urban sector is forced to devalue because of the new competition from cheaper imports. Therefore, agriculture demand decreases from a substitution effect and an income effect. Overall, this implies a small gain in rural welfare which is in part offset by a small loss in urban welfare summing to only a small gain in total welfare of about 0.2 per cent of the total base GDP in the year 2002.

Three sets of scenario are used by OECD to assess the impact.[7] The first set revolves round agricultural trade liberalisation in India without and with higher world agricultural prices. The second set concentrates on domestic policy issues such as possible responses to exogenous increases in crop yields and reduction in fertiliser subsidy. The third set is concerned with food subsidy policy. The outcome of these scenarios are simulated using a computable general equilibrium model of the Indian economy. The model has 17 commodity sectors and uses an econometrically estimated supply model for agriculture, which is disaggregated into rice, wheat, coarse cereals and other crops. Its key features are (a) trade quotas are imposed on some sectors (b) wages adjust partially to food prices in the medium run and are determined by market clearing in the long run and (c) it incorporates an econometrically estimated system of equations describing rice and wheat procurement. The base year for the model is 1983-84. The results are reproduced below.

"The trade liberalisation scenarios confirm that industrial protection is responsible for most of the taxation of agriculture while the effects of restrictions on agricultural trade may be large for some commodities, their overall effect on agriculture is small. In addition, since processed agricultural commodities are highly protected compared to the unprocessed commodities, extending trade liberalisation to the former has a large adverse impact on agriculture, resulting in decrease in agricultural prices fuels non-agricultural expansion and the combined effect of these is an increase in the real incomes for all the groups. However, in the long run, these gains are smaller and become negligible for large farmers. When industrial protection is also removed, a large devaluation is needed to keep the balance of payments constant. GDP falls in the medium and the long run. The accompanying removal of constraints in the agricultural trade results in increased price transmission. Elasticities for all unprocessed agricultural commodities except coarse cereals, trade in which is negligible. But, for the other crops, removal of protection and devaluation tend to counter balance each other and price changes little". (pp.13-14).

"However, these gains are undone by the increase in food prices for all but the medium and large farmers. While liberalisation has a desired effect of improving farm incentives, it does little for the urban and the rural poor. This points to a major policy dilemma. The growth enhancing efficiency gains expected from liberalisation are operative only in the long run" (P.14). Measures are required to protect the poor while these gains take effect.

The technical change scenarios demonstrate the key role of price flexibility in determining the distribution of gains from technical change. The observed low output elasticity of labour demand in agriculture suggests that higher food prices affect the poor while the gain from employment resulting from the supply response is likely to be less.

"The fertiliser subsidy scenario confirms in a general equilibrium system, what has long been argued in a partial equilibrium framework. The bulk of the subsidy accrues not to the agricultural sector but to the fertiliser sector. A novel finding emerging from food subsidy scenarios is an increase in procurement and subsidised sales, if financed by an increase in indirect taxes, results in lower real incomes for all households including the recipients of the increase in subsidised sales. However, if the increase is financed by an increase in direct taxation of large farmers and urban capitalists, it results in substantial benefits for the recipient household groups. Thus, the distortionary costs of increased indirect taxation are larger at the margin than the marginal increase in income for the groups receiving the subsidy." (P.15).

In brief while globalisation may benefit the large farmers in India as a result of rise in the world prices and through access to the markets of developed countries, its distribution effects are likely to be adverse to the poor. Measures will be needed to protect the poor against such effects, it may be advisable to go slow on Globalisation.

SUMMARY AND CONCLUSIONS

This paper sought to capture the effects of domestic liberalisation on agricultural exports by comparing the post-liberalisation period 1990-91 to 1992-93 with pre-liberalisation period 1988-89. The findings are as follows :

As compared to the past trends there is a reversal of decline in trend in the share of agricultural exports in the post-liberalisation period. The rate of growth of the post-liberalisation period compared to the pre-liberalisation period is not however much higher than the growth rate of 8.30 per cent observed between 1970-71 and 1989-90. Agricultural imports declined at a faster rate as compared to the long term trend. The post-liberalisation period is marked by an increase in growth rate of net exports of agricultural commodities. Considering variations in exports of agricultural commodities, there was a decline in the rate of growth of traditional commodities, like Tea, Coffee and Spices and an increase in the rate of growth of commodities like Fish and fish preparations. In respect of most commodities, the percentage increase in value terms in Dollars is less than the percentage increase in quantity since the international prices appeared to have declined. Coffee, Tea and mate and Spices show a decline in values in the post-liberalisation period as compared to pre-liberalisation. Though exports in the post-liberalisation period appear to be related to production, there is no statistically significant relationship between production and exports except in the case of sugar. Exports are marked by high instability as measured by co-efficient of variation much more than instability in production and prices. In the absence of sustained growth of agricultural productivity, export promotion becomes difficult because of the competing interest of consumers and farmers and industrialists. Adhocism in exports is likely to benefit the traders much more than the producers and consumers.

As regards Globalisation and the impact of GATT Uruguay Round Negotiations on Indian agricultural exports, large farmers may benefit in the short run by the rise in world prices as Indian agricultural products may become more competitive. But this is however, conditioned by the policies of developed countries with regard to non-tariff barriers. The short-term impact of Globalisation is likely to be adverse on the poor. The poor will suffer much more by the rise in food prices and their employment gains will be small due to low elasticities of employment to output in agriculture.

Notes

1. Agricultural Trade Liberalisation and India, Ed., by Shankar Subramaniam; Development Centre Studies, Paris, P.26.
2. Ramesh Chand and S.C. Tewari, "Growth and Instability of Indian Exports and Imports of Agricultural Commodities", Indian Journal of Agricultural Economics, April-June, 1991, Vol. XLVI, No. 2, P.159.
3. Ratna Reddy, V., and Badri Narayanan, K. : "Trade Experience of Indian

Agriculture : Behaviour of Net Export Supply Functions for Dominant Commodities", Indian Journal of Agricultural Economics, January-March, 1992, Vol.XLVII., No. 1, P.49.

4. R.I. Singh, V. Prasad and S.M. Dingar : "Indian Agricultural Policy in the Context of New Trade and Industrial Policy", Indian Journal of Agricultural Economics, July-Sept. 1992, Vol. XLVII, No.3, pp. 357-359.
5. "India's Exports to Eastern Europe and former USSR - A Study of Past Trends", Export Import Bank of India, Occasional Paper No. 19, June 1993, P.3.
6. "India's Exports to Eastern Europe and former USSR - A Study of Past Trends", Op.cit., P.3.
7. OECD, Development Centre Studies ; Agricultural Trade Liberalisation and India by Shankar Subramanian, 1993, pp.13-41.

* This section is based on the OECD publication, Trade Liberalisation : Global Economic Implications by Ian Goldin, Odin Knudsen and Dominique van der Mensbrugghe. (1993).

6

Rural Poverty and Economic Reforms

Opportunities and Constraints*

THIS paper (1) reviews the trends in rural poverty in A.P. for the Pre-economic reform period and highlights the problems in rural poverty at the beginning of economic reform; (2) Reviews the opportunities and constraints of the Economic reform to poverty alleviation in AP and provides an empirical examination of the changing scene; and (3) Presents an outlook for the poor in the medium term.

I. TRENDS IN RURAL POVERTY: AN ANALYSIS

I.1. Review of Trends

Montek Ahluwalia's (1978) pioneering study provides estimates of trends in rural poverty for A.P. for the period 1956-57 to 1983-84. In this study the poverty line chosen was Rs. 15.5 for rural areas at 1960-61 prices. In 1956-57 the incidence of poverty was 53.5 per cent. In 1960s, except for a sharp dip in 1964-65, the incidence fluctuated around 45 per cent. It showed a falling trend only in the 1970s.

A comparison of the incidence of rural poverty in A.P.

---

* A Case Study of Andhra Pradesh

with All-India shows a distinct pattern. For the period 1959-60 to 1961-62, the incidence of rural poverty in A.P. exceeded All-India levels. From 1963-64 onwards and up to 1973-74, it was less than the All-India incidence. This pattern is found to be related to the changing poverty line of A.P. in relation to All India. For the first period (1959-60 to 1961-62), the poverty line of A.P. was higher than for All India; in the second period starting with 1963-64, it was lower. This suggests that the lower incidence of rural poverty in A.P. compared to All-India is related, in part, to lower levels of the consumer price index for agricultural labour (CPIAL).

A.P. was unique in showing not only a trend decline in the incidence of rural poverty, but statistically a significant decline (Ahluwalia 1978).

For the period since 1970-71, we have estimates for discrete five year intervals. These are presented in Table-1 for A.P. and All-India.

The estimates differ widely ranging from 20.92 (Expert Group) to 40.76 (CESS) as in 1987-88. The wide differences between the two estimates is due to difference in the sample chosen; the CESS uses the state sample while the expert group uses the central sample. The Planning Commission's estimate and the estimate of Minhas and others are closer to each other. In our judgement the estimate of expert group for A.P. is an under-estimate, and does not match other correlates of rural poverty. For instance as per the expert group, A.P. obtains fourth rank in the incidence of poverty among the major states, as in 1987-88. But its ranking percapita of NSDP was 7th; unemployment rate was 8th. The rank of incidence of rural poverty (9th) as seen by the Planning Commission and Minhas and others matches other correlates of poverty better.

TABLE – 1

Recent Estimates of Rural Poverty in Andhra Pradesh

(Percentage of Persons)

	1964-65	*1970-71*	*1972-73*	*1977-78*	*1983-84*	*1987-88*
Mahendra Dev (1988)						
Andhra Pradesh	41.2		46.7	30.6	19.4	NA
All-India	0.4		50.4	44.2	35.9	NA
Sudhakara Reddy (1991)						
Andhra Pradesh	NA		NA	63.54	NA	40.78
Minhas et. al. (1991)						
Andhra Pradesh		51.57	NA	NA	34.92	31.56
All-India		58.75	NA	NA	50.77	48.69
Planning Commission (1988)						
Andhra Pradesh		NA	NA	45.4	38.7	33.8
All-India		NA	NA	51.2	40.4	33.4
Report of the Expert Group (1993)						
Andhra Pradesh			48.41	38.11	26.53	20.92
All-India			56.44	53.67	45.61	39.06

However, in all the estimates except for the Planning Commission's estimate for 1987-88, the incidence of rural poverty in A.P. shows a decisive decline and is lower than All-India. The rate of decline in the incidence of poverty is also higher in A.P. As in the earlier period starting in 1962-63, this period is also characterised by lower CPIAL and consequently, a lower poverty line for A.P. Rural poverty in A.P. as in 1987-88 was only one-half of the estimate for All-India by the expert group and 60 per cent of the estimate by Minhas and others. It is only in the Planning Commission estimate that both are equal. The poverty line used by the Planning Commission for Andhra Pradesh was same as All-

India poverty line which was Rs. 130/-. The state specific poverty line used by the expert group committee was the lowest i.e. around Rs. 92/-.

I.2. Agricultural Growth and Rural Poverty in A.P.

Agricultural growth has a potential to reduce the rural poverty, provided, the growth rate of Agricultural production exceeds the growth rate of population and of labour force.

During the period from 1955-56 to 1966-67 the growth rate of agricultural production was less than the corresponding growth rate of labour force or population. This was the period during which there was no significant decline in the incidence of rural poverty. The second period 1967-68 to 1978-79, was associated with Green Revolution. There was an increase in productivity of rice, the major crop, during this period. The growth rate per annum was 3.13 per cent for all crops and 3.89 per cent for foodgrains (Table-2).

TABLE – 2

Growth Rates (Log-Linear) Agricultural Production in Andhra Pradesh 1955-56 to 1992-93

Item	*1955-56 to 1966-67*	*1967-68 to 1978-79**	*1980-81 to 1992-93***
Foodgrains	2.21	3.89	1.2
All Crops	1.71	3.13	2.5

* Agro-Economic Research Centre, Andhra University, Waltair.

** IDPS, MVP Colony, Visakhapatnam

This was higher than the growth rate of labour force and in population. Conditions were created for tightening of the labour market and also increase in Real Wage rate. In this period there was a significant decline in the incidence of rural poverty. The third period, i.e. 1980-81 to 1992-93 was marked by tapering of the spread of Green Revolution, and a lower rate of growth of irrigation. Taking all crops, the rate of growth of agricultural production during this period was only slightly higher than the rate of growth of rural labour force. The rate of growth of foodgrain production was less than the rate of growth of population and labour force. It is surprising that during this period also there was significant decline in the incidence of rural poverty. Growth cannot account for this decline. We have to examine the bearing of poverty alleviation programmes initiated by the Central Government and the State Government since 1980 on the incidence of rural poverty during this period.

I.3. Poverty Alleviation Programmes and Rural Poverty

Public intervention for poverty alleviation included programmes for (a) access to land and water for the poor (b) asset and skill development and access to institutional credit; (c) employment and minimum wages (d) basic needs covering food, public distribution system, shelter, and other requirements for the identified rural poor; and (e) Social security.

The earliest of the public intervention, for poverty alleviation was provision of access to land through land reforms. Of the various programmes, intermediary abolition alone benefited the peasant. Under the land ceiling legislation only 3.03 per cent of the total area owned was declared surplus. Of this less than one-half was redistributed. The surplus distributed formed only 1.43 per cent of the total owned area. Beneficiaries formed only 7.61 per cent of the total owners of below one hectare including, the landless. The total lack of records of rights of tenants and overall insecure tenancies rendered Tenancy Legislation ineffective. In terms of magnitude, the extent of waste land distributed to the land-poor in A.P. was large; between 1969 and 1987; 1.5 million hectares were distributed. There is little available information on the extent to which waste land distribution benefited the poor.

Deprivation of tribals of their land leading to support to the growing Naxalite movement should be considered an important issue for public policy. Tribal deprivation took two major forms: alienation of land, and declining access to forests, a source of tribal livelihood. Government action towards the tribals moved in cycles of indifference and drift (Subba Reddy 1988, 1989).

Public intervention to enable the rural poor to cross the poverty line through development of assets and skills was started during the Fifth Plan period and has assumed importance since 1980. In Andhra Pradesh around 2.5 million rural families, or 60 per cent of the rural poor, were covered under IRDP between 1980 and 1990. Funds utilised per beneficiary family, both subsidy and credit together were of the order of Rs. 4,000 (CMIE 1991).

The TRYSEM programme, in relation to its contribution to self-employment, does not present an encouraging picture (Hussain and Prakash 1988). Its coverage is also small in relation to need and it is not well integrated with on-going development programmes.

A special programme for development of women and children, DWCRA, was taken up in A.P. in the three districts of Adilabad, Cuddapah and Srikakulam as a sub-plan of IRDP in 1983-84. It was extended to two more districts in 1986-87 — Anantapur and Mahabubnagar. Where linkages were established with purchase units, such as tribal welfare hostels in the case of dress making, as in Adilabad district, the units were relatively successful. Promotion of the banking habit through introduction of pass books has been noted as a positive feature.

Public intervention in access to institutional credit for the poor has been assigned a critical role. Ghosh and Patel (1991), in a state-wise examination of access to institutional credit for marginal and small farmers, based on data provided by credit institution for 1986-87, show that A.P. position is better than the All-India position for Cooperatives, regional rural banks, and scheduled commercial banks. This is not, however, very comforting. What needs to be recognised is that only one-fifths of the marginal and small farmers get farm credit from Co-operatives; only 4 per cent from rural regional banks; and only 16 per cent from commercial banks.

With regard to access to institutional credit for agricultural labour households, the debt and investment survey, NSS 37th Round, 1982, reveals a continued poor access of institutional credit for households with assets of less than Rs. 10,000/- to which most of the rural labour households belong. Landlords and money lenders are the major loaning agencies. The poorest continue to be the most disadvantaged in the credit market.

Employment programmes were implemented on a small scale until the beginning of 1980. They were expanded in the Sixth Plan period under the National Rural Employment Programme (NREP) and the Rural Landless Employment Generating Programme (RLEGP). These programmes were modified into Jawahar Rozgar Yojana (JRY) in 1989-90.

The shift from NREP to JRY contributed to interest among elected representatives and to more widespread participation. Not less than 80 per cent of the funds allocated in each district after setting a part 6 per cent for the Indira Awas Yojana (a housing programme for the poor and destitute among SCs and STs on a 100 per cent subsidy) are distributed among village Panchayats in the district.

As of 1989-90, the total resources utilised under JRY in A.P. amounted to Rs. 183 crore and employment generated was 71 million man days (Government of A.P. 1990) – roughly seven man days on the average for 10 million usually employed casual labourers. Assuming 45 days of unemployment under JRY in 1989-90, this covered 15 per cent of the unemployment. This should be considered a significant creation of additional employment.

In the Seventh Plan, the outlay on rural housing was the highest among all the States – as much as 37 per cent of total outlay of Rs. 577 crore on rural housing in All-India was in Andhra Pradesh. Around 14 per cent of rural labour households and 20 per cent of SC households were provided with pucca houses by 1988. This was no mean achievement.

Drinking water supply continues to be a problem. Particularly in the dry and tribal villages. In the canal irrigated villages rural labour needs improved access to protected water supply. The maintenance of hand pump, tube wells leaves much to be desired. The performance of A.P. with regard to the special nutrition programme is found to be poor, not only absolutely but also in relation to All-India averages. Further, A.P. was the only state to introduce and quickly withdraw noon-meal programme, during the Sixth Plan.

The key issues of health policy relate to (1) healthy infrastructure, (2) Primary health care, and (3) integration of the health system with the rest of the social system, including nutrition. A World Bank evaluation study in some districts of A.P. (Subba Rao 1987) showed that progress in immunisation and oral dehydration therapy (ORT) is critical for reduction of infant mortality. It commented on the current inadequacies of the IDS: (1) relative failure to reach children below three years and pregnant and lactating women; (2) poor health and nutrition programmes; and (3) neglect of home visits and community participation.

Until 1983, as in most other parts of the country public

distribution of foodgrains did not cover the rural poor. But the *Two Rupees A Kilo Rice Scheme*, a widespread and popular programme directed to the rural poor introduced by the Telugu Desam Government in 1983, made for a difference.

The public distribution system has changed both qualitatively and quantitatively in A.P. since 1983 with the introduction of the two rupees a kilo scheme. Under the scheme families having an income of Rs. 6,000/- and below per annum, having up to 1.5 acres of wet land under assured water sources, 2.5 acres of wet land under other irrigation source like tanks, wells, etc., three acres of dry land under commercial crops, and five acres of land under other crops, were given green cards, currently called white card. Green card holders are eligible to draw five kgs. of rice per capita per month, subject to a maximum of 25 kg per household per month from the fair price shops. The non-poor are given yellow cards and they are not eligible for rice. The total off-take of foodgrain from the central pool rose from 6.26 lakh tonnes in 1983 to 18.40 lakh tonnes in 1986. The off-take in Andhra Pradesh in 1986 was only slightly less than in Kerala and Maharashtra. There has been extensive coverage of rural areas under the public distribution system and rural fair price shops.

The impact of the two rupees per Kg. rice scheme on the poor depends upon a number of factors; the extent of quota availed; the share of subsidised foodgrain in the total consumption of foodgrains; the price of rice in the open market, and the extent to which the open market price differs from what it would be in the absence of intervention. Notwithstanding several leakages, the benefits to the rural poor from the two rupees a kg. Rice scheme are significant. Though a large percentage of non-poor are included, only a small percentage of poor even in rural areas are outside the purview of the green card system. This accounts for the appeal of this programme. Other gains, such as the improvement of the bargaining power of labourers in the labour market, are also attributed to the public distribution system.

I.4. Growth Versus Public Intervention

Despite a large coverage of the order of 60 per cent of the beneficiaries, sustained benefits from IRDP have been of a low order. Yet the plea for total withdrawal of IRDP and its substitution by NREP is defeatist and misleading. Continuing unequal distribution of land and other assets in rural areas results in wide inequalities in benefits. Employment programmes, however effective, cannot correct these inequalities. Further, there has been little absorption of the landless and land-poor in the urban-industrial sector, even while the surpluses of rich and middle farmers get shifted outside the rural sector. Under these circumstances, IRDP has a role in obtaining a better share in the new assets created in the rural sector, especially in allied occupations such as dairy, poultry, sericulture, pisciculture and horticulture for the land-poor groups, and in easing the pressure on the hired labour market. As allied occupations expand, new opportunities are created in service occupations. What is required again is a closer co-ordination of IRDP programmes with remunerative development opportunities in these areas.

A.P.'s public distribution system in rural areas has been most popular, yet it has suffered on several counts:

(1) It covered the large majority of the poor, within rural areas, no doubt, but it could not exclude the non-poor from its purview. In the Seventh Plan period, only one-fourth of the benefits accrued to the poor. Repeated efforts to eliminate bogus cards did not bear fruit. Sharper targeting continues to be an issue.

(2) The rising subsidies at a fixed supply price have put enormous strain on resources; it is reported that

expenditure on irrigation and power was not at the desired level because of the rising cost on public distribution. This again suggests a need for sharper targeting.

(3) If improved nutrition is the objective, trends in cereal consumption among subsidy users do not show that this is being achieved. Nutrition programmes directed to vulnerable sections should supplement a better targeted public distribution programme.

Despite inadequacies in the implementation of rural poverty alleviation programmes the contribution of IRDP, employment, public distribution system, housing and social security to the reduction in the rural poverty was quite significant during the period when growth rate was poor. Our estimates in an earlier paper (EPW, 1995) showed that the total benefits for poor households after several adjustments for leakages etc. per annum during the VII Plan period were as follows (Parthasarathy, 1995, EPW, Oct., 14-21, pp. 2584).

IRDP	: 50 crores
Employment	: 58 crores
POs	: 47 crores
Housing	: 8 crores
Social Security	: 4 crores

The percapita benefits for rural people during the VII Plan period was estimated as Rs. 7.75 per month. The P.C.I. of the rural poor in 1987-88 was Rs. 85/- per month. The P.C.I. of the rural poor would have been less by the Rs. 9/- in the absence of public intervention.

The data show that employment programmes confer more benefits on the poor than IRDP. The percentage benefiting among agricultural labour from IRDP assistance exceeds the corresponding percentage among self-employed. In terms of beneficiaries the maximum number of beneficiaries are from PDS. By caste group SCs are far better than all in respect of IRDP assistance. The landless and near landless proportion benefiting from IRDP and public works is not much more than for other landed categories. By per capita expenditure class the poorest of the poor are better represented than other groups in respect of public works.

I.5 Regional and Other Aspects of Incidence of Rural Poverty and the Characteristics of Rural Poverty at the beginning of Economic Reform

The CESS study based on state samples (Sudhakar Reddy, 1991) throws considerable light on the district wise incidence of poverty and the changes between 1977-78, and 1987-88. Based on district-wise data we provide in Table-3 regional distribution of incidence of rural poverty in Andhra Pradesh.

TABLE – 3

Regional Distribution of Incidence of Rural Poverty

	1977-78	*1987-88*	*Percentage Decline*
North Coastal Andhra	73.81	48.73	-33.69%
South Coastal Andhra	53.83	32.89	-38.86%
Rayalaseema	67.59	49.37	-26.66%
Telangana	66.88	44.65	-33.24%

Source: S. Sudhakar Reddy, "Poverty and Agricultural Growth in Rural Ads. P.", Sept. 1991.

Data for Coastal Andhra is presented under two groups, North Coastal Andhra, bordering Orissa, the former zamindari area depending on tank irrigation. South Coastal Andhra covers the deltas of Godavari, Krishna and pennar, Rayalaseema comprises of drought prone districts. Telangana is the semi-fuedal area with intense naxalite movement, which was formerly under Nizam's rule.

The incidence of rural poverty as per 77-78 was the highest in North Coastal Andhra and the least in South Coastal Andhra. Rayalaseema and Telangana record similar levels of poverty. All regions show a decline in poverty, but the decrease is the least in Rayalaseema and the highest in South Coastal Andhra. In 1987-88, the incidence of poverty was highest in drought prone Rayalaseema (See Table-3).

Poverty levels by occupation are shown in Table-4.

TABLE – 4

Poverty Levels by Occupations

	1977-78	*1987-88*	*Percentage Decline*
Self-employed in non-Agriculture	60.91	34.75	-42.89%
Agricultural labour	75.94	54.19	-28.54%
Other labour	59.80	43.38	-16.42%
Self-employed in Agriculture	53.79	28.38	-47.24%
Others	41.31	24.64	-59.55%

Source: S. Sudhakar Reddy, "Poverty and Agricultural growth in Rural A.P.", Sept., 1991.

Agricultural labour recorded the highest level of poverty as in 1977-78 and the least incidence of poverty is among those classified as others, i.e. service categories. In 1987-88 there was decline in poverty in every occupational group. The highest rate of decline was seen among service and trade categories and the least decline was among the labour categories.

As a consequence of these trends, the concentration of rural poor was much more in the backward regions of Rayalaseema and Telangana (Table 5A), and much more among Agricultural Labourers in 1987-88 as compared to 1977-78 (Table 5B.)

TABLE – 5A

Regional Distribution of Poor Persons

	1977-78	*1987-88*	*Percentage Difference*
North Coastal Andhra	13.85	9.57	-30.90
South Coastal Andhra	24.48	25.23	+3.08
Rayalaseema	22.57	24.05	+6.56
Telangana	39.10	40.65	+3.96

TABLE – 5B

Occupational Distribution of Poor

	1977-78	*1987-88*	*Percentage Difference*
Self-employed in non-Agriculture	14.91	10.92	-26.76
Agricultural labour	39.77	56.35	+41.69
Other labour	4.93	6.26	+26.98
Self-employed in Agriculture	36.95	22.54	-39.00
Others	3.44	3.93	+14.24

Source: S. Sudhakar Reddy, "Poverty and Agricultural growth in Rural A.P.", Sept., 1991.

Table-6 shows the incidence of rural poverty by the level of irrigation. Five districts i.e. East Godavari, West Godavari, Krishna, Nizamabad and Nellore with 67.24 per cent as compared to bottom five districts, mostly located in Telangana and Rayalaseema with 16.64 per cent irrigation record less incidence of poverty and a greater rate of decline (Table-6).

TABLE – 6

Changes in Poverty by Level of Irrigation

	Percentage of Irrigation	*Incidence of Rural Poverty*		*Percentage Decline*
		1977-78	*1987-88*	
Top 5 Districts by level of Irrigation: East Godavari, West Godavari, Krishna, Nizamabad, Nellore	67.24	54.12	30.85	-42.99
Bottom 5 Districts by level of Irrigation Mahaboobnagar, Rangareddy, Ananthapur, Kurnool, Adilabad.	16.64	76.71	54.87	-28.47

Sources: 1) Statistical abstract of A.P. 1990.
2) S. Sudhakar Reddy (1991), Op.cit.

1.6. Level of Social Development in Andhra Pradesh at the beginning of Economic Reforms

The level of social development is critical for utilising opportunities provided by economic reform. Literacy provides conditions for learning of skills required for new occupations generated as a consequence of economic reform. Women's literacy is particularly important as it contributes to better enrolment of children in the school, better nutrition and reduced fertility rate. Health for all is also critical for raising the level of productivity of labour. Maternal and child care contribute to reduced infant mortality and thereby reduce fertility.

Only three states Bihar, Rajasthan and Uttar Pradesh show a lesser rate of literacy level than Andhra Pradesh as in 1991. Taking male literacy only Bihar, Rajasthan and Uttar Pradesh show a lesser rate of literacy than Andhra Pradesh. States with lower level of per capita income than Andhra Pradesh record much higher literacy rate. Orissa records only a per capita income of Rs. 3077 in 1991, as against Andhra's Rs. 4728. Yet, Andhra's literacy rate is lower than that of Orissa. Among the agricultural labourers the literacy rates are the lowest. As in 1987-88 agricultural labour households in rural areas formed 39.5 per cent, next only to Tamilnadu which recorded 40.2 per cent. Female work participation rates are the highest in rural Andhra Pradesh. High participation rates, coupled with low literacy rates among them result in poor enrolment of children in the school as the elder children take care of the babies when mothers go out for work. This situation contributes to high dropout rates and cumulatively contributes to high rate of illiteracy.

The trends in literacy rates as seen from Table-7A for Andhra Pradesh, show only a slow Progress. Even while the percentage of literacy has increased the absolute number of illiterates has risen both for males and females. As compared to 1961, 1991 showed more than 50 lakh additional male illiterates and more than 80 lakh additional female illiterates (Table-7A.)

TABLE – 7A

Trends in Literacy Rates in Andhra Pradesh

(In percentage)

	1961	*1971*	*1981*	*1991*	*Women's Literacy as % Male Literacy*
Males	30.2	33.2	39.3	46.05	
Females	12.0	15.8	20.4	27.31	59.31
Illiterates (in lakhs)					
Males	126.79	147.06	164.67	181.92	
Females	156.79	181.08	210.48	238.28	

The districts with high level of irrigation show much higher percentage of literacy than with districts with lower level of irrigation (Table-7B).

TABLE – 7B

Literacy Levels by Quality of Irrigation

	Literacy Rate		*Female Literacy as % of Male Literacy*
	1981	*1991*	
High Irrigation Districts			
A Predominantly Canal Irrigation (East Godavari, West Godavari, Krishna)	25.66	43.41	76.22
Lower Canal Irrigation (Nellore, Nizamabad)	13.40	34.97	59.16
Low Irrigation Districts			
Predominantly Canal Irrigation (Kurnool)	17.07	32.53	48.91
Low Canal Irrigation (Mahaboobnagar, Rangareddy, Adilabad, Nizamabad, Ananthapur)	11.45	31.49	50.21

Within high irrigation category canal irrigated districts, the deltas of the East Godavari, West Godavari and Krishna districts show significantly the highest level of literacy among districts with high levels of irrigation, Nellore and Nizamabad districts with low canal irrigation percentages record lower literacy levels. These also show a higher incidence of poverty as compared to districts with predominantly canal irrigation. Even agricultural labourers show better level of literacy rates in canal irrigated areas as compared to other areas because of access to schools in better irrigated areas. It may be noted that the incidence of rural poverty is the lowest in these districts. The poorer districts in the dry areas no doubt record the highest percentage of illiteracy as well as the highest levels of poverty. The percentage disparities in literacy rates between canal irrigated districts and others show an increase over a period.

Indicators of health and demography are shown in Table-8A for Andhra Pradesh.

TABLE – 8A

Demographic indicators

	1992			*1993*		
	Rural	*Urban*	*Combined*	*Rural*	*Urban*	*Combined*
Crude Birth Rate per 1000 population	25.1	22.3	24.1	31.5	28.4	30.8
Crude Death Rate per 1000 population	10.1	6.0	9.2	11.2	7.2	10.4
Infant Mortality Rate Per 1000 live births	78	42	71	83	54	77

Urban areas show a better picture as compared to rural areas in respect of demographic indicators. Crude birth rates and crude death rates are lower in urban areas, and infant mortality rates are also lower. The percentage rate of decline in infant mortality is higher for urban areas as compared to rural areas. This is due to better access of urban areas to medical facilities. For 1992 Andhra Pradesh picture appears to be better as compared to All-India in respect of three demographic indicators viz. Birth rate, death rate, and infant mortality rate (Table-8B).

TABLE – 8B

3 Year Moving Average of Birth Rates, Death Rates and Infant Mortality Rates in Andhra Pradesh and All-India: 1981-83 and 1990-92

	All-India			*Andhra Pradesh*		
	1981-83	*1990-92*	*% Decline*	*1981-83*	*1990-92*	*% Decline*
Birth rate	33.8	29.6	-12.42	31.2	25.6	-17.94
Death Rate	12.1	9.9	-18.18	10.7	9.3	-13.08
Infant Mortality	107.00	80.00	-25.23	81.0	71.0	-12.34

Source: Sample Registration Bulletin.

But the rate of decline in infant mortality rate between 1981-83 and 1990-92 was only one half of the corresponding decline for All-India. The level of infant mortality in Andhra Pradesh is also much higher than for Tamil Nadu and Kerala. Kerala's infant mortality rate is only one-fourth of that of Andhra Pradesh. Tamil Nadu's infant mortality is around 80% of infant mortality rate of Andhra Pradesh (Table-8C). These show that health development requires much attention in A.P.

TABLE – 8C

Infant Mortality in Andhra Pradesh, compared to other South-Indian States as in 1990-92

State	*Birth rate*	*Death rate*	*Infant Mortality rate*	*Incidence of Rural Poverty*	*Proportion of hunger (1983)*
Andhra Pradesh	25.6	9.3	71.0	20.92	15.51
Tamil Nadu	21.0	8.6	58.0	45.80	17.42
Karnataka	27.0	8.5	73.0	32.82	18.74
Kerala	18.5	6.1	17.0	29.10	18.97

In brief at the beginning of the economic reform, Andhra Pradesh confronted the problem of low social development; especially in literacy and health. The level of social development in Andhra Pradesh does not match the low poverty levels noted by the Expert Group (1992). It has also to reckon with the problem of hard core poverty in rainfed areas and among agricultural labourers.

II. OPPORTUNITIES AND CONSTRAINTS OF ECONOMIC REFORMS

II.1: Review

1. The opportunities opened by the economic reforms have been listed as follows:

The flow of foreign investment supplements domestic investment with a consequential higher rate of growth. This has the potential to expand employment opportunities for the poor. We may call this the growth effect of economic reforms.

1. Economic reforms remove distortions in relative prices by considerably reducing subsidies which are essentially for capital. Such removal of distortions in relative prices, shifts production from capital intensive to labour intensive goods. By eliminating tariffs, economic reforms contribute to domestic efficiency by exposure of domestic industry to international competition. There will also be a shift of domestic industries from import substitution to export promotion, by exchange rate adjustment which reduces the over valuation of the rupee. Economic reforms promote export trade and thereby promotes employment. This we may call the allocation effect.

2. Economic reform is associated with globalisation and entry of India into WTO. India receives benefits by removal of subsidies for agricultural commodities by developed countries with rise in international prices. It also benefits from the adoption of MFN clause in Textiles. The growth in agriculture will benefit small peasants and agricultural labourers and there by reduces poverty. This we may call the trade effect.

3. A commitment to economic reforms to the reduction

of fiscal deficit and the consequent reduction in deficit financing could contribute to a lesser rate of inflation. The poor will gain by reduced inflation rate. This we may call the reduced inflation effect.

We could summarise the opportunities of economic reforms as:

1. Growth
2. Allocation
3. Trade and
4. Reduced inflation

CONSTRAINTS: Each of these opportunities has a constraint:

1. Growth

Market opened up for foreign investment is not an unmixed blessing. MNC's investment pattern need not conform to the most desired pattern for the country. MNC's investments in soft drinks, fast foods etc. distort the allocation of resources. Their technology is likely to be most sophisticated and much more labour displacing. Even if growth is achieved, jobs may not grow. We may be in a situation of job less growth. This is not conducive to poverty eradication.

2. Allocation

A blanket removal of subsidies is not in the interest of the poor. Market prices are not always in the interest of optimum allocation of resources. Backward areas, socially backward castes and vulnerable groups of the society need protection of the state. The policy of 'no subsidy' has contributed to the suffering of the handloom weavers as Janatha cloth subsidy has been removed. Free exports of cotton and cotton yarn have led to abnormal prices of cotton yarn used as input by handloom weavers. This led to loss of employment for many weavers in Andhra Pradesh as they could not manage their business with the abnormal prices of hank yarn. This is only a specific case of general constraint to the expansion of the unorganised sector which has to compete with the organised sector under unregulated market conditions.

3. Trade

The benefits of trade to the poor will depend upon not only with opportunities of trade created by higher prices but also infrastructural facilities within the country and restrictive trade regulations such as non-tariff barriers by the developed countries. That unregulated trade does not always help the poor as illustrated by the conditions of handloom weavers.

4. Reduced Inflation

Though there is a commitment in economic reform to reduce fiscal deficit, we have not been able to reduce it to the targeted levels. Further, the objective of reduction of fiscal deficit is sought to be achieved more by cutting expenditure under social welfare sector and plan expenditure on capital works. The cuts in social welfare sector affect the poor states and the poorer people most. The cuts in capital expenditure, affect growth rate, and consequently affect the employment for the poor.

Conclusion

This preceding review of constraints, suggests that even though economic reform opens up opportunities for poverty alleviation, these opportunities are available only under specific conditions.

II.2 Empirical Examination

Growth

We saw earlier that the growth caused by economic reform

was expected to be higher. The realities are examined with reference to empirical data for the pre-reform and post-reform periods. The initial years of reform were marked by stabilisation programmes. These sought to reduce fiscal deficit and cut the total expenditure, mainly social expenditure and capital expenditure. Further, in order to reduce the balance of payment deficit, imports were severely out. Both these-reduction of agriculture expenditure and import cuts affected growth rates in NSDP and per capita NSDP (See Table-9).

TABLE – 9

Growth Rates of Net State Domestic Product in Andhra Pradesh: Pre-reform and post-reform periods

(At constant prices, 1980-81)

Year	*Growth rate in A.P.*		*Growth rate in All-India*	
	NSDP	*Per capita*	*NSDP*	*Per capita*
Pre-reform Period				
1987-88(*)	9.77	7.89	4.12	1.60
1988-89	15.57	13.52	11.18	8.31
1989-90	4.67	2.91	7.06	4.91
Post-reform Period				
1990-91	1.56	-3.37	4.72	2.45
1991-92	2.53	0.51	0.52	-2.08
1992-93	-2.23	-3.97	4.41	2.72
1993-94	5.17	3.38	4.13	2.52

Source: Survey of Economic Trends, State Plan 1995-96, Vol. VII, Page 22.

(*) Growth Rate over the period of 1986-87 and 1987-88.

Further, agriculture production index for A.P. during the years 1991-92 & 1992-93 was the lowest since 1988-89. Since most poor people in rural areas are engaged in agriculture, the low rate of agricultural growth which was less than the growth rate of labour force, should have contributed to reduction of incomes of the poor people.

Even industrial sector, registered manufacturing as well as unregistered manufacturing growth rates were less than the growth rates of labour force suggesting the growth could not have contributed to employment and incomes of poor during the post reform period.

Table-10 gives the details of the general index of industrial production. It has growth only at the rate of 2.2 per cent per annum during the post-reform period. Manufacturing growth rate stagnated at the pre-reform period level. The preceding review shows that growth rates either in agriculture or in industry could not have contributed to increase in employment and increase in income for the poor during the post-reform period.

TABLE – 10

Index Numbers of Industrial Production, A.P.

(Base : 1970-71=100)

	Mining & Quarrying	*Manufacture*	*Electricity*	*General Index*
Pre-reform period				
Triennium Average for the year ending 1989-90	489.6	315.1	502.2	353.53
Post-reform period				
1991-92	570.70	348.54	633.50	405.10
1992-93	624.43	284.50	625.50	356.90
1993-94	685.40	315.30	690.80	394.80
Average for the Triennium ending 1993-94	626.84	316.11	649.93	385.66
Rate of growth per annum between pre-reform & post-reform period	6.37	Negligible	6.66	2.20

Source: Survey of Economic Trends and State Plan 1995-96.

The preceding survey about industrial production relates to both rural land urban areas together. Since trends in rural poverty are associated with what is happening in rural areas, we need to have a break-up of the trends in production by rural and urban. Such a break-up is available only for 1980-81 in National Account Statistics[1] that too for All-India. In 1980-81 the rural share of NSDP at All-India level was 58.91 per cent. The per capita rural NSDP was Rs. 1245/- as against Rs. 2887/- for urban and Rs. 1625/- for total. The ratio of rural per capita to total and urban was 77 per cent for the former and 43 per cent for the latter. What happened to the rural areas between 1981 and 1994-95 would depend, upon mainly 3 factors.

a) Growth rate of population

b) Growth rate of agricultural production and rural industries in particular, and

c) Terms of trade between rural and urban areas

Growth rate of population in the rural areas was 1.7 per cent per annum. The urban population rate was 3.66 per cent per annum. This suggests that 15 per cent of rural population migrated to urban areas. Normally migration should help to contribute to improve the income for remaining population under conditions of disguised unemployment.

The growth rate of the primary sector between pre-reform and post-reform period was 0.99 per cent per annum in A.P. which is less than the rate of growth of rural labour force of 1.7 per cent. If unregistered manufacturing is mainly located in rural areas, post-reform period gives a growth rate of around 2 per cent which is slightly above the rate of growth of rural labour force. If NSDP from primary production and unregistered manufacturing is aggregated together, we obtain a growth rate of 1.08 which is less than the rate of growth of rural labour force.

The index numbers of wholesale price of agricultural commodities in A.P. for the pre-reform and post-reform periods are examined. (Table-11). The examination shows that the index of wholesale price of agricultural commodities rose sharply during the post-reform period. The index number with 1970-71 as the base in 1990 was 404.1. This rose to 678.2 in March, 1994.

TABLE – 11

Index numbers of wholesale prices of agricultural commodities and wholesale prices of industrial commodities

Year	*Index No. of Agricultural Commodities	** Index No. of Industrial Commodities (base 1982-82=100) Cotton Cloth	Fertilisers	Cement	Iron & Steel
Pre-reform period					
1987	138.41	122	108	139	138
1988	148.28	129	105	127	158
1989	163.70	135	99	141	176
1990	184.10	153	99	162	196
Post-reform period					
1991	219.41	168	99	185	208
1992	281.32	197	128	217	215
1993	257.50	206	182	209	217
1994	308.97	241	180	211	262

Source: * Government of Andhra Pradesh, Survey of Economic Trends in A.P., Vol. VII, March 1987.

** Economic Survey 1994-95, All India Data, Government of India.

This shows the rate of growth of prices agricultural commodities was much higher in the post-reform period as compared to the pre-reform period. We examine the trends in the prices of agriculture commodities in relation to the index of industrial commodities which are bought by the agriculturists. The prices of cotton cloth, fertilisers, cement and iron and steel are chosen for this purpose. In general the latter part of the 80's and early 90's show a rise in terms of trade in favour of agriculture. The post-reform period recorded a price rise in agricultural commodities by 68.20 per cent as compared to the pre-reform period. While cotton cloth prices rose by 58.07 per cent, fertilisers prices by 43.35 per cent, cement prices 44.46 per cent and iron and steel 35.03 per cent. Both in respect of articles of consumption as well as inputs used in agriculture, the relative price movements show a gain for the agriculturists in the post reform period. But the question is whether this gain benefited the poor in rural areas. We saw earlier that there is a concentration of poor among agricultural labourers who do not sell agricultural products, but sell only labour power. Even small producers are net buyers of foodgrains. The issue of benefits to the poor through the rise in the price of agricultural commodities is discussed in the section on inflation.

The money wage rate shows a rise of 8.12 per cent for males where the CIPAL Index for the same period rose by 12.31 per cent. The male workers suffered a loss in the real wages during the post-reform period. The female workers appear to have gained during this period. They too should have lost in the subsequent year since CIPAL Index rose by 36.15 per cent; the highest ever seen in the CIPAL index (Table-12).

Sector wise plan expenditure is shown in Table-13. The total expenditure at constant prices falls below the target expenditure. Expenditure in social services was most affected. As compared to Seventh Five Year plan period average of 343.51 crores of rupees expenditure on social service sector was only 263.36 crores of rupees (Triennium average for the period 1991-92 to 1993-94). This must have affected, in particular, programmes of health and education directed to the needs of the poor.

TABLE – 12

Consumer Price Index Numbers of Industrial Workers, Urban Non-Manual Employers and Agricultural Labourers: A.P.

Month/Year	CPI Nos. for Industrial Workers 1960:100	Growth rate (p.a.)	CPI Nos. for Urban Non-Manual Employers 1960:100	Growth rate (p.a.)	CPI Nos. for Agricultural Labour 1960-61:100		Growth rate (p.a.)	Average money wage rate for field labour		
								Male	Female	Year
Pre-Reform Period:										
March 1985	575	-	562	-	448)		-			
March 1986	617	7.30	599	6.58	459)		2.46	11.09	8.30	1985-86
March 1987	666	7.94	640	6.84	481)	508	4.79	12.77	8.84	1986-87
March 1988	749	12.46	731	14.22	543)		12.89	13.26	9.62	1987-88
March 1989	803	7.21	781	6.84	610)		12.34	14.62	10.64	1988-89
Post-Reform Period:										
March 1990	851	5.98	848	8.58	601)		-1.47	16.98	11.99	1989-90
March 1991	959	12.69	951	12.15	675)		12.31	18.38	19.00	1990-91
March 1992	1135	18.35	1086	14.41	919)	811	38.15	NA	NA	
March 1993	1194	5.20	1169	7.44	925)		0.65	NA	NA	
March 1994	1300	8.88	1263	8.04	937)		1.30	NA	NA	

Source: Survey of Economic Trends and State Plan 1995-96 volume VII P. 33.
S. Sudhakar Reddy (September, 1991)

TABLE – 13

Sectorwise Plan Expenditure: Pre-reform and post-reform period

(At constant prices of VII Plan Period)

Major Sector	*VII Plan period Annual Average*	*1991-92*	*1992-93*	*1993-94*	*Triennium Average*
1. Irrigation	281.46	266.84	340.76	469.85	359.15
2. Energy	208.87	322.19	435.35	370.34	375.96
3. Social Service	343.51	250.17	283.02	356.89	263.36
4. Others	361.41	324.46	433.32	535.86	431.21
Total	1,195.32	1,163.66	1,492.45	1,632.94	1,429.68
Growth rate over VII Plan average		-0.67	4.54	5.34	3.64

Source: Survey of Economic Trends and State Plan 1995-96, Vol. VII. Pp. 42-43.

Items of plan expenditure for pre-reform and post-reform period, which are relevant to the employment and income of the poor, are given in Table-14. For the post-reform period the expenditure is seen at constant prices of VIIth Plan period. Comparison at constant prices of VIIth Plan expenditure shows short falls in respect of dairy development, handlooms, village and small industries, general education, public health, housing, welfare of SCs and STs and Social Welfare.

Rate of Inflation: Pre and Post-Reform Periods

Economic reform, by reducing fiscal deficit, is expected to reduce the rate of inflation. The second year of economic reform was marked by double digit inflation rate. During the 3rd year inflation rate was accelerated as a consequence of fall in agricultural production and also rise in the prices of agricultural commodities. The worst affected by inflation rate

TABLE – 14

Expenditure in pre-reform and post-reform periods in A.P.

(Rs. in lakhs)

Items	VIIth Plan (1985-90) Annual Average	Average of three Annual Plans 1991-92 to 1993-94		Growth Rate per annum at constant prices
		Current Prices	Constant Prices of VIIth Plan	
1. Seri-Culture	351.8	783	491.22	8.70
2. Dairy Development	188.03	98	61.48	-24.38
3. Rural Development	10,320.8	18,981	11,907.78	3.64
4. Land Reforms	294.4	1,134	711.42	24.68
5. Minor Irrigation	3,565.8	6,892	4,323.71	4.94
6. Handlooms	1,265.4	1,915.3	1,201.38	-1.29
7. Village and small scale industries	406.8	427.0	267.88	-9.92
8. Roads	2,580.0	14,950.3	9,379.11	38.08
9. General Education	5,349.4	4,496.3	2,820.76	-14.78
10. Public Health	1,778.4	1,815.3	1,138.64	-10.55
11. Housing	7,200.00	8,368.7	5,250.12	-7.59
12. Water supply and sanitation	6,151.8	10,884.0	6,828.10	2.64
13. Labour and Labour Welfare	561.8	1,422.0	892.10	12.25
14. Welfare of SCs and STs and BCs	7,415.6	6,982.7	4,380.6	-12.33
15. Social Welfare	712.8	431.0	270.39	-21.52
16. Women and child welfare	707.0	1,175.7	737.58	1.06
17. Other Social Services	193.6	498.3	312.61	12.73

Source: Survey of Economic Trends and State Plan 1995-96, Vol. VII, pp. 48-50.

was agricultural labourers in Andhra Pradesh who form around 60 per cent of the total poor. Consumer price index for agricultural labour rose by 36.15 per cent in March 1992 as compared to March 1991, the highest ever witnessed. It was also the highest among all indices. Insights could be got on the sufferings of the people by looking at the trends of average retail price for some of the important items of mass consumption at selected centres in Andhra Pradesh (see Table-15).

TABLE – 15

Average Retail Prices of Selected Items at Vijayawada Centre

(Price per kg. in Rs.)

Items	*1987**	*1990*	*1993*	*Difference between*		*Rate of growth*	
				1987-90	*1990-93*	*1987-90*	*1990-93*
Rice	2.66	3.94	5.95	1.28	2.01	13.99	14.73
Jowar**	1.83	2.74	4.11	0.91	1.37	14.40	14.47
Taurdal	9.90	12.95	16.91	3.05	3.96	9.36	9.30
Bengalgram	5.69	10.63	15.13	4.94	4.50	23.16	12.49
Onions	2.56	2.98	4.56	0.42	1.58	5.19	15.23
Groundnut	24.05	23.33	31.50	-0.72	8.17	-1.00	10.53
Sugar	4.85	5.25	8.13	0.40	2.88	26.77	15.69
Tamarind	7.61	13.62	20.78	6.01	7.16	21.41	15.12
Chillies	11.25	14.19	17.96	2.94	3.77	8.05	8.17
Gur	4.39	8.01	13.54	3.62	5.53	22.20	19.12
Mutton	32.00	43.20	60.04	11.20	16.84	10.52	11.16

* Prices at Rajahmundry Centre

** Prices at Adoni Centre

Source: Statistical Abstract, Andhra Pradesh 1993.

Rice which is the staple food of the poor in Andhra Pradesh recorded annual growth rate of 14.73 per cent during the period 1990-91. The retail price of rice rose by Rs.2/- per kg. between

1990-93. Jowar also witnessed a similar rate of rise. Groundnut oil prices showed very sharp rise in the post-reform period, a difference of Rs. 8/- per kg. between 1990-93. Similarly tamarind, another article of mass consumption showed a rise by Rs. 7/- during the post-reform period over and above Rs. 6/- addition in the pre-reform period. The abnormal rise in the prices of goods of mass consumption has contributed to the erosion in the real income of wage earners.

Employment

The elasticity of employment both in agriculture and non-agricultural sector in A.P. has been showing a considerable decline since 1980. Between the two, agricultural sector shows much poorer elasticity. A number of factors which have been operating within the agricultural sector contribute to the declining elasticity. The maintenance of plough-cattle has declined over a period and tractorisation has increased at a rapid pace. Secondly, area under high yielding varieties has come to a saturation point. Thirdly, the rate of growth of irrigation has declined. Fourthly, there has been a shift away from labour intensive crops like rice to social forestry and fish culture. As a result, labour use per hectare of net sown area has declined from 420 man days in 1977-78 to 379 in 1987-88 (Vaidyanathan, 1986).

We do not have comparable data for the post-reform period but we can reasonably assume that the trends witnessed in 1980s should have continued in the early 1990s also. What prevented a considerable fall in the income for the poor during the 1980s was the step up of employment programmes on public account. The compensation for the fall in private employment by rise in public employment appears limited during the post-reform period. The data surprisingly shows a decline in unemployment rate for rural males as well as rural females both usual status as well as weekly status. A similar decline is recorded for urban females. The urban males show a stagnation in weekly status unemployment and a decline in usual status unemployment rate. But the trend does not match well with the increase in poverty seen in the next section.

Occupational Shifts: Post-Reform Period

For the post-reform period we have data only for 1990-91. These data are shown in Table-16.

For 1987-88 and 1990-91[2], the data shows slight shift of population from the agriculture sector to other sectors in percentage terms. The shift is mainly to tertiary sector; there is a decline in the secondary sector also. Within the tertiary sector the gainers are 'banking and finance' and 'public administration'.

Trends within Rural Areas

What is much more important is to observe the trends within rural areas and to examine this bearing on rural poverty. The relevant data are presented in Table-17.

The rural urban break up shows the primary sector's share in population records a small decline in 1990-91 as compared to 1987-88. The secondary sector in rural area shows a decline both in absolute numbers as well as in percentages. The rate of increase in tertiary sector is also not very significant in rural areas as compared to the urban areas. Thus the gainers of occupational shifts are mostly urban areas.

TABLE – 16

Net Domestic Product of A.P. by Industry and Working Population by Sectors 1987-88, 1990-91

Industry	*1987-88*		*1990-91*	
	Working Population %	*NSDP Rs. (Crores)*	*Working Population %*	*NSDP Rs. (Crores)*
1. Agriculture, Forestry and Fishing	67.75	39.87	66.04	39.82
2. Mining and Quarrying	0.99	0.80	(1 to 2)	0.90
3. Manufacturing	10.16			
a) Registered		7.35		7.49
b) Unregistered		1.73		4.13
			12.84	
4. Electricity, Gas and Water supply	0.22	0.52	(3 to 5)	1.18
5. Construction	2.89	5.60		4.86
6. Trade, Hotels and Restaurants	7.14	16.98		16.57
7. Transport, Storage and Communications	2.39			
a) Railways		0.56		0.56
b) Transport by other Means and Storage		3.46		3.29
c) Communications		0.66		0.67
			21.12	
8. Financing, Insurance, Real Estate and Business Services			(6 to 9)	
a) Banking and Insurance		4.29		6.10
b) Real Estate Ownership of dwelling, and Business services		4.88		4.50
9. Community, Social and Personal Services	8.60			
a) Public Administration		4.20		4.68
b) Other Services		6.02		5.23
Total	(100.00) (27.45) millions	(100.00) (9542.39)	(100.00) *(32.86) millions	(100.00) (11602.12)

Source: Statistical Abstract 1992, A.P., p. 207.
Sarvekshana for 1990-1991 & 1987-88 for occupational data (Figures in Brackets are Absolutes).

(*) The figure is revised by supplying the work participation rate of NSS to Census population of 1991. The work participation rates as per Census are lower and workers as per Census number only around 30 millions.

TABLE – 17

Percentage Distribution of Working Persons by Sector and by Residence 1987-88 and 1990-91 in A.P.

Year	Primary			Secondary			Tertiary		
	Rural	*Urban*	*Total*	*Rural*	*Urban*	*Total*	*Rural*	*Urban*	*Total*
1987-88	65.39 (17.95)	2.95 (0.81)	68.34 (18.76)	8.38 (2.30)	4.92 (1.35)	13.30 (3.65)	9.65 (2.65)	8.67 (2.38)	18.32 (5.03)
1990-91	66.3 (20.80)	2.71 (0.89)	66.00 (21.69)	7.18 (2.36)	5.66 (1.86)	12.84 (4.22)	10.16 (3.34)	10.95 (3.60)	21.01 (6.94)

Source: Derived from Sarvekshana, September 1990, 58th Issue, Jan-Mar 1994, and 53rd Issue, Oct-Dec 1992.

Figures in Brackets are absolutes in millions.

Trends in Per Capita NSDP

Trends in per capita NSDP in the primary sector have a bearing on rural poverty since the primary sector has the largest concentration of rural poor. The trends are presented for the pre- reform period and post-reform period in Table-18. The post-reform period is marked by near stagnation in the per capita NSDP of primary sector. Similar stagnation is seen in tertiary and secondary sectors also. As a result the overall levels of per capita NSDP shows little progress during the post-reform period. This could be attributed to reduced growth rates of NSDP during the post-reform period. Given the widening of inequalities of income, the stagnation of percapita NSDP in primary sector should have contributed to more poverty.

TABLE – 18

Trends in Population NSDP and per capita NSDP: A.P.

(At constant prices, 1980-81)

Year	*Primary Percapita NSDP (Rs.)*	*Secondary Percapita NSDP (Rs.)*	*Tertiary Percapita NSDP (Rs.)*	*Total Percapita NSDP (Rs.)*
Pre-reform period				
1980-81	947	1,794	2,526	1,380
1987-88	967	1,893	3,164	1,535
Post-reform period				
1990-91	1,167	2,163	2,982	1,754
1991-92	1,174	2,063	2,988	1,788
1992-93	1,134	1,824	2,886	1,717
1993-94	1,169	1,844	2,975	1,775

Source: 1. Statistical Abstract: A.P. 1992

2. Survey of Economic Trends and State Plan, Vol. VII, 1995-96.

Occupational Shifts by Gender

Within the rural areas Table-19 shows distribution of population by sectors and by sex for the years 1987-88 and 1990-91. Between the two years females witnessed a larger percentage rise in primary sector as compared to males. Within the rural areas the percentage of rise of females in the primary sector is more than that of males. Within the secondary sector, total females show a rate of rise far less than that of males in urban areas. Within the rural areas, males and females together show a decline in the secondary sector suggesting trends in rural deindustrialisation. In the tertiary sector, there is a positive change for males and females in both rural and urban areas. However the rate of change is less for females. Negative rates of growth in secondary sector for rural males suggest that rural people did not benefit from the occupational shifts in the post-reform period. There is a strong suggestion that rural poverty has risen in the post-reform period.

TABLE – 19

Distribution of Working Population by Sectors and by Sex for 1987-88 and 1990-91

(In Millions)

Year	*Primary*			*Secondary*			*Tertiary*		
	Rural	*Urban*	*Total*	*Rural*	*Urban*	*Total*	*Rural*	*Urban*	*Total*
Males									
1987-88	10.05	0.42	10.47	1.45	0.96	2.41	1.84	1.90	2.74
1990-91	10.53	0.44	10.97	1.18	1.46	2.64	2.41	2.92	5.33
Ratio	1.05	1.17	1.05	-0.81	1.52	1.09	1.31	1.54	1.94
Females:									
1987-88	7.90	0.39	8.29	0.88	0.39	1.24	0.81	0.48	1.29
1990-91	10.27	0.48	10.72	1.18	0.40	1.58	0.93	0.68	1.61
Ratio	1.29	1.15	1.29	1.39	1.02	1.27	1.15	1.42	1.06

Source: 1990-91 - For percentage distribution of workers see Sarvekshana Jan-March 1994 and for population - See statistical abstract.

1987-88 - For percentage distribution of workers see Sarvekshana Sept. 1990 and for estimated persons see Sarvekshana 53rd issue Oct-Dec 1992.

Incidence of Rural Poverty in 1990-91 in Andhra Pradesh

The National Sample Survey Organisation (NSSO) provides data on distribution of persons by Monthly Percapita Expenditure class (MPCE) for the year 1990-91 based on its 46th round data. The distribution of persons over MPCE class in rural areas per 1000 is shown in Table-20.

TABLE – 20

Per '000 Distribution of Households over MPCE Classes in A.P. in Rural and Urban Areas 1990-91

MPCE Classes (Rs.)	*Households*	*MPCE Classes (Rs.)*	*Households*
00-65	7	00-90	35
65-80	34	90-110	29
80-95	39		
95-110	128	110-135	56
110-125	80	135-160	64
125-140	113	160-185	115
140-160	98	185-215	95
160-180	82	215-255	111
180-215	191	255-310	145
215-280	119	310-385	178
280-385	58	385-520	93
385 and above	51	520-700	39
		700 above	40
All Classes	1,000	All Classes	1,000
Average monthly per capita expenditure	186.96	Average monthly per capita expenditure	296.66
State poverty line	114	State poverty line	187
All India	142	All India	179

Source: Sarvekshana, 58th Issue, Jan.-March, 1994, P. 69.

The incidence of rural poverty in 1991 was 22.9 per cent, when the state specific poverty line for 1987-88 as adjusted is applied to the distribution of monthly percapita expenditure of 1990-91. This shows an increase of 2 per cent over 1987-88. Adjusting the All-India poverty line for 1987-88 and applying it to the data for 1990-91[3] we get an incidence of poverty of 49.9 per cent. Similar adjustments made for arriving at urban poverty shows a rise in urban poverty by 20.5 per cent when Planning Commission norm is applied and a fall to

30.5 per cent when the Expert Group norm is applied. We do not have data for period subsequent to 1990-91 for either unemployment or poverty. But, considering that the prices of goods of mass consumption have increased at a faster rate and considering also the fact that many poor have been forced to buy in the open market as a result of weak functioning of the P.D.S., the 1991-92 incidence of rural poverty should have been much higher than that of 1990-91.

III. OUTLOOK FOR THE RURAL POOR IN THE MEDIUM TERM

It was seen earlier that in the short-term rural poor have suffered losses of income and incidence of rural poverty has increased. This result is understandable, since stabilisation programme affected very badly growth rates and plan expenditure on social services and on capital works.

Growth, Demand and Supply Constraints

In the medium term, however, the outlook for the rural poor depends upon the extent of rise in the growth rate, changes in the elasticity of employment to output, the rate of inflation especially of wage goods, the rate growth of rural population and rural urban migration. The growth rate should be a minimum of 5 per cent if all the additional labour force has to be absorbed; given the elasticity of employment to output is around 0.4. Domestic rate of investment will not be adequate for us to obtain even this minimum growth rate, given the rise in capital output ratios and much will depend upon the flow of direct foreign investment. High growth rate alone is not adequate to benefit the rural poor. High growth rate must be achieved in those sectors in which rural poor are concentrated i.e., agriculture and rural industries. But a high growth rate of more than 5 per cent based only on foodgrains faces demand constraint and should be growth based mainly on dairy, poultry, sericulture etc. for which income elasticity of demand is high. But as long as the rural poor are illiterate and lack of access to land, they do not directly benefit from shift to commercialisation or allied products. Since their incomes do not rise a shift to commercial products results in demand constraints within the rural sector. Prices of such products fall with increase in supply in the absence of external demand.

Need for Group Action by the Poor

A small peasant with less than a hectare will not gain from pesticide spraying if he alone sprays and the neighbours do not spray. This becomes critical in view of the shift to crops like vegetables, fruits and flowers, in which both water management and pesticide spraying become important. The gains from globalisation could be got from small farmers only with institution building based on group activity.

Displacement Effects of Growth

Secondly it needs to be recognised growth will not only be employment generating but also employment displacement. Several instances could be cited, handloom weavers are displaced by power looms. The artisional fisherman are displaced by trollers. As a result besides the traditional rural poor new poor groups are generated. Those require protection until they are in a position to get new jobs. They must also be given training for new jobs.

Competition of the Poor with Big Industry and Producers

The entry of big business, domestic as well as foreign into agro-processing and into rural areas will mean that the poor in traditional industry will have to compete with these groups in the input market as well as product market. The basket maker would have to compete with paper mill for bamboo. In this competition the former cannot hope to win. Without support from public agencies to obtain for him a share of bamboo for his business; similarly, the cobbler has to compete with Bata company. Even though cobbler's products are priced low, he cannot match the aggressive advertisement of Bata in the market. So he looses in the battle. The cobbler needs to be helped with appropriate techniques to improve his product and also be assisted to market his products. The outlook for the rural poor in the medium term depends upon the success of public intervention on the behalf of traditional artisans.

Backward Areas and Backwash Effects of Market Forces

We saw earlier the poverty is getting more and more concentrated in rain fed areas and areas with low quality irrigation. Market forces should normally result in flow of capital to backward areas because interest rates are high. But capital will not flow to the backward areas, instead, it will flow to cities like Hyderabad and Vizag for taking advantages of economies of agglomeration. Further backward areas lack infrastructural facilities and cost for private industries per unit will be high. In view of this it will be necessary for the Government to ensure flow of capital to backward areas through subsidies and prevent concentration of industries by public action. The extent to which economic reform will benefit the poor will depend upon the success of public action in inducing the market flow of capital to backward areas.

Elasticity of Employment to Output

The elasticity of employment to output in agriculture has been coming down in recent years. It said to be around 0.4. Currently, divergent trends were with regard to elasticities of employment to output. In Rayalaseema, the shift from millets to ground nuts and horticulture, increase the levels of employment per hectare. But in south coastal Andhra the shift from paddy farms to fish farms has reduced the level of employment per hectare in crop production. The rapid replacement of bullocks by tractors in canal irrigated regions has reduced the need for the permanent farm servants. Initially tractors were not labour displacing (since they were associated with growth of irrigation). In recent years, however, with HYVs saturation, decline in the rate of growth of irrigation, have become labour displacing. The outlook for the poor in the medium term will depend upon the extent to which those displaced in agriculture are given skills in non-agricultural occupations in processing, package, grading, transporting, etc. The extent to which poor could benefit from vocational education will depend upon social development, especially, literacy.

Access to Institutional Credit to Poor

As people drift into unorganised sector and into self-employment or casual labour, the need for improved access to institutional credit will be greater than in the past. One important aspect of institution building is building of credit institutions to meet the requirements of the poor and unorganised. In this context, the Thrift and Credit Societies organised on group basis for women (See Parthasarathy, "Economic Impact of Women's Thrift and Credit Societies", 1995), have been found to serve a useful function. In the dark environment of credit indiscipline, the Women's Thrift and Credit Societies have emerged as torch-bearers of thrift and self-reliance. In performing this function, they also emerge as training grounds for economic democracy for women. But, their success essentially depends upon commitment with which the sponsoring organisation establishes a system and makes it successful. Government assistance may help, but it is not the key factor. The key factor is the role of voluntary organisation which sponsors the group, nurtures it and makes it a self-reliant Thrift and Credit society. The role of enlightened citizens in promoting such voluntary organisations becomes important. But, there is a limit to the success of these organisations in the absence of income-generating activities. Income-generating activities for the members have to meet the constraints of marketing (see Parthasarathy, "Group Lending by Mahila Mandals in the BCT Area, Yelamanchili, Visakhapatnam Dt.", (mimeo) 1993). The tie-up of group activities of women with organised purchasing agencies has been found to be helpful. It is here that government could help promote marketing products of unorganised sector. It should be made obligatory on the part of all public sector employees, who farm the privileged section, to purchase part of consumption requirements from unorganised sectors. Similarly, it must be made obligatory on schools to use the products of unorganised sector for uniform material. This may sound unnecessary and wasteful interference with market and consumer preferences. But, where the trade-off is joblessness and starvation for the many petty producers versus a little discomfort to the privileged sections in the organised sectors, this has to be accepted as a measure towards redistribution of incomes from organised to unorganised sectors.

Reforms in Land Market

Structural adjustments have resulted in pressures from certain sections for relaxing all constraints on land market. There is a plea for relaxing ceiling laws and for unlimited flow of private investments into agriculture and land acquisition. This may be considered desirable if the labour has opportunities outside agriculture and land. In the absence of such opportunities, revoking the ceiling law is bound to displace many marginal and small peasants and accelerate the trends towards casualisation of labour. Such trends will result in a situation where less than 25 per cent alone within agriculture (the present position is 25 per cent of the holders belong to the semi-medium, medium and large farms category) could benefit from the changes brought about by structural adjustment. The success of structural adjustment in Korea, Taiwan, People's Republic of China etc. is attributed to the successful land reforms preceding the New Economic Policy. A widely dispersed agricultural growth benefiting the mass of peasants shifting their consumption patterns to higher levels will be necessary for the emergence and growth of non-farm activities. Even if there is no programme for a fresh piece of land reform, it will be necessary to ensure that current programmes on the statute books are not disturbed.

Terms of Trade and Exports

Economic reform associated with globalisation benefits agriculture essentially in two ways. Firstly domestic prices will be more in conformity with international business and this will benefit agricultural producers. Secondly removal of tariffs will reduce the protection to domestic industry, and will improve domestic terms of trade. Both there will induce the growth of agriculture and there will be perculation of benefits to the rural poor. What is missing in this type of argument is the impact of rise in agricultural prices and cost of living index of the agricultural labourers. The poor need protection through PDS. The outlook for the poor in the medium term will depend upon the extent to which PDS is strengthened.

Industrial Projects and Rehabilitation for the Poor

Many industrial projects are likely to deprive the poor agriculturists of the land. The agriculturists are expected to make sacrifice for the benefit of wider community through industrialisation of the country. It is unfair to deprive the poor agriculturists of his right to occupation and right to life for what is called vaguely 'public purpose'. Since many mineral projects are likely to be located in tribal areas, the tribals are likely to be the worst sufferers. If the newly created poor are not to suffer because of State action, it is necessary to formulate proper rehabilitation plan. A national policy for rehabilitation for displaced person is essential.

Safetynet is a limited concept in relation to the poor in unorganised sector. As a part of the New Industrial Policy, a National Renewal Fund was established vide the Government Resolution on 3rd Feb., 1992 which has three important objects: (a) to cover retraining cost for redeployment of labour in the course of modernisation and upgradation of technology; (b) to provide compensation to employees affected by closure or restructuring of industrial units; and finally, (c) to offer investment funds for mostly self-employment generation in both the organised and unorganised sectors. But the unorganised sector has not so far benefited from this programme (Amit Bhaduri, 1993).

Countries with massive proportion of workers in the unorganised sector have to reckon with the fact that the numbers of these are likely to rise as a consequence of structural adjustments. Safetynets and structural adjustments with human face could hardly bring solutions to their problems. A new approach to development in which the petty producers are made the agents of social transformation through their own organisations which will bring them economies of scale of production, technology, credit and marketing will be found necessary. The newly set up Panchayat Raj institution should help to promote this process. It is unfortunate that in the euphoria of liberalisation and globalisation we are made to forget the most fundamental task, i.e., institution building for mobilisation of the rural urban masses within the unorganised sector for growth, employment and poverty alleviation.

Notes

1. National Account Statistics, CSO 1993, P. 217.
2. Strictly speaking 1990-91 data are not comparable with 1987-88 since the farmer is based on a small sample.
3. The poverty line as per adjustment in 1990-91 was 142 as against 115 in 1987-88 for the rural, and 179 in 1990-91 as against 152 in 1987-88 for urban. This is according to Planning Commission norm. As per expert group, State specific poverty line was 92 in 1987-88 for rural areas and 114 in 1990-91. For the urban areas the poverty line was 159 for 1987-88 and 187 in 1990-91. The adjustments are made by using the CIPAL index for rural and cost of living index for Hyderabad for urban areas.

References

Ahluwalia, Montek (1978): "Rural Poverty and Agricultural Performance in India", *The Journal of Development Studies.*

Bhaduri, A. (1993): "Structural Adjustment, Labour Market and Employment in India", *ARTEP Working Papers.*

Central Statistical Organisation, Department of Statistics, Ministry of Planning and Programme Implementation, Government of India, *National Accounts Statistics, 1993.*

Government of Andhra Pradesh, *Survey of Economic Trends and State Plan*, 1995-96, Vol. VII.

Government of India, *Economic Survey, 1994-95.*

National Sample Survey Organisation, Department of Statistics, Ministry of Planning, Government of India, *"Sarvekshana"*, Sept. 1990 and Jan.-Mar. 1994.

Parthasarathy. G., (1985): "Growth, Stability and Equity within the Agrarian Sector of Andhra Pradesh", Presidential Address to the Third Annual Conference of the Andhra Pradesh Economic Association, January, 19.

Parthasarathy, G., (1993): "Group Lending by Mahila Mandals in the BCT Area," Yelamanchili, Visakhapatnam Dist. Mimeo.

Parthasarathy, G., (1995): "Economic Impact of Womens Thrift and Credit Societies," Institute of Development and Planning Studies, Visakhapatnam.

Parthasarathy, G., (1995): "Public Intervention and Rural Poverty: Case of Non-Sustainable Reduction in Andhra Pradesh", *Economic and Political Weekly*, Oct. 14-21.

Parthasarathy G., (1995): "The Unorganised Sector in the Indian Economy and Structural Adjustment", Centre for Economic and Social Studies.

Parthasarathy, G., (1995): "Employment and Unemployment in Andhra Pradesh; Trends and Dimensions", *Economic and Political Weekly*, April, 15.

Subba Rao, K.: (1987): "Improving Nutrition in India: Policy and Programme and their Impact", World Bank.

Sudhakar Reddy, S.: (1991): "Poverty and Agricultural Growth in Rural Andhra Pradesh: Sinter District Analysis", CESS, Mimeograph No. 1.

Sudhakar Reddy, S.: (1991): "Effects of Irrigation on Levels of Living, Labour Force Participation and Wages: A Case Study of Rural Andhra Pradesh", CESS Mimeograph No. 2, Hyderabad.

Sudhakar Reddy, S.: (1991): "Effects of Agricultural Growth on Labour Force Participation, Unemployment and poverty: The Case of Rural Andhra Pradesh", Mimeograph, Hyderabad.

Vaidyanathan, A.: (1986): "Labour Use in Rural India: A Study of Spatial and Temporal Variations", *Economic and Political Weekly*, Dec. 27.

7

Employment and Unemployment of Youth

Introduction

YOUTH is a prized human resource of any nation and it is important to understand the socio-economic conditions and problems of youth, especially in the changing economic structure for formulating policies for productively mobilising the immense youth power for development. This paper aims to examine: (i) the growth and pattern of employment among youth; (ii) the extent of unemployment among youth; (iii) the changes in the structure of employment of youth; and (iv) the regional dimensions of youth unemployment rates.

The study is based on the NSSO data on employment and unemployment, especially the 38th Round (1983), the 50th Round (1993-94) and the 53rd Round (1997).

The paper is organised as follows. Section II defines youth and provides details of the dimensions of youth in India. Section III examines the growth of employment of youth. Section IV analyses the changes in the structure of employment. Section V deals with regional dimensions of unemployment among youth followed by a brief summary in Section VI.

This paper has been co-authored by K.A. Nirmala.

II. Dimensions of Youth

Youth is defined differently in different countries. In terms of age-group, youth is defined to be in between 15-35 years in India, 15-30 years in Bangladesh, 15-29 years in Sri Lanka, 16-40 years in Nepal and 14-25 years in China (Thamarajakshi, 1987). The International Labour Organisation (ILO, 1985) defines youth in the age-group 15-24 years. In this study, population in the age-group 15-29 years is considered as youth, as these years mainly form the transitional stage from educational to work environments.

Age-group-wise population, workers and labour force are estimated for the 1997 projected census population (population projections as given in the Ninth Plan document) by considering the age-wise proportions as per the NSS 53rd Round. NSS absolutes are not considered as they are underestimates. The dimensions of population, labour force and workers by usual principal status+subsidiary status (UPS+SS) for children, youth and non-youth (30+population) and total population are furnished in Table 1. The total youth population is 256.39 millions as in 1997, i.e., about 27 per cent of the total population of 949.89 millions. Of the total youth population, 124.09 millions are females and male youth are estimated to be 132.30 millions. The sex ratio for the total population is 921 while among the youth population, it is slightly better as there are 938 females per 1000 males. The 30+ population form about 37 per cent of the total population.

There are 134.92 million youth workers, i.e., a work participation rate (WPR) of 52.62 by UPS+SS. The WPR for the 30+ population is 66.38 per cent and for the total population, it is 40.21 per cent only. A little over one-third of the total workers and the total labour force are in the age-group of 15-29 years.

TABLE – 1

Age-wise Distribution of Population, Workforce and Labour Force, UPS+SS : All-India 1997

(millions)

	0-14	*15-29*	*29+*	*Total*
Population	340.59 (35.86)	256.39 (26.99)	352.86 (37.15)	949.89 (100.00)
Workforce	12.82 (3.36)	134.92 (35.32)	234.24 (61.32)	381.98 (100.00)
Total Labour Force	13.11 (3.37)	140.75 (36.21)	234..88 (60.43)	388.71 (100.00)

Note : Figures in Brackets are Percentages to Total.

Source : Derived by adjusting the 1997 projected census population to the age-wise proportions of NSSO, 53rd Round (1997).

An examination of the rural-urban data indicates that 72.55 per cent of the youth population lives in the rural areas, a little less than the total population of 74.28 per cent (Table 2). Youth workers in the rural areas form 36 per cent of total workers while in the urban areas, they form about one-third of the total urban workers. Youth form 36.47 per cent and 35.27 per cent of the total labour force in rural and urban areas, respectively. Among females, the proportion of labour force in the total labour force is about 35 per cent, both in rural and urban areas, but male youth in rural areas form a little higher proportion of the total labour force compared to urban youth.

TABLE – 2

Age-wise and Sex-wise Distribution of Population, Workforce and Labour Force for Rural and Urban Areas, UPS+SS, All-India, 1997

	Rural				Urban			
	0-14	*-29*	*29+*	*Total*	*0-14*	*15-29*	*29+*	*Total*
Male								
Population	138.95	95.98	131.82	366.77	42.07	36.32	49.18	127.58
Workforce	6.22	73.24	122.27	201.72	1.12	22.08	43.21	66.47
Total Labour Force	6.41	75.59	122.49	204.29	1.17	24.4	43.47	69.15
Female								
Population	122.43	90.04	126.38	338.87	37.14	34.05	45.48	116.67
Workforce	4.97	34.59	58.98	98.61	0.51	5.01	9.78	15.28
Total Labour Force	5.01	35.13	59.05	99.29	0.52	5.63	9.87	15.98
Person								
Population	261.38	186.02	258.2	705.64	79.21	70.37	94.66	244.25
Workforce	11.19	107.83	181.25	300.33	1.63	27.09	52.99	81.75
Total Labour Force	11.42	110.72	181.54	303.58	1.69	30.03	53.34	85.13

Source: Same as for Table 1.

III. Employment Growth in 1980s and 1990s

The Eighth Plan document summarises the employment growth during the decade 1977-78 and 1987-88. During the decade, employment increased at about 2 per cent per annum with relatively higher rates in urban areas over rural areas and male employment growth over female employment growth. Sector-wise, all major sectors except agriculture experienced over 3 per cent per annum growth of employment. However, there was deceleration of growth between 1983 and 1987-88 over 1977-78 and 1983, in all sectors except agriculture. Decelaration in the rate of employment has been particularly sharp in the organised sector. Despite a slow and declining rate of employment growth in the aggregate, employment of the educated has shown a relatively high and accelerating growth, particularly among women. Sharma (1997) examined the growth of employment from 1977-78 to 1993-94. Even during this period the UPS employment growth exhibits the same feature as between 1977-78 and 1987-88. But the details of employment growth given in the Eighth Plan document and those discussed by Sharma (1997) were for the total population. In this section, we examine the growth of employment for youth and all ages between 1983 and 1997. During this period the long-term growth-rate of employment at the All-India level was 1.78 per cent per annum for the total population while youth employment grew by 1.44 per cent per annum only (Table 3). Urban employment growth was better over rural areas for all groups except male youth. Rural male youth employment grew at 1.87 per cent per annum, while in urban areas the growth was only 1.64 per cent. In general, growth of youth employment was lower than the total employment growth and female employment growth was lower than male employment growth. An examination of the growth-rates for the two sub-periods, i.e., 1983 to 1993-94 and 1993-94 to 1997, shows wide variations in the growth-rates of female employment, both in rural and urban areas. Between 1993-94 and 1997, female employment of youth recorded negative growth-rates. Even in urban areas, the growth-rates declined sharply between 1993-94 and 1997 over the previous sub-period. The growth rate of female employment in rural areas show a continuous slide. Sharma (1997) provides growth-rates for 1977-78 to 1983. The negative growth of female employment in the post-reform period indicate that reforms had an adverse effect on rural female employment.

TABLE – 3

Growth of Employment (UPS): 1983 to 1997

(per cent per annum)

	1983 to 1993-94		*1993-94 to 1997*		*1983 to 1997*	
	Youth	*All*	*Youth*	*All*	*Youth*	*All*
RM	1.71	1.96	1.85	1.50	1.87	1.97
RF	0.61	1.04	-0.65	-0.44	0.29	0.69
RP	1.37	1.68	1.14	0.95	1.41	1.59
UM	1.57	2.50	1.44	2.30	1.64	2.62
UF	1.45	2.31	0.66	0.19	1.33	1.86
UP	1.55	2.46	1.32	1.94	1.59	2.49
All-India	1.41	1.86	1.18	1.18	1.44	1.79

Note : RM = Rural male; RF = Rural female; RP = Rural persons; UM = Urban male; UF = Urban female; UP = Urban persons; 'All' indicates all ages.

Source : (a) NSSO Reports of 38th, 50th and 53rd Rounds.

(b) Population estimates are based on 1981 and 1991 censuses and population projections provided in Government of India - Economic Surveys and Ninth Plan document.

Sector-wise Growth of Employment

During the 80s, tertiary sector employment in general showed impressive growth-rates over the other two sector, i.e., primary and secondary. This is found both in youth employment and all age-groups through the growth-rate of youth is lower compared to all ages (see Table 4). In the rural areas, male tertiary employment grew faster and in the urban areas, females. Correspondingly urban females recorded negative growth in the primary sector both among youth and all ages. During the 90s, the primary sector recorded negative growth-rates both for males and females in urban areas while in rural areas there is a perceptible growth in the 90s as compared to the 80s. The secondary sector showed modest growth-rates between 1983 and 1993-94. Urban growth-rates

TABLE – 4

Sector-wise Growth-rates Between 1983 and 1997

(per cent per annum)

	Primary sector		*Secondary sector*		*Tertiary sector*	
	Youth	*All*	*Youth*	*All*	*Youth*	*All*
1983 to 1993-94						
RM	0.58	0.88	1.99	2.19	2.98	3.02
RF	-0.34	0.22	1.86	1.59	1.84	1.23
RP	0.29	0.67	1999	2.04	2.71	2.73
UM	-0.05	0.77	0.81	1.47	1.2	2.25
UF	-1.79	-0.89	0.53	1.25	2.41	3.15
UP	-0.64	0.2	0.75	1.44	1.4	1.02
All-India	0.25	0.65	1.42	1.76	1.96	2.54
1993-94 to 1997						
RM	3.12	3.11	0.27	0.51	3.5	0.67
RF	1.03	1.42	-3.03	-3.64	-6.56	-7.29
RP	2.44	2.58	-0.65	-0.47	2.58	-0.38
UM	-2.27	-0.33	3.00	34.02	2.4	3.21
UF	-6.46	-1.96	6.47	3.37	0.36	0.8
UP	-3.47	-0.85	3.64	3.91	2.01	2.84
All-India	2.25	2.46	1.28	1.6	2.27	1.46
1983 to 1997						
RM	1.34	1.58	1.64	1.87	3.34	2.56
RF	0.03	0.58	0.57	0.18	-0.51	-1.19
RP	0.92	1.26	1.37	1.46	2.87	2.03
UM	-0.7	0.51	1.49	2.3	1.63	2.68
UF	-3.27	-1.26	2.23	1.94	1.99	2.7
UP	-1.5	-0.09	1.62	2.24	1.68	2.69
All-India	0.84	1.21	1.49	1.84	2.19	2.41

Source : NSSO Reports of 38th, 50th and 53rd Rounds.

were lower than rural growth-rates. In the latter period, secondary employment showed a sudden fall in rural areas and a sudden rise in urban areas. In fact, rural females registered negative growth-rates. In the urban areas, secondary-sector employment grew at a faster rate registering a maximum rate of 6.5 per cent for urban female youth. Sector-wise long-term growth-rates, i.e., between 1983 and 1997 showed negative rates in the urban primary employment for all ages. Secondary and tertiary employment indicate positive growth-rates except tertiary employment of rural females. The tertiary-sector employment for rural females, both among youth and all ages, declined drastically in the 90s with a negative growth of -6.5 per cent for youth and -7.3 per cent for all females.

IV. Changes in Employment and Unemployment Pattern

A number of writers have examined the changes in the structure of economy and their implications on employment and unemployment pattern. Visaria and Minhas (1996) use the quinquennial data of 1972-73, 1977-78, 1983 and 1987-88 for this purpose. Mathur (1998) considered the period 1983 to 1994 for similar examination. Sharma (1997) also examined data for the period 1977-78 to 1993-94. The variables that they covered included work-participation rates, sectoral distribution of labour and activity status. But all these studies do not focus on youth and, secondly, they do not cover the period 1994-97. Studies on youth were undertaken in a seminar conducted by the IIPS, Bombay, in collaboration with the Indian Association for the Study of Population. But the papers mostly dealt with the period the 80s and do not throw light on the changes due to economic reforms in the 90s. In this section, we examine the changes between 1983 and 1997. The changes would be influenced by the peculiar conditions of the year of enquiry. The 1983 survey was conducted during the calendar year following the near-severe drought of 1982 of about 104 million hectares, i.e, 32 per cent of the cropped area. The year 1993-94 was a good agricultural year. The 1997 survey, again, like 1983, was conducted for a calendar year which covered crop years 1996-97 and 1997-98. The crop year 1996-97 was an agriculturally bad year while 1997-98 was a good agricultural year.

1. Changes in Work Participation Rates

Work Participation Rates (WPRs) are measured by UPS and UPS + SS for youth and the 15+ population. The WPRs in general exhibit a declining trend and the WPRs of youth are lower compared to the 15+ population by both measures, both in rural and in urban areas (Table 5). The highest WPRs were registered by the rural males. The WPR of the 15+ rural males was found to be between 85 and 87 per cent. By the UPS measure, the employment scenario of male youth as well as the 15+ population remained rather stable between 1993-94 and 1997, in both rural and urban areas. The WPR of rural male youth was 83 per cent (PS + SS) in 1983 which declined to 76 per cent by 1997. The sharpest fall was among urban male youth. The WPRs of urban female youth rose slightly in 1993-94 over 1983 and then declined sharply by 1997 by the PS + SS measure. This was mostly due to the increasing enrolment of females in educational institutions. According to the 1997 survey, 53 per cent of urban females and 22 per cent of rural females in the age-group 15-19 years attended educational institutions. In the age-groups 20-24 and 25-29, around 60 per cent attended to 'domestic duties only'. Correspondingly, in rural areas, among the females in the age-group 20-29 years, only about 40 per cent are registered as attending 'domestic duties only'. In rural areas, females combine the collection of firewood and other articles for household consumption, with their domestic duties.

TABLE – 5

Work Participation Rates by UPS + SS for Youth and 15+ Population

	UPS		*UPS + SS*	
	Youth	*15+*	*Youth*	*15+*
1983				
RM	78.9	85.6	82.7	87.7
RF	36.1	37.3	49.7	N.A.
RP	57.4	61.4	66.1	N.A.
UM	64.0	76.9	66.6	78.4
UF	14.5	18.0	18.7	22.5
UP	40.6	49.0	44.0	N.A.
Total	N.A.	N.A.	N.A.	N.A.
1993-94				
RM	74.0	84.6	77.5	86.4
RF	31.2	34.6	44.7	48.6
RP	52.8	59.9	61.3	67.8
UM	60.1	75.8	61.9	76.8
UF	13.3	17.5	19.8	22.3
UP	38.0	48.1	40.7	50.9
Total	48.8	N.A.	55.8	N.A.
1997				
RM	74.1	84.7	76.3	85.8
RF	29.3	33.1	38.4	43.2
RP	52.4	59.6	58.0	65.1
UM	59.8	75.8	60.8	76.4
UF	12.4	15.8	14.7	18.6
UP	36.8	46.8	38.5	48.5
Total	48.2	56.1	52.7	N.A.

Source: Same as Table 4.

2. Sector-wise Changes in Employment

Development should bring about a decline in the primary sector and increase in the secondary and tertiary sectors, both in terms of income as well as labour force. In the Indian context, however, while there was a decline in the share of agricultural income, the decline in the labour force in agriculture was very slow. The share of income from agriculture at the all-India level declined from about 40 per cent in the 80s to about 30 per cent in the 90s. The labour force decline in agriculture over about one-and-half decades starting with 1983 has been quite small. Decline in the primary sector was perceptible in the 80s but, since 1991, there has been an upward trend in the primary sector, with a corresponding decline in the secondary sector.

Our major concern in this section is the sector-wise employment of youth. In both rural and urban areas, the proportion of youth in the primary sector was slightly less than for all ages in all the three rounds (Table 6). This is found to be true both among males as well as females. The tertiary sector also exhibits the same phenomenon, but in the secondary sector, this position was reversed. Youth recorded a higher proportion in the secondary sector and the gap between the two groups in respect of the absorption in the secondary sector is increasing in the case of urban youth. In the rural primary sector, all groups recorded a fall in 1993-94 and again increased in 1997 but the rise was sharper for the total population compared to the youth population. In urban areas, primary-sector employment declined in all groups. The secondary-sector employment exhibited a rise-and-fall pattern for all groups in rural areas and in urban areas it is the reverse. Urban female youth registered the sharpest rise between 1993-94 and 1997. In the tertiary sector, there was a sharp rise of urban females between 1983 and 1993-94, but again declined slightly by 1997 but urban males registered a rising trend. The trends in rural areas indicate that rural non-farm employment increased during the 80s but in the 90s there was a decline.

TABLE – 6

Change in Sectoral Division of Employment (UPS)

	Primary sector		*Secondary sector*		*Tertiary sector*		*Total*	
	Youth	*All*	*Youth*	*All*	*Youth*	*All*	*Youth*	*All*
1983								
RM	76.8	77.3	11.7	10.4	11.5	12.4	100	100
RF	86.4	86.4	9.3	8.0	4.4	5.7	100	100
RP	79.8	80.1	11.0	10.0	9.2	10.3	100	100
UM	9.4	9.8	37.4	34.6	53.2	55.7	100	100
UF	24.9	25.6	37.3	31.0	37.9	43.4	100	100
UP	12.0	12.6	37.4	34.0	50.6	53.5	100	100
Total	N.A.	N.A.	N.A.	N.A.	N.A.	N.A.	N.A.	N.A.
1993-94								
RM	72.9	73.7	13.0	11.4	14.1	14.1	100	100
RF	83.3	84.7	11.3	9.1	5.4	6.2	100	100
RP	76.0	76.9	12.6	10.7	11.4	12.4	100	100
UM	8.4	8.7	36.8	33.2	54.7	58.1	100	100
UF	18.7	19.3	36.2	29.7	45.1	51.0	100	100
UP	10.1	10.6	36.6	32.6	53.3	56.8	100	100
Total	62.2	62.5	17.6	15.5	20.2	22.0	100	100
1997								
RM	73.87	5.6	11.8	10.6	14.5	13.7	100	100
RF	86.0	87.8	10.0	7.7	4.1	4.5	100	100
RP	77.1	78.9	11.2	9.8	11.6	11.3	100	100
UM	7.1	7.6	37.9	34.3	55	58.1	100	100
UF	13.4	16.4	43.7	32.7	42.9	50.9	100	100
UP	8.1	9.0	38.8	34.1	53.1	57.0	100	100
Total	62.6	63.4	17.04	15.15	20.32	21.46	100	100

Source: Same as for Table 4.

3. Changes in Status of Employment

Self-employment among youth is found to be consistantly lower compared to the total population, for all social groups. Regular employment is also not favourable to youth and casualisation of youth is found to be higher compared to total population both in urban and rural areas (Table 7). In general, a little over 50 per cent of the workers are self-employed. Regular employment forms less than 10 per cent in the rural areas. Casual labour proportions increased between 1983 and

1993-94 but again there was a slight decline by 1997. In 1997, urban female youth seemed to be doing better than male youth. Their proportion in regular employment increased and was higher than that of all females. Likewise, the casual labour proportion declined and was lower than all females.

TABLE – 7

Changes in Status of Employment (UPS)

	Self-employed		*Regular employed*		*Casual labour*		*Total*	
	Youth	*All*	*Youth*	*All*	*Youth*	*All*	*Youth*	*All*
1983								
RM	56.3	60.0	9.9	10.1	33.8	29.9	100	100
RF	49.7	54.2	3.8	3.5	46.5	42.2	100	100
RP	54.2	58.2	8.0	8.1	37.8	33.7	100	100
UM	39.9	40.4	39.8	44.8	20.4	15.3	100	100
UF	34.7	37.4	30.9	31.7	34.3	31.0	100	100
UP	39.1	39.8	38.2	42.1	22.7	18.1	100	100
Total	51.1	54.5	14.2	15.0	34.7	30.5	100	100
1993-94								
RM	54.1	56.7	7.4	8.7	38.5	34.5	100	100
RF	46.7	50.9	4.0	3.6	48.6	45.5	100	100
RP	52.0	55.0	6.4	7.3	41.6	37.7	100	100
UM	41.6	41.1	35.7	42.6	22.8	16.2	100	100
UF	34.7	36.5	35.8	35.9	29.8	27.7	100	100
UP	40.3	40.3	35.6	41.5	23.9	18.2	100	100
Total	49.6	51.9	12.5	14.7	37.9	33.5	100	100
1997								
RM	56.3	59.0	7.2	7.4	36.5	33.6	100	100
RF	51.2	51.8	2.5	2.7	46.3	45.5	100	100
RP	55.0	57.0	5.9	6.2	39.2	36.9	100	100
UM	39.4	39.7	36.1	41.9	24.5	18.4	100	100
UF	33.0	33.3	37.9	36.0	29.1	30.6	100	100
UP	38.4	38.7	36.4	40.9	25.2	20.4	100	100
Total	51.5	52.9	12.3	13.9	36.2	33.2	100	100

Source: Same as for Table 4.

4. Changes in Unemployment

Table 8 provides unemployment rates for youth and all ages by usual principal status and current weekly status. Usual status which pertains to a long period over a year does not capture unemployment adequately. Current weekly status captures intermittent unemployment or seasonal unemployment better than usual status. A much more comprehensive measure of unemployment is provided through the current daily status approach but unfortunately, the 1997 survey does not provide details of daily status unemployment.

TABLE – 8

Changes in Unemployment

	1983		*1993-94*		*1997*	
	Youth	*All*	*Youth*	*All*	*Youth*	*All*
Usual principal status						
RM	4.7	2.1	4.8	2.0	2.1	0.9
RF	2.8	1.4	3.2	1.4	3.8	1.6
RP	4.1	1.9	4.4	1.8	3.4	1.3
UM	12.3	5.9	10.8	4.5	10.0	4.0
UF	15.5	8.1	19.4	8.2	13.2	5.1
UP	12.8	6.2	12.4	5.2	10.4	4.2
Current weekly status						
RM	N.A.	3.7	5.8	3.0	4.3	2.0
RF	N.A.	4.3	4.8	3.0	3.4	1.8
RP	N.A.	3.9	5.4	3.0	4.1	2.0
UM	N.A.	6.7	11.4	5.2	10.2	4.3
UF	N.A.	7.5	18.5	8.4	12.6	5.8
UP	N.A.	6.8	12.8	5.8	10.6	4.5

Source: Same as for Table 4.

In general, the data indicate a declining trend of unemployment. The unemployment rates both among youth and all age-groups particularly within rural areas, are small by the usual status measure. In the urban areas, unemployment rates are much higher as compared to rural areas both among youth and all age-groups. They are more than three times in the urban areas as compared to rural areas. Though the unemployment rates for youth declined along with the unemployment rates of the total population, they remain high between 10 and 13 per cent. The highest unemployment rate is among female youth, especially the urban female youth seem to be the worst sufferers. In rural areas, it is higher among males than among females but just the opposite in urban areas. In absolute numbers, the unemployed youth amount to 6.43 millions forming 87.36 per cent in total unemployed.

(i) Educated Unemployment of Youth

The educated seek employment mainly in the public/private organised sector. But the organised sector employment has grown at a rate of 0.56 per cent for males and 1 per cent for the total during the 1990s. These rates of employment may be compared with the past, i.e., 80s. In the 80s, growth-rate of employment in the organised sector was 1.58 per cent. This came down to 1 per cent in the 90s. In 1997, employment in the organised sector was only 28.2 millions while the total workforce during the year was 381 millions. The organised sector accounted for only 7.3 per cent of the total work force.

The supply of labour to the organised sector comes mainly from the educated. The rate of growth of student enrolment in 'general' and 'professional/special higher' education was 4.82 per cent for the 80s and 4.47 for the 90s (UGC, 1997). This may be compared with the demand from the organised sector for the educated which is growing only at the rate of 1 per cent. Education of females has grown at a faster rate than the education of males during the 90s. The growth rate of enrolment in 'general education' was 4.10 per cent for males and 6.71 for females. The corresponding figure for 'professional/special higher education' was -0.32 for males and 1.14 for females. Thus, professional education has grown at a much slower rate than general education.

In a study on education and employment of youth, Parasuraman (1989) found that one-third of all chronic unemployment in the age-group of 15-29 is accounted for by the educated, in that age-group. With the growth in the number of educated youth, the educated unemployed is bound to increase.

We do not have data for unemployment for youth separately by levels of education. But unemployment rates for the educated aged 15 years and above presented in Table-9 pcrmit broad conclusion. Unemployment rates are positively correlated to levels of education, i.e., at higher levels of education, there are higher levels of unemployment. The most striking conclusion that could be drawn from the data is that rural areas experience a higher degree of educated unemployment as compared to urban areas. The highly educated among rural males and females face higher rate of unemployment as compared to urban males and females. A comparison of unemployment rates by education between 1983 and 1993-94 show, in general, that the rates have increased in the case of higher educated females in particular.

TABLE – 9

Unemployment Rates for the 15+ Population by Educational Level

	Not literate	*Literate upto primary*	*Middle*	*Secondary*	*Higher secondary*	*Graduate & above*	*Secondary & above*
Usual principal status							
RM	0.3	0.8	3	6.7	9.8	13.2	8.8
RF	0.2	1	5.3	19.9	29.1	34.6	24.9
UM	1.1	2.5	5.7	6.3	8.5	6.4	6.9
UF	0.4	4.5	15.7	20	22.2	20.6	20.6
Current weekly status							
RM	1.8	1.9	3.8	6.5	9	12.2	8.3
RF	2.2	2.6	5.3	14.5	24.3	32	19.8
UM	2.2	3.5	6.4	6.6	9.1	6.3	7
UF	2.2	4.8	14.3	17.6	21.6	20.2	19.6

Source: NSSO 1993-94 Report, 50th Round.

The 'graduate and above' category unemployment rates are 12 and 32 per cent for rural males and females and 6.3 and 20 per cent for urban males and females, respectively. Thus, between males and females also, there is a difference in the extent of educated unemployment. The 'not literate' record the least degree of unemployment, both in rural and urban areas. We have the distribution of unemployed by levels of education (Table-10). The illiterate and below primary form only about 10 per cent in rural areas and less than 10 per cent in urban areas.

TABLE – 10

Percentage Distribution of Unemployed (UPS) Youth by Education Levels, All-India: 1993-94

	Not literate	*Below primary*	*Primary middle & secondary*	*Higher secondary & above*	*All*
RM	6.1	3.4	54.7	35.8	100
RF	13.1	3.6	48.5	34.8	100
RP	7.5	3.4	53.3	35.6	100
UM	4.5	4.6	54.3	36.7	100
UF	2.1	2.2	43.2	52.4	100
UP	3.7	3.9	51.2	41.1	100

Source: NSSO 1993-94 Report, 50th Round.

(ii) Structural Adjustment and Differentiation Among Youth

The emerging pattern of foreign investment and the choice of capital-intensive techniques by the MNCs contribute to an accelerated growth of dualism in the labour market, weaken the linkages between the industrial sector and the rural/agricultural sector, and arrest the growth of local autonomous enterprise in small scale industry (Parthasarathy, 1999). The MNCs managed to achieve a break through in the vicious circle of low-wage-high-turnover-low-productivity-low-wages in a section of urban and industrial markets, particularly in the information technology sector. But this is at the expense of the overall degree of participation of the labour force in wage employment. Increased labour productivity and rising real wages contribute to a rise in the living standards for a small proportion of youth with high technical qualifications while the wage opportunities for the unskilled, semi-proletarian peasantry are reduced. Besides, the low income elasticity of demand for agricultural produce in general, and local produce in particular, implicit in the capital-intensive growth of the modern sector, also restrains growth of demand for output of the peasant producer. Thus, the emerging pattern of foreign investment tends to reduce both the complementary links between urban and rural sector and speeding up of development stimuli from the modern to traditional sector. It tends to produce an impoverished agriculture without fostering its absorption in capitalist agriculture. The pattern of consumption associated with capital-intensive production also works to the disadvantage of the labour-intensive small-scale industry since the income elasticity of demand for its products will be lower than what it should be in the case of a labour-intensive type of economy.

V. Regional Dimensions of Youth Unemployment

In this section, we present regional dimensions of the work participation rates of youth, and unemployment rates for youth. The final part of the section reviews the factors that are relevant to an explanation of variations in unemployment rates. The data of this section is drawn from 1993-94 NSSO Report since regional dimensions of youth unemployment rates are not available in 1997 data.

1. Regional Dimensions of Unemployment Rates Among Youth

The NSSO Report 1993-94 provides unemployment rates for the age-group 15-29 state-wise by four different approaches, i.e., current weekly status (CWS), usual principal status, (UPS + SS), and current daily status. We use the data provided under two approaches, viz., CWS, UPS+SS approach. The state-wise data are classified by the level of unemployment rates. Four levels are chosen for presenting the data on UPS + SS and three levels for presenting data on CWS (Tables 11a and 11b). The levels chosen are: (1) below 25 per 1000; (2) 25-50 per 1000; (3) 50-100 per 1000; (4) above 100 per 1000. By the CWS, the unemployment rate for rural males ranged between 18 in Rajasthan and 220 in Goa. Goa, Assam and Kerala top the list of states with high unemployment rates (Table 11a). Eight states recorded unemployment rate of 'below 50', six States between 50-100, and three States above 100. States recording high unemployment rate for rural male youth also recorded high unemployment rate for female youth. The number of states recording unemployment rate of below 50 per thousand were 11 in the case of females as against eight in the case of males. Correspondingly, three of the states, viz., Bihar, Haryana, and Maharashtra which recorded more than 50 per 1000 among rural males do not figure among the rural females. As compared to unemployment rates among rural males and rural females, urban male and urban females youth record much higher rates of unemployment. While only three states figure under more than 100 per thousand unemployment rate for rural males and rural females, 10 states record more than 100 per 1000 unemployment rate for urban males. In the case of urban females, 16 out of 17 states record more than 100 per 1000. The only exception is Rajasthan. Such high unemployment rates among urban female youth needs an explanation. Urban female youth suffer from several disadvantages in the labour market. Access to the job market is limited and the mobility is also much restricted due to domestic responsibilities. Educated unemployment of females in the urban areas is found to be more than 2½ times the corresponding rate for males.

TABLE – 11A

Unemployment Rates Among Youth, CWS: 1993-94

(Per 1000 persons)

	Unemployment Rate of below 50 per 1000
RM	A.P.(38) Gujarat(40) J&K(48) Karnataka(40) M.P.(35) Punjab(34) Rajasthan(18) UP(38) Total no. of states are 8.
RF	A.P.(24) Bihar(29) Gujarat(29) Haryana(32) J&K(22) Karnataka(20) M.P.(19) Maharashtra(37) Punjab(41) Rajasthan(5) Tamil Nadu(43). Total no. of states are 11.
RP	A.P.(33) Gujarat(36) J&K(39) Karnataka(32) M.P.(29) Punjab(35) Rajasthan(13) U.P.(47). Total no. of states are 8.
UM	Nil
UF	Rajasthan(26)
UP	Rajasthan(47)
	Unemployment Rate of 50 to 100 per 1000
RM	Bihar(66) Haryana(85) Maharashtra(65) Orissa(87) T.Nadu(85) W.Bengal(79). Total no. of states are 6.
RF	Orissa(60) U.P.(86) W.Bengal(71). Total no. of states are 3.
RP	Bihar(60) Haryana(17) Maharashtra(54) Orissa(79) T.Nadu(67) W.Bengal(77). Total no. of states are 6.
UM	A.P.(94) Gujarat(77) Haryana(84) Karnataka(85) Punjab(73) Rajasthan(53) U.P.(95). Total no. of states are 7.
UF	Nil
UP	Gujarat(88) Haryana(93) Punjab(81) U.P.(97). Total no. of states are 4.
	Unemployment Rate of above 100 per 1000
RM	Assam(134) Goa(220) Kerala(182). Total no. of states are 3.
RF	Assam(214) Goa(444) Kerala(329). Total no. of states are 3.
RP	Assam(153) Goa(294) Kerala(227). Total no. of states are 3.
UM	Assam(156) Bihar(204) Goa(141) J&K(190) Kerala(204) M.P.(150) Maharashtra(114) Orissa(198) T.Nadu(116) W.Bengal(192). Total no. of states are 10.
UF	A.P.(121) Assam(453) Bihar(296) Goa(482) Gujarat(143) Haryana(153) J&K(291) Karnataka(158) Kerala(416) M.P.(152) Maharashtra(151) Orissa(165) Punjab(156) T.Nadu(182) U.P.(102) W.Bengal(343). Total no. of states are 16.
UP	A.P.(100) Assam(228) Bihar(214) Goa(221) J&K(214) Karnataka(103) Kerala(268) M.P.(151) Maharashtra(122) Orissa(192) T.Nadu(135) W.Bengal(228). Total no. of states are 12.

The UPS+SS approach results in less unemployment rate compared to the CWS approach. Six states recorded unemployment rate below 25 per 1000 in the UPS+SS among rural males. Among rural females also, the total number of states which recorded less than 25 per thousand unemployment rate is more. Urban areas recorded a much higher rate of unemployment in all the states as compared to rural areas. The total number of states recording unemployment rates ranging above 100 was nine for urban males and 13 for urban females as against 3 for rural males and 3 for rural females.

The top unemployment states for rural youth by both the approaches are Assam, Goa and Kerala. Of these, both Kerala and Goa share some common characteristics. Illiteracy is low in these two states. While rural non-farm employment is of the high order. In Goa, out of 1000 households classified by principal industries, as many as 646 are engaged in non-agricultural industries. In Kerala, 450 out of 1000 are engaged in non-agricultural industry. The two states have also a high percentage of non-cultivating households; 604 out of 1000 in Goa, 694 in Kerala. Assam, however, is seen to be different from kerala and Goa.

TABLE – 11B

Unemployment Rates Among Youth, UPS + SS, 1993-94

(Per 1000 persons)

	Unemployment rate of below 25 per 1000
RM	A.P.(17) J&K(25) Karnataka(22) M.P.(17) Rajasthan(10) U.P.(20). Total no. of states are 6.
RF	A.P.(2) Bihar(19) Gujarat(8) Haryana(9) J&K(11) Karnataka(10) M.P.(2) Maharashtra(6) Orissa(18) Rajasthan(3) T.Nadu(17) U.P.(8) Total no. of states are 12.
RP	A.P.(10) Gujarat(19) J&K(19) Karnataka(17) M.P.(11) Maharashtra(20) Rajasthan(7) U.P.(17). Total no. of states are 8.
UM	Nil
UF	Rajasthan(13)
UP	Nil

	Unemployment rates of 25-50 among youth per 1000
RM	Bihar(50) Gujarat(27) Haryana(35) Maharashtra(32) Orissa(43) Punjab(29) T.Nadu(49) W.Bengal(42). Total no. of states are 8.
RF	Punjab(37) W.Bengal(30). Total no. of states are 2.
RP	Bihar(43) Haryana(26) Orissa(34) Punjab(31) T.Nadu(35) W.Bengal(39). Total no. of states are 6.
UM	Rajasthan(43)
UF	U.P.(33)
UP	Rajasthan(37)
	Unemployment rates of 50-100 among youth per 1000
RM	Nil
RF	Nil
RP	Nil
UM	A.P.(67) Gujarat(67) Haryana(56) Karnataka(70) Punjab(68) T.Nadu(98) U.P.(80). Total no. of states are 7.
UF	A.P.(95) Haryana(78). Total no. of states are 2.
UP	A.P.(74) Gujarat(71) Haryana(59) Karnataka(86) Punjab(79) U.P.(74). Total no. of states are 6.
	Unemployment rates of above 100 per 1000
RM	Assam(118) Goa(163) Kerala(156). Total no. of states are 3.
RF	Assam(160) Goa(329) Kerala(290). Total no. of states are 3.
RP	Assam(128) Goa(224) Kerala(200). Total no. of states are 3.
UM	Assam(159) Bihar(181) Goa(141) J&K(173) Kerala(171) M.P.(132) Maharashtra(110) Orissa(168) W.Bengal(163). Total no. of states are 9.
UF	Assam(461) Bihar(249) Goa(442) Gujarat(105) J&K(237) Karnataka(128) Kerala(392) M.P.(118) Maharashtra(120) Orissa(159) Punjab(173) T.Nadu(153) W.Bengal(298). Total no. of states are 13.
UP	Assam(236) Bihar(190) Goa(212) J&K(189) Kerala(240) M.P.(130) Maharashtra(105) Orissa(167) T.Nadu(115) W.Bengal(195). Total no. of states are 10.

Note : Figures within brackets are unemployment rates per 1000 for the state concerned.

Source : NSSO 1993-94 Report, 50th Round, pp. 139-144.

2. *Regional Dimensions of Work participation Rates Among Youth*

For studying the regional dimensions of work participation rates, we have to rely upon the data of 1993-94 since such data by age distribution are not available for the states for 1997. The data are examined for three age-groups among youth for 1993-94, i.e., 15-19, 20-24 and 25-29. For 1983, the data were available for the 15-29 age-group. Age-specific UPS + SS work participation ratio for rural males and rural females for urban males and urban females are studied separately. The regional variations of work participation rates are not significant for males but they are much more significant for females. The 1993-94 work participation rates of females in the age-group 15-19 varied between 6.8 in Kerala and 67.1 in A.P. The classification of states by low, medium and high female participation rates is shown in table 12. States with less than 250 workers per thousand population are classified as low participation states; 250-500 are classified as medium participation states; and above 500 are classified under high participation states.

Our examination of female participation rates age-wise among youth reveals the following: Work participation rates among urban female youth are much lower than rural females in all states. Female participation rates in the age-group 15-19 are low in the north-eastern states of Assam and West Bengal, the northern states of Bihar and Uttar Pradesh, the north-west state of Punjab and the western state of Goa. In Goa and Kerala, female participation rates are low because they are enrolled in schools. In urban areas, all the states recorded less than 250 participation per thousand in the age-group 15-19. In the age-group 20-24, only one state Tamil Nadu, recorded medium participation rates. In the age-group 25-29 also, Andhra Pradesh, Karnataka, Tamil Nadu in the south, Rajasthan in the north, and Maharashtra in the west recorded medium rates.

TABLE - 12

Classification of States by Female Work Participation Rate (UPS)

	1983	*1993-94*		
	15-29	*15-19*	*20-24*	*25-29*
		Rural		
Below 25 per cent	Assam Kerala, Punjab	Assam, Bihar, Kerala, U.P., West Bengal	Assam, Bihar	Nil
25-50 per cent	Bihar, Haryana, Kerala, Orissa, Punjab, U.P., West Bengal	Gujarat, Haryana, Orissa	Goa, Haryana, Orissa, Punjab, W.Bengal	Assam, Bihar, Goa, Kerala Punjab,U.P. W. Bengal
Above 50 per cent	A.P., Goa, Gujarat, Karnataka, M.P., Maharashtra, Rajasthan, Tamil Nadu	A.P., Karnataka, Maharashtra, Rajasthan, Tamil Nadu	A.P., Gujarat, Karnataka, M.P., Maharashtra, Rajasthan, T. Nadu	A.P., Gujarat, Haryana, Karnataka, M.P., Maharashtra Orissa, Rajasthan, T.N.
		Urban		
Below 25 per cent	A.P., Assam, Bihar, Gujarat, Haryana, Kerala, M.P., Maharashtra, Orissa, Punjab, U.P., W. Bengal	All states	All states except Tamil Nadu	Nil
25-50 per cent	Karnataka, Rajasthan, T.N.	Nil	Tamil Nadu	Karnataka, Maharashtra Rajasthan, T.N.
Above 50 per cent	Nil	Nil	Nil	Nil

Source: NSSO, 1983 & 1993-94 Reports.

The 1983 data also suggest lower participation rates in urban areas as compared to rural areas. Comparison is not possible with 1983 because 1983 presents for the entire youth age-group 15-29 while 1993-94 data presents it age-group-wise. Though a direct comparison is not possible, we could summerise from the data presented that few states like Maharashtra have recorded better participation rates in 1993-94 as compared to 1983.

3. Unemployment Among Youth as Ratio of Overall Unemployment: State-wise Analysis

(i) Current Weekly Status (CWS)

It was seen earlier that at the all-India level unemployment among youth exceeds by far the unemployment of all ages. We use the state-wise data in this section to examine the position of youth unemployment in relation to overall unemployment. Firstly, we use the CWS approach. The data are drawn from the NSSO Report 1993-94 for both the variables, state-wise data on youth unemployment and unemployment among all ages. In every state, unemployment among youth exceeded the overall unemployment rate (Table 13). The minimum ratio of youth unemployment to overall unemployment is 1.22 in Andhra Pradesh. The maximum is found to be in Kerala 2.6 followed by Assam 2.42, Jammu and Kashmir 2.4 and Bihar 2.0, for rural areas. Urban ratios are found to be invariably higher than the corresponding rural ratios. For instance, urban Andhra Pradesh recorded an unemployment ratio of youth to all of 1.96 against 1.22 in rural areas. Similarly in Bihar, urban ratio is 2.64 as against 2.00 in rural areas. Only in Haryana the urban ratio was marginally lower than the rural ratio. The highest urban ratio was for J&K 2.7. Rajasthan, A.P. and Tamil Nadu recorded a ratio of 2.2 each. West Bengal recorded a ratio of 2.3.

TABLE – 13

Youth Unemployment Rate as a Ratio of Overall Unemployment Rate by Alternative Approaches for Rural and Urban Persons, 1993-94

State	*Current weekly status*		*Usual status: principal and subsidiary*	
	Rural	*Urban*	*Rural*	*Urban*
Andhra Pradesh	1.2	2	2.5	2.5
Assam	2.4	2.5	2.5	2.7
Bihar	2	2.6	2.7	2.7
Goa	1.5	2	2.5	2.1
Gujarat	1.6	2	2.1	2.2
Haryana	2	1.4	2.4	2.3
J & K	2.4	2.7	2.7	2.9
Karnataka	2	2.1	2.4	2.4
Kerala	2.6	2.4	2.9	2.8
Madhya Pradesh	1.6	2.2	2.2	2.6
Maharashtra	2.1	2.4	2.6	2.4
Orissa	1.8	2.3	2.4	2.6
Punjab	1.8	2.2	2.4	2.3
Rajasthan	1.9	2.2	2.3	2.6
Tamil Nadu	1.9	2.2	2.7	2.3
Uttar Pradesh	1.7	2.2	2.4	2.6
West Bengal	1.8	2.3	2.2	2.5
All-India	1.7	2.5	2.4	2.4

Source: NSSO, 1993-94 Report (50th Round).

(ii) Usual Principal and Subsidiary Status Approach (UP+SS)

The usual status approach as distinguished from the weekly status approach, has a long reference period of one year and therefore, the unemployment rates are generally lower than under the CWS approach. Under this approach, unemployment for all as well as for youth is lower than the corresponding CWS unemployment rates. When youth unemployment is seen as a ratio of all in rural areas, the ratio is found to be higher.

For instance, the ratio of youth in the over-all unemployment rate under the CWS approach for Andhra Pradesh is 1.2 for rural areas. But under this approach, it is 2.5. For Goa, it is 2.5 as against 1.54 under CWS approach. J&K also records a higher ratio. In general, urban ratios are found to be higher than the corresponding rural ratios for most of the states. The urban ratios ranged between 2.1 in Goa and 2.9 in J&K while the rural ratios ranged between 2.2 in West Bengal and 2.7 in J&K.

4. *Explanation of Variations in Youth Unemployment Rates: Regression Results*

We sought to explain the variations in youth-unemployment rates in rural and urban areas through regression analysis (Tables 1 and 2 in Appendix) and the results are as follows:

(i) Rural Areas

We chose to regress the youth unemployment rates (y) with the following variables: (1) levels of illiteracy (XI); (2) percentage of population having secondary and higher education (X2); (3) growth rate of agricultural output (X3); (4) per cent of non-farm employment (X4) and (5) per capita expenditure on rural development. Illiteracy was chosen as one of the independent variables as this is expected to show a negative relation to unemployment since illiterates have less staying power because of their poverty. The secondary-and-higher educated population is expected to have a positive relationship with the unemployment rate since they belong to relatively better strata of society and have more staying power. Growth of agricultural output is expected to have a negative relationship with unemployment and also non-farm employment. An increase in the per capita expenditure on rural development may increase the work opportunities in rural areas thereby reducing unemployment.

The regression equation is as follows:

$$Y = 32.6234 - 0.4186\ XI - 0.3786\ X2 - 0.4308\ X3 + 0.0259\ X4$$
$$(3.1640) \quad (0.8185) \quad (1.4712) \quad (0.1836)$$

$R^2 = 0.7836$

Note: Figures in brackets are 't' values.

Though the four independent variables together explain 78 per cent of variation in the unemployment rate, only one variable, i.e., the levels of illiteracy alone, is statistically significant. 1 per cent rise in illiteracy leads to a 0.42 per cent reduction in youth unemployment The growth rate of agriculture has the expected negative sign indicating a rise in output growth and leads to a reduction in unemployment but is not statistically significant as also is non-farm employment.

(ii) Urban Areas

Unemployment rate in the urban areas may be influenced by the following factors: growth of the manufacturing sector (X1), growth of the tertiary sector (X2), growth of urban population (X3) and per cent of secondary and higher-educated persons (X4). Growth of the manufacturing and tertiary sectors will lead to expansion of employment and, thereby, reduce unemployment. Growth of urban population as a result of rural urban migration may adversely affect the urban labour market and raise unemployment rates. To examine the effect of these factors on unemployment, a linear regression is estimated and the regression equation is as follows:

$$Y = 199.938 - 43.149\ X1^{*} + 8.432\ X2 + 32.614\ X3 + 18.438\ X4^{*}$$
$$(3.0971) \quad (0.6748) \quad (1.6517) \quad (3.0403)$$

$R^2 = 0.5726$

Note: Figures in brackets are 't' values.

The results show that though all the independent variables together explain 57 per cent of the variation in the unemployment rate only the coefficients of growth of manufacturing and percentage of higher-and secondary-educated persons are statistically significant. The coefficient for X1 has a negative sign indicating that a 1 per cent rise in rate of growth of manufacturing will lead to a 4.31 per cent reduction in the youth unemployment, and the coefficient of X4 has a positive sign which indicates that a 1 per cent rise in the secondary-and higher-educated persons unemployment rises by 1.8 per cent. The proportion of secondary-and higher-educated persons was not found to be significant in rural areas but in urban areas this is significant. Thus, in urban areas the problem of youth unemployment is educated unemployment.

VI. Major Findings

The study has focussed on three time periods, 1983, 1993-94 and 1997. The major change noticed is reversal of trends in growth-rates of employment in the agricultural sector within rural areas. The annual employment growth in the agricultural sector among youth between 1983 over 1993-94 was 0.29 per cent. This has increased to 2.44 per cent between 1993-94 and 1997. Correspondingly, there was a decline in the employment growth of the secondary and tertiary sectors in rural areas. The secondary sector in rural areas was marked by negative growth for youth and all. This is mainly due to a sharp decline in the rate of growth of female employment in the secondary and tertiary sectors.

In the urban areas, both the secondary-and tertiary-sector employment have grown at a higher rate between 1993-94 and 1997 as compared to 1980s. Such results have several implications for the activity status of workers in rural areas. Self-employment, which was found to decline between 1983 and 1993-94 in rural areas, has shown an increase in 1997 for both male and female youth and all ages. Regular employment which declined in the 80s continued to decline in the 90s also. Casual labour, which was increasingly in the

80s showed a decline in 90s among youth and all. But the increase in self-employment results in more disguised unemployment as the size of landholding declines.

Unemployment among rural youth and all by UPS showed a continuous decline. In urban areas, where unemployment rates are much higher, there was a decline in youth unemployment between 1983 and 1993-94 and 1997 by the UPS and CWS also. What is important is youth unemployment rates continued to be higher by several multiples of unemployment for all. The figures of decline in unemployment must be considered in the context of developing economies in which the time criterion does not adequately capture unemployment. Further, we should also recognise the fact that 1997 showed an increase in self-employment and, for self-employed people, the measurement of unemployment is much more difficult. Unemployment among youth is mostly educated unemployment. The growth of the organised sector which absorbs most of the educated, is not keeping pace with the growth in persons acquiring higher education. With the emerging pattern of foreign investment and the choice of capital intensive techniques by the MNCs, dualism in the labour market is growing with scope only for the small proportion of highly skilled persons at very high wages.

Regional dimensions of youth unemployment rates have shown wide variations across states. These variations are sought to be explained by regression analysis of cross-sectional data. Cross-sectional analysis of states has shown that states with the highest illiteracy rates show the least unemployment and illiteracy explains the variations in unemployment of states much better than any other variables. Hence, a reduction in unemployment rates should not be a matter of comfort.

Urban regression results suggest that the rate of growth of manufacturing is much more critical for reducing unemployment among youth in urban areas than the growth of the tertiary sector. Secondary education is found to be positively correlated with urban youth unemployment. This may be the result of a mismatch between education and jobs and suggest the need for imparting technical skills to the youth. The study brings to sharp focus unemployment rates of youth, particularly female unemployment rates which are much higher than overall unemployment rates. The shockingly high rates of youth unemployment has dangerous implications for the stability of society and need to be reduced.

APPENDIX

TABLE – 1

Variables Considered for Regression-Rural

State	*Unempl. rates CWS per 100*	*Illiteracy rates per 100 annum*	*Proportion of sec. and higher persons(%)*	*Growth rates of agri. output % per annum*	*% of non-farm workers*
Andhra Pradesh	3.3	65	4.7	3.08	20.7
Assam	15.3	39.8	8	2.15	20.8
Bihar	6	66.5	6.5	2.08	15.7
Gujarat	3.6	51.2	8.8	11.96	21.3
Haryana	7	52.9	9.4	4.7	28.1
J&K	3.9	50.9	7.9	0.33	24.2
Karnataka	3.2	56.20	7	3.92	18.8
Kerala	22.7	16.5	16.1	2.24	43.6
Madhya Pradesh	2.9	64.7	4.2	4.71	10.2
Maharashtra	5.4	48.5	7.6	2.87	17.4
Orissa	7.9	58.6	4.3	1.15	19.1
Punjab	3.5	49.5	11.5	3.87	25.3
Rajasthan	1.3	68.2	3.7	5.02	20.1
Tamil Nadu	6.7	46.2	8.6	4.59	29.5
Uttar Pradesh	4.7	63.1	6.3	2.83	20
West Bengal	7.7	50.1	5.1	5.39	36.7

Sources: 1. NSSO, 1993-94 Report;
2. G.S. Bhalla and Gurmail Singh (1997)

TABLE – 2

Variables Considered for Regression-Urban

States	*Unempl. rates CWS*	*Growth-rates between 1983-84 & 1993-94 NSDP (constant prices)*		*Growth rate of urban population 1981-91*	*Secondary and higher educated persons (%)*
		Manufacturing	*Tertiary Sector*		
Andhra Pradesh	100	4.38	5.69	3.66	19.8
Bihar	214	3.31	4.76	2.67	22
Goa	221	8.08	7.58	3.15	28
Gujarat	88	7.08	6.68	3	24.2
Haryana	93	7.56	7.14	3.67	25
Karnataka	103	5.86	7.34	2.63	25.9
Kerala	268	6.01	6.19	4.88	25.4
Madhya Pradesh	151	5.76	6.1	3.78	22.2
Maharashtra	122	6.92	8.6	3.34	26.8
Orissa	192	4.1	5.95	3.14	22.8
Punjab	81	7.46	3.95	2.57	28.2
Rajasthan	47	6.27	7.87	3.39	18.9
Tamil Nadu	135	5.53	7.39	1.81	21.3
Uttar Pradesh	97	5.2	5.28	3.33	20.5
West Bengal	228	4.16	5.43	2.62	24.7

Source: NSSO 1993-94 Report; CMIE, Indian Social Sectors, 1996; EPW Research Foundation (1997); National Accounts Statistics of India, 1950-51 to 1995-96.

References

Bhalla, G.S. and Gurmail Singh (1997), "Recent Development in Indian Agricultural, A State Level Analysis", Economic & Political Weekly, Vol. 32, No. 13.

ILO (1985), A Contribution to a Discussion Paper on Entry of Youths into Working Life in Asia and Pacific, Tenth Conference of Asian and Pacific Labour Ministers, Melbourne.

Mathur, Ashok (1998), "Employment, Equity and Growth", The Indian Journal of Labour Economics, Vol. 41, No. 1, January-March."

NSSO (1998), Sarvekshana, Journal of the National Sample Survey Organisation, Government of India, New Delhi. Vol. 11, No. 4, April.

——— (1990), Sarvekshana, Vol. 14, No. 1, Issue no. 44, July-September.

——— (1990), Sarvekshana, Vol. 14, No. 2, Issue no. 45, October-December.

——— (1997), Employment and Unemployment in India, 1993-94, NSS Fiftieth Round (July 1993 - June 1994). National Sample Survey Organisation, New Delhi.

——— (1998), Household Consumer Expenditure and Employment Situation in India, 1997, NSS 53rd Round, January-December.

Parasuraman, S. (1989), "Education, Employment and Training - An Exploration into the Present and Future Position of Youth in India", in P.S. Nair, et al. (eds.), Indian Youth: A Profile, Mittal Publications, New Delhi.

Parthasarathy, G. (1999), "Neo-Colonialism, Transnational Corporation and Basic Development Issues", in Chalam, K.S. (ed.), Readings in Political Economy, Orient Longman.

Sharma, A.N. (1997), Trends in the Structure and Pattern of Employment and Unemployment in India, Working Paper Series, No.E/188/97, Institute of Economic Growth, Delhi.

Thamarajakshi, R (1987), Youth Employment in Asian Countries, Asian Employment Programme, Working Papers, ILO-ARTEP.

UGC (1997), "Statistical Data on Growth of the Higher Education System in India (1947-1996)", Journal of Higher Education, Vol. 20, No. 4, Winter.

Visaria, P. and B.S. Minhas (1996), "Evolving on Employment Policies for the 1990s", in Kapila, Uma (ed.), Indian Economy Since Independence, Academic Foundation, New Delhi.

Published in "New Economic Policy and Vulnerable Sections", IDPS, Jaipur, 1994.

8

Unorganised Sector & Public Policy

(in the Context of Structural Adjustment)

The Theme

THE division of economy into two sectors has a long heritage. Arthur Lewis in a seminal article, back in 1950s, propounded the theory of dualism. His version of dualism differs from an earlier version of Boeke in which a segmented society is explained by fundamental and permanent differences in economic behaviour. This has long been dismissed as untenable by many critics. The socio-economic duality of Arthur Lewis was popular in the 1950s and 1960s. Lewis and others see the cities with their modern industries as dynamic centres from which the static character of the rural order, characterised by stagnating agriculture with very low labour productivity can gradually be overcome. It was assumed in the Lewis model that unorganised sector with surplus labour will gradually disappear as the surplus labour gets absorbed in organised sector.

In the last few decades, the Indian situation at least does not conform to the Lewis model. The organised sector failed to absorb the labour engaged in the unorganised sector. The Lewis model, which is drawn from the experience of the capitalist countries in which the share of agriculture and the share of unorganised sector showed a spectacular decline was not found to be true of many developing countries, including India. The late-comer developing countries faced an entirely new situation of development. Borrowed technology from developed countries was labour displacing. The change in industrial structure was also not favourable to the absorption of labour from unorganised sector. The information and knowledge revolution put a premium on educational skills of the labour force and absorption of blue collar workers as against the white collar workers has been less in the current stage of industrial development. Even in developed countries the share of blue collar workers has been going down.

It is not only mainstream theory that visualised absorption of unorganised sector in the growing urban industrial sector; but, Marxian theory also anticipated the destruction of pre-capitalist structures as a result of aggressive growth of capitalism. In Marxian theory, the small fish is eaten by the big fish. Capitalist accumulation will sweep away the non-capitalist and pre-capitalist village and small industries. The labour in such industries will enter into the ranks of proletariat. Those who cannot get absorbed will enter the ranks of immiserised unemployed labour. Social transformation takes place through a revolution generated by the conflict. Neither in Marxian theory nor in Classical Economic Theory, the unorganised sector has a permanent place in the economy.

The situation we witness currently in India is quite different. The share of unorganised sector in National Income has been declining but the number in the unorganised sector continues to swell. Five decades of post-independent capitalist growth has not been able to absorb the labour force in unorganised sector. There is a need for direct support to unorganised sector besides defending it against appropriation by organised sector for improving employment, productivity and incomes of the poor. We address in the lecture the issues of relative efficiency of the organised vis-a-vis the unorganised sector, the exploitation of the unorganised sector by the organised, and the big gap between profession and performance in relation to public support to the unorganised sector. The lecture also focuses on the adverse implications of structural adjustments for the unorganised sector and finally concludes with an appeal for public policy which goes beyond safety nets and adjustments with a human face.

Conceptualization of Unorganised Sector

There is much controversy on the concept of unorganised sector. It is sometimes defined as the sector which is not recorded under any Factory Legislation. In this sense, it is derived as a residual after deducting the registered labour force from the total labour force. Since the small and village industry is not generally registered, the unorganised sector is identified with the small and village industry sector. But this is not appropriate. The method will not cover the unorganised part in service sector. Further, not all industries defined as 'small' by the Government are unregistered. Some are registered under Factories Act. A more meaningful use of the concept of unorganised sector is its identification with pre-capitalistic structure of production while organised sector is related to capitalist structure. In this sense, the unorganised sector is comprised of own account workers, and also casual labour employed in establishments. The latter do not have access to the benefits of social security. The unorganised sector is sometimes also identified with the informal sector though such an identification is not without controversy.

The term 'informal sector' was first launched by Hart (1971). He describes the informal sector as that part of the Urban Labour Force which falls outside the organised labour market. The concept has been further refined by a mission of International Labour Office (ILO), which studied the employment situation in Kenya within the framework of the World Employment Programme (Breman, 1994, pp.1-4).

In the earlier writings, the approach to unorganised sector was negative. The sector was considered unproductive which would disappear with development. Recent literature shows that activities in the unorganised/informal sector are economically efficient and profitable. Though they are characterised by low capital intensity, low level of productivity, a small and usually poor clientele, a low level of formal schooling, intermediate technology, preponderence of family labour and ownership and ease of entrance and last but not the least lack of support and recognition on the part of Government.

The concept of informal sector is usually applied to urban system. This ignores the production relations within agriculture. The large, medium and semi-medium farms on which modern methods of management have been introduced, may be considered under organised sector within agriculture. Further these need to be distinguished from the self-employed small, marginal farmers and casual laborers. Only the latter category, and not the whole of agriculture needs to be considered under informal sector. Further, the inclusion of modern small scale industry and powerlooms in the unorganised sector may not be considered appropriate.

Magnitude, Trends and Composition of Employment within Organised and Unorganised Sectors

In this paper, as a first step, the employment in the unorganised sector is derived as a residual after deducting the employment in the organised sector from the total labour force given in Census data. The estimates of organised sector employment, are recorded in the Economic Surveys prepared by Finance Ministry. The details of organised sector are available for period 1981 onwards for every year in the pre-budget Economic Surveys. For the years 1961, 1967, 1971 and 1974, the figures are obtained from Fifth Plan draft. The trends of employment in organised and unorganised sector are shown in Table-1.

TABLE – 1

Trends in Employment in Organised and Unorganised Sectors 1961 to 1991

(In Million)

Year	*Organised*	*Unorganised*	*Total*	*Share of Unorganised Sector Employment*
1961	14.60	174.10	188.70	92.26
1971	20.20	206.70	226.90	91.10
1974	22.50	NA		
1981	22.90	214.00	236.90	90.33
1983	24.01	264.00	288.00	91.67
1987-88	25.70	268.00	293.70	91.25
1991	26.70	259.38	286.08	90.66

Note : It may be noted that work participation rates as per the NSS are higher than for Census.

Sources :

1. Five Year Plan Draft, 1978-83, Planning Commission.
2. Economic Survey, 1994-95.
3. Draft Five Year Plan, 1978-83.
4. Sarvekshana, Vol. III, No. 1, July, 1979 — Unorganised sector employment is got by deducting the workers in the organised sector from the total workers.

As in 1991, the share of unorganised sector in Indian economy was as high as 90.66 per cent. There has been very little decline in the share since 1961. Employment in the unorganised sector over the period of 3 decades grew at an annual rate of 1.1. per cent. In absolute terms the additions to employment in the unorganised sector per annum during the three decades was 2.68 millions. Employment in the organised sector has not grown at a rate high enough to reduce the rate of growth of organised sector.

The share of employment in organised sector in 1981 was only 9.70 per cent, this may be compared with corresponding share of net domestic product of 30 per cent (Table-2). Between 1980-81 and 1990-91, the share of organised sector in NDP increased further from 29.97 to 36.14 per cent. But the share in employment showed a decline from 9.70 to 9.37 per cent. This shows the inability of the organised sector (even in the context of growth) to absorb the growing labour force. Between 1981 and 1991, the annual addition to labour force as per the demographic censuses was 4.9 million. Out of this, absorption of organised sector was only 0.38 millions or around 8 per cent of labour force.

TABLE – 2

Net Domestic Product by Organised and Unorganised Sectors at Current Prices

Year	*Organised*	*Unorganised*	*Total*	*Share of Unorganised to Total*
1980-81	33073	77267	110340	70.03
1985-86	72952	134610	207562	64.85
1986-87	84652	145555	230207	63.23
1987-88	96755	164755	261510	63.00
1988-89	114624	199895	314519	63.56
1989-90	131644	228049	359693	63.40
1990-91	151749	268030	419779	63.85

Source : National Accounts Statistics, 1993, pp.203-04.

We show the share of organised and unorganised sectors in NDP for 1991 by industry division (Table-3): Electricity, gas and Water, Railway Transport, Communication, Public

Administration and Defence are exclusively within the organised sector. A major percentage of production in manufacturing, financial services, bank services are within the organised sector. The unorganised sector accounts for much of agricultural production, bulk of trade and construction, major proportion of transport other than railways, and storage.

TABLE – 3

Share of Organised and Unorganised Sectors in the NDP by Industry (1990-91)

(Rs. in crores)

	Industry	*Organised*	*Un-organised Sector*	*Total*	*Share of organised Sector in Total*	*Share of unorganised Sector*
1.	Agriculture, Forestry & Fishing	4486	135385	139871	3.21	96.79
	1.1 Agriculture	3287	126229	129516	2.54	97.46
	1.2 Forestry & Logging	1196	5898	7094	16.86	83.14
	1.3 Fishing	3	3258	3261	0.09	99.91
2	Mining & Quarrying	7254	767	8021	90.44	9.56
3	Manufacturing	45928	30098	76026	60.41	39.59
	3.1 Registered	45928	—	45928	100.00	—
	3.2 Unregistered	—	30098	30098	—	100.00
4	Electricity, Gas & Water	4031	—	4031	100.00	—
5	Construction	11816	13893	25709	45.96	54.04
6	Trade, Hotels, Restaurants	4083	53026	57109	7.15	92.85
	6.1 Trade	3659	50442	54101	6.76	93.34
	6.2 Hotels and Restaurants	424	2584	3008	14.10	85.90

Contd...

...Contd...

7	Transport, Storage & Communications	12881	12156	25037	51.45	48.55
	7.1 Railways	4368	—	4368	100.00	—
	7.2 Transport by other means	4660	11963	16623	28.03	71.07
	7.3 Storage	184	193	377	48.81	51.19
	7.4 Communications	3669	—	3669	100.00	—
8	Financing, Insurance, Real Estate & Business Services	19006	13857	32863	57.83	42.17
	8.1 Banking & Insurance	18836	2389	21225	88.74	11.26
	8.2 Real Estate & Business Services	170	11468	11638	1.46	98.54
9	Community, Social and Personal Services	42264	8848	51112	82.69	17.31
	9.1 Public Admn. & Defence	24336	—	24336	100.00	—
	9.2 Other Services	17928	8848	26776	66.96	33.04
	Total	151749	268030	419779	36.15	63.85
Total (Non-Agr.)		147263	132645	27908	52.61	47.39

Source : National Accounts Statistics, 1993

The preceding analysis is based on data, which show the entire crop production sector and the entire SIS as unorganised. But this position does not seem to be warranted in the light of the changes in rural economy following green revolution. A new class of farmers well integrated with the outside world has emerged following the green revolution. It is appropriate to consider this class under the organised sector, whereas small and marginal farmers and agricultural labourers are treated under unorganised sector. The organised sector thus covers semi-medium, medium and large holdings. Out of 185 million employed in agricultural sector as per 1990-91, 139 million are in the unorganised sector. Out of these, agricultural labourers form the majority. They are mainly drawn from small and marginal farmer families. Their growth reflects the trends towards the break up of pre-capitalistic structure within agriculture and simultaneously the growth of the capitalist class within agriculture (Table-4).

TABLE – 4

Trends in the Number of Workers in the Organised and Unorganised Sectors

(Millions)

Item	*1979-80/ 1980-81*	*1990-91/ 1989-90*	*% Change over the Decade*	*% Share of Un-organised Sector*
(1)	*(2)*	*(3)*	*(4)*	*(5)*
I. UNORGANISED SECTOR				
1. Agriculture:				
a) Marginal farmers	47.00	48.00		
b) Small farmers (*)	15.00	16.00		32.24
c) Agricultural labour	56.00	75.00	33.93	36.76
Total	118.00	139.00	17.80	70.00
2. Non-Agriculture: Traditional: (**)				
a) Khadi	1.12	1.40		
b) Village Industry	1.61	3.21		
c) Handloom	6.15	7.60		
d) Sericulture	1.60	5.00		
e) Handicrafts	2.00	4.21		
f) Coir-Fibre Works	0.60	0.50		
Total	13.08*	21.92*	90.37	11.04

Contd...

(...contd...)

3 Other Non-Agricultural Labour	28.67	25.05		12.62
4 Own Account Workers in Trade and Services	14.33	12.52		6.36
Total	43.00	37.57	12.47	18.98
Total of Unorganised Sector	174.20	198.49	1.32	
II. ORGANISED SECTOR				
1. Agriculture: Medium, Semi-Medium land holding	40.00	46.00	15.00	52.59
2 Non-Agricultural Labour:				
a) Public Sector Employees	15.60	18.00		20.58
b) Private Sector Employees in Establishments with more than 10 workers	7.40	7.00		8.00
c) Powerlooms	1.10	4.50		5.15
d) Modern Small Scale Industry	6.70	11.96		13.67
Total of Non-Agricultural Labour	30.80	41.46	41.88	
Total of Organised Sector	70.80	87.46	26.69	47.40
Grand Total of Unorganised and Organised Sectors	245.00	286.00	16.53	100.00

* This includes both Household Industry and Non-Factory Non-Household Industry.

Estimated from the household data and the Census data on Cultivation.

** Data from VII Plan Report 1990-91.

Note : The total number of employees in unregistered manufacturing was 18.4 million according to 1980 census. These formed 32 per cent of the total non-agricultural workers. Substantial number of non-agricultural workers are in the tertiary sector. See for details "Employment in Unorganised Manufacturing as per 1980 census, Data Base of the Unorganised Manufacturing Industry : An Appraisal", Small Scale Enterprises in Industrial Development.

If employment in the unorganised sector is classified under precapitalist structures of production and the emerging casual labour class (both agriculture and non-agricultural labour), it is equally distributed.

The non-household non-factory industry shows the highest rate of growth during the period 1961-81. The household industry shows a negative rate of growth. Factory sector which showed a high rate of growth during the period 1961-81, shows a deceleration during the period 1981-91.

The entire employment in the public sector is considered under organised sector because of job security and social security benefits that the employees are enjoying. In 1991 employment in the public sector was 18 million as against seven million in the organised private sector. If modern and small scale industries and powerlooms are added to this total, employment in the private organised sector could be around 24 million as against 18 million workers in the organised public sector, making a total of 42 million in the organised sector within non-agriculture as against a total of 54 million in the unorganised sector.

Our adjustments of the components of unorganised sector from around 90 to around 70 per cent in the organised sector from 10 to 30 per cent or roughly 90 million in a total of 285 million.

Within non-agriculture, there has been a shift towards non-factory, non-household sector employment. Household sector's share has steadily declined since 1961. Factory sector employment, which grew at a higher rate of 4.7 per cent per annum from 1961, showed a perceptible decline to 0.04 per cent per annum in the 80s (Table-5). Since 1983-84, organised private sector contributed very little to employment. Whatever employment growth we found during this period is attributed to public sector. Thus, the organised sector's capacity to absorb the labour weakened considerably in 1980s.

TABLE – 5

Distribution of Worker in Manufacturing Establishments 1961-91.

(In 000s)

				Rate of Growth	
	1961	*1981*	*1991*	*1961-81*	*1981-91*
All-manufacturing	17523 (100.00)	25175 (100.00)	28671 (100.00)	1.83	1.31
Household	9651 (55.08)	7743 (30.75)	6804 (23.73)	-1.09	-1.28
Factory	3050 (17.40)	7715 (30.65)	7743 (27.01)	4.75	0.04
Non-factory & Non-household	4822 (27.52)	9717 (38.6)	14124 (49.26)	3.57	3.81

Source: IJLE, Vol. 37. No. 3, July-Sept. 1994, See also Ramaswamy, p.339, EPW, Feb. 26, 1994

The preponderance of self-employed in total labour could be seen from Table-6A and the trends from Table-6B. Regular labour formed over 14 per cent of total labour. When the labour composition is considered by rural and urban, within the rural sector, regular labour formed only 8 per cent as against 40 per cent in the urban sector. As regards the trends, a decline in regular employment in both rural and urban areas for both the sexes, and an increase marked by casualisation are observable in urban areas.

TABLE – 6A

Absolute Number of Workers by Self-Employed, Regular and Casual Labour Status — 1987-88

(Millions)

	Rural			*Urban*			*Total*		
	Male	*Female*	*Total*	*Male*	*Female*	*Total*	*Male*	*Female*	*Total*
Self-Employed	89.31	52.80	142.11	17.75	5.51	23.26	107.06	58.31	165.37
Regular Labour	15.31 (10.04)	3.17 (3.66)	18.48 (7.73)	18.61 (43.65)	3.21 (27.46)	21.82 (40.17)	33.92 (17.39)	6.38 (6.48)	40.30 (13.73)
Casual Labour	47.85	30.73	78.58	6.27	2.97	9.24	54.12	33.70	87.82
Total	152.47 (100)	86.70 (100)	239.17 (100)	42.63 (100)	11.69 (100)	54.32 (100)	195.10 (100)	98.39 (100)	293.49 (100)

Note : Figures in brackets are the percentages to total.
Source : Sarvekshana.

TABLE – 6B

Trends in Employment

Year	*Employment Status* *Self-Employed*	 *Regular Employee*	 *Casual Labour*
Rural Males			
1972-73	659	121	220
1977-78	628	106	266
1983	605	103	292
1987-88	586	100	314
Rural Females			
1972-73	645	41	314
1977-78	621	28	351
1983	619	28	353
1987-88	609	37	355
Urban Males			
1972-73	392	507	101
1977-78	404	464	132
1983	409	437	154
1987-88	416	437	147
Urban Females			
1972-73	484	279	237
1977-78	495	249	256
1983	458	258	284
1987-88	471	275	254

Source: Sarvekshana, Sept. 7, 1990, p.92.

Relative Efficiency — Unorganised Sector vis-a-vis Organised Sector

The NDP per worker in the organised sector is more than three times the corresponding productivity within the unorganised sector (Table-7). Even if agriculture is not considered, productivity in organised sector is much higher than in unorganised sector. Does it imply that organised sector is more efficient? It may not be appropriate to draw such an inference. In a capital scarce economy, capital-output ratios provide a better norm for judging relative efficiency as compared to labour-output ratios.

TABLE – 7

Net Domestic Product Per Worker in Organised and Unorganised Sectors — 1987-88 by Industry

Industry	*Organised*	*Unorganised to Unorganised*	*Ratio of Organised*
Agriculture	28100	4435	6.33
Mining and Quarrying	46900	3306	14.19
Manufacturing	46740	7303	6.40
Electricity, Gas and Water	27310	Nil	Nil
Construction	63760	3135	20.33
Trade	95950	3238	29.63
Transport, Storage and Communication	25490	10640	2.40
Finance, Insurance, Real Estate, etc.	93690	71438	1.31
Community, Social and Personal Services	27170	3985	6.82
Total	37640	10110	3.72
All Non-Agricultural Sector	38182	23483	1.63

As we do not have data on capital stock by industry, we could use the data on capital stock for registered and unregistered manufacturing units. The total capital stock used in the organised manufacturing sector is 125118 crores of rupees as against 51141 crores of rupees in unorganised sector in 1987-88. Per worker capital stock is as high as Rs.201803 lakh in registered manufacturing as against Rs.20486 lakh in unregistered manufacturing. Thus, the organised manufacturing sector uses 10 times the capital stock per worker when compared to the unorganised manufacturing sector. It is this which gives an advantage to the organised sector. A number of scholars examined the relative efficiency in the past and we may consider their findings.

Dhar and Lydall "Relative Efficiency of Modern Small Scale Industries in India" by Bishwanath Goldar, in K.B. Suri (Ed.) 1988, p. 97 show that capital output ratios in units employing 20 or more persons are not higher. Rather, in certain cases, they are lower. But this is with reference to small scale units in the modern sector. Hajra (1965) in a study, using the data of CMI for 1955-58 came to similar conclusions.. Sandesara in his studies and 1969 using CMI data for 28 industries for the period 1953-58 found again negative association between size and capital-output ratios. He concluded that small scale industries neither generated more employment nor more output per unit of capital compared to large scale units. Mehta in a study published in 1969 using the ASI data for 1960-63 however found that capital-output ratios rose with size. The conflict between the results of Mehta and the earlier studies of Sandesara and Dhar and Lydall could be explained in terms of methods used. Mehta used only fixed capital whereas Sandesara, Dhar and Lydall also covered working capital.

A major limitation of the studies based on the CMI/ASI data is that they cover only those small scale units which are registered as factories under Factories Act [p. 99, Goldar (Ed. Suri)]. These cover only 11 per cent of the sample units though they cover 55 per cent of output [p. 61, Suri (Ed.)]. A later study by Bhavani (1980) which uses the census of small scale industrial units comes to conclusions similar to those of Dhar and Lydall [Goldar in Suri (Ed.)p.100]. Goldar using two factor frontier production functions, arrives at the conclusion that small scale industries are relatively efficient in those industries in which the difference in capital-labour ratio between large scale and small scale units is relatively small. They can not be relied upon to generate large amount of employment under these conditions. Where they had substantial advantage in employment generation, they are relatively inefficient and where they are efficient they do not have much advantage in employment generation [Goldar in Suri (Ed.) p. 111]. Goldar further finds that small scale units are less efficient in the use of capital in almost all (35 out of 37) industries. Estimates of relative efficiency indicate that in a fairly large number of units, small scale units are relatively inefficient compared to large scale units. The relative efficiency index is found to be positively related to size, and the proportion of small scale units using power are negatively related to the ratio of closing stock to consumption of raw materials and the ratio of short term bank credit to inventories [Goldar in Suri (Ed.) p. 117]. The finding of a negative relationship between short-term bank borrowings and efficiency in small scale industries is somewhat surprising suggesting that subsidised credit involves some cost in terms of efficiency.

While there is almost conclusive evidence that modern small scale industry is no different from large scale industry in economising capital use, there is little evidence on the relative efficiency of traditional small industry vis-a-vis large scale industry. The virtual absence of serious academic research is altogether intriguing. In fact, there are only two studies of note that have examined this question in the Indian context. One, undertaken by the Project Appraisal Division of the Planning Commission (1979) and the other done for the World

Bank by Dipak Mazumdar (1984) (Sanjiv Misra, 1993, p. 90). The Planning Commission study indicated that whereas fixed capital cost per unit of output was the highest in the mill sector and the lowest in the handloom sector, employment per unit of output was the highest in the handloom sector and the lowest in the mill sector. The data also showed that the cost of production of handloom cloth per metre was actually lower than that of mill made cloth by 17 per cent in the case of coarse cloth and 5 per cent less in the case of finer than medium cloth. The Planning Commission linear programming exercise indicated that, at actual factor cost for coarse and lower medium varieties cloth, handlooms were the preferred mode of production. With a low capital constraint, the optimal solution indicated an equal sharing of output between the two sectors, the share of powerloom sector rising as the constraint of capital was progressively eased. As a policy prescription, the study recommended a virtual reservation of all varieties of coarse and lower medium cloth for the handloom and finer varieties for the powerloom sector.

Mujumdar's study for the World Bank (1984) presents the data on output per worker and capital per unit of labour and per unit of output for the three sectors, namely, handloom, powerloom and mill. Output per worker per day was 5.4 metres for handloom, 16.8 metres for powerloom and 42.5 metres for mill. Capital cost per metre of cloth works out to Rs. 1054 for handloom and Rs. 467 for powerloom, when fixed capital alone was considered (similar details for mill are not available). If working capital is also included capital costs workout to Rs. 614 for handloom, Rs. 625 for powerloom and Rs. 447 for mill. Dipak's data has shown that production of cloth on powerlooms is the preferred technique over a wide range of interest rates, i.e., between 13.2 per cent and 46.05 per cent. A market interest rate lower than 13.2 per cent would make mill production more profitable than powerloom production, whereas beyond an interest rate of 46.05 per cent, it would be more profitable to produce on handlooms rather than on powerlooms (Misra, p. 94).

While the evidence from micro-data on capital-output ratio is fragmented, sketchy and partial, the evidence in the NSA data suggests lower capital-output ratios for the unorganised manufacturing sector as a whole, as compared to the organised manufacturing sector.

It should also be noted that research focus so far has been mainly on technical efficiency but not allocative efficiency. Even if small scale units are inferior in terms of technical efficiency, they may be far superior in allocative efficiency, so that economic efficiency of small scale units may be as high as that of large units.

Earlier Policies to Strengthen the Unorganised Sector : A Critique

Earlier policies to strengthen the unorganised sector may be classified under the following heads: (1) fiscal, i.e., discriminatory excise tax, (2) product subsidies, (3) input quotas, (4) marketing, (5) technical support, and (6) reservations. None of these policies has been a success in strengthening the unorganised sector. Discriminatory excise taxes have failed to benefit the handloom sector. The powerlooms gained at the expense of handlooms and also purchase of hank yarn intended for handlooms was appropriated by powerlooms (L.C. Jain, EPW, August 27, 1983). The importance of tax evasion on powerloom cloth in tilting the scales of competitive advantage in favour of powerlooms vis-a-vis the mills has not received adequate attention (Misra, 1993, p. 101). Discriminatory excise taxes together with the obligation on textile mills to supply controlled cloth have shifted the advantage from textile mills to powerlooms. L.C. Jain commented in 1983 the loss of employment of weavers is unimaginable and one half of those who lost their jobs are women since women are also engaged in handloom weaving industry (EPW, August 27, 1983).

Production subsidy has been the other instrument of public policy. The 1985 textile policy has also provided for the production of Janata cloth by the handloom sector through the provision of subsidies devoted to the production of Janata cloth. Overall the total subsidy support to handloom weavers would be of the order of Rs. 200 crore at present (Report of the Committee to Review the Progress of Implementation of Textile Policy of June 1985, January 1990, p.51). The IRMA (Institute of Rural Management) Report entitled "A Study of Interventions in the Handloom Industry" has the following to say on the Janata scheme "Even in the worst of states, the scheme has helped the weavers get steady earnings, distinctly higher than other state-aided weavers, but not always even a minimum starvation wage — we could not discern any conscious attempt anywhere, to use the scheme to bring relief to the poorest weaver. It is suggested that the organisations could have full freedom to price the Janata products as they find suitable and that the allocation of production should clearly be for the poorest weavers" (IRMA Report, 1989, p.44) (see also Abid Hussain Committee's Report, p. 66).

Input quotas have been found necessary in the case of unorganised sector since the sector is found to lose in competition with the organised sector because of aggressive marketing strategies of the latter.

Under the 1985 Textile Policy, spinning mills are required to produce 50 per cent of their total marketable output as hank yarn. But the actual delivery of hank yarn amounts to 40 per cent of total hank yarn produced. This has raised two different kinds of problems. Firstly, there are widespread complaints of diversion of hank yarn to powerlooms. Secondly, the demand for yarn by handlooms is for specific qualities and counts, and there is a mismatch between the yarn supplied and yarn demanded. Further, yarn prices are found to rise to abnormal heights (Abid Hussain Committee Report, pp.45-46). The role played by the organisations such as the National Handloom Development Corporation (NHDC), the State-Level Handloom Development Corporations and Apex Handloom Organisations in achieving stability of prices leaves much to be desired.

Weavers' Co-operatives have been the chosen agent for assistance in marketing of handloom products. But it is disquieting to note that the weavers co-operatives at various levels in general could not deliver the goods for a variety of reasons. Unfortunately, a major chunk of production and marketing activities in the handloom sector is still in private hands. Further, over half of all registered weavers' co-operatives in the country have time and again been reported to have been lagging behind. Broadly speaking, the weavers' co-operative sector registered slow pace of progress vis-a-vis the private sector. Lack of co-operative character is said to be one of the main reasons. Further, they do not have the liquid cash for maintaining inventories and they often have inadequate and halting supplies of inputs like, dyes chemicals, yarn, etc. They are also obliged to depend upon private spinning mills and dyes manufacturers. (Rao A.U., Management of Handloom Co-operatives, Vaikunt Mehta National Institute of Co-operative Management, 1978, pp. 34-35). One of the main prescriptions of the 1985 Textile Policy is reservation of 22 varieties of fabrics for handloom weavers. This has been rendered null and void by the stay order granted by various High Courts and the Supreme Court (Abid Hussain's Committee Report, p. 93. See also VIII Plan Report, p. 139).

The experience in respect of other traditional industries has not been different. There has been a decline in the growth of handloom and village industries. Changing consumer preferences and produce preference against khadi have been the factors. A large number of artisans' co-operatives engaged in village industries have continued to be dormant. The wages of artisans are found to be lower than those observed for the farm sector (VIII Plan pp. 136-37).

Up to the end of VII Plan, the implementation of various schemes for promotion and development of handicrafts has not been able to provide assistance to large sections of craftsmen insofar as production and related inputs are concerned. Marketing of their produce is still left largely to private trade. Consequently, the programmes have not made any discernible impact on their earnings and standard of living. Their potential in terms of employment and exports are also limited. (VIII Plan, p. 141).

The Political Economy of Unorganised Industry

Organised sector and unorganised sector are not two water tight compartments. In fact, the organised sector exercises its hold on the unorganised sector through several mechanisms. In the Calcutta Sandal Industry, four big companies purchase almost the entire goods produced by 2000 petty producers. The monopoly control on the market has reduced the production sites of Sandal markets into Sweat houses (Manjit Singh, "the Political Economy of Unorganised Industry," 1990, p. 43). The squeezing of coir production in Kerala is carried out by the big merchant-exporters, who impose their own terms on the purchase market. In 1979, only two big merchants controlled 35 per cent of the total market. From the history of the coir mat and matting industry of Kerala, Issac (1982) concludes that as long as there is scope for absolute surplus appropriation, capital will not aim at relative surplus appropriation through increasing labour productivity (Manjit Singh, Ibid., p. 44). The Growth of the Lace Industry of Narsapur, studied by Mies (1982), is reminiscent of the three centuries old British putting-out system, sometimes also termed capitalist domestic industry (Manjit Singh, Ibid., p. 44). The Lace industry has expanded due to boost from the export market. The entire control over workers by the exporters is maintained through agents and their sub-agent. (Manjit Singh, Ibid., p.45). In the Beedi industry, Mysore, there has been a change over from workshop to put-out system to meet the threat of strike from workers (Manjit Singh, Ibid., p. 46). This development contrasts with the classical development of capitalism in industry, where domestic workers, once brought into the workshops, were pushed into Factory production and not back to domestic work. The carpet industry of Bhadohi is another example of a traditional industry, organised on the basis of putting-out work to domestic weavers and controlled by the merchant manufacturers. (Manjit Singh, p. 47).

The lace, beedi and carpet industry present parallel examples of the putting-out system, carried out under the dominance of merchant-manufacturing capital and characterised by traditional methods of production. On the other hand matchsticks, fireworks and agarbati are organised on the basis of workshops. Here the capital-wage relations are more visible. The means of production are owned by the employer while the workers own nothing except their labour power. These workshops constitute the biggest 'slaughter house' of children. (Manjit Singh, p. 48).

The garment export industry of Madras employed three times the workers in the non-factory sector as compared to its employees in factory sector. Here merchant capital is seen to be dominant. The Jari Industry of Surat is another example of putting out system in which independent producers are also found (p. 50). The Cotton Hosiery Industry in Calcutta illustrate the case in which the workers supply not only their labour power but also small machines in the service of capital. (Manjit Singh, p. 50). The merchant-manufacturers bought yarn from the market and advanced this yarn to the knitting units.

Manjit Singh classified the unorganised industries into four broad categories on the basis of the labour process. (1) Industries using traditional skill and traditional instruments of labour; (2) Though the place of work is the home of worker, there is a detailed division of labour and labour is formally subsumed under capital. Merchant-manufacture plays a key role; (3) Workers are brought to the workshops and are made to work under the direct supervision of the manufactures; and (4) Those where the production process has changed from manufacture to 'machinofacture' or factory form. Merchant-manufacturing capital thrives owing to the decentralised nature of the production process.

Ancillary industries or sub-contracts have been another method by which organised sector exercises its power over the unorganised sector. Notwithstanding the fact that small industries have gained technical and market support by being ancillaries, the general experience has been that the organised sector used sub-contracts for exploiting the unorganised sector [Sucha Singh Gill, p. 173, G.K. Chadha (ed.)].

In conclusion, the unique evolution of capitalism in the colonial context has resulted in lack of progress of industries in the unorganised sector to organised sector. Further, industries in the organised sector have failed to step up labour productivity.

Inadequate Public Support to Unorganised Sector

If organised private sector is found to squeeze the unorganised sector through appropriation of absolute surplus, public support to the unorganised sector has been inadequate

TABLE — 9

Output, Employment, Exports and Plan Outlay by Type of Industry in 1989-90 within VSI Sector

Type of Industry	*Production (crores)*	*Percentage*	*Employment (millions)*	*Percentage*	*Exports (crores)*	*Percentage*	*VII Plan Outlay (crores)*	*Percentage*	*Productivity Per Worker*
Modern small scale industries	92080 (15478)	80.55	12.0	24.77	7626.00	51.50	1120.51	40.71	76,733.33 (12,898.33)
Powerlooms	9865	8.63	4.5	9.29	—	—	11.77	0.42	21,922.22
Khadi cloth	203	0.18	11.41	23.55	1.39	0.01	636.25	23.11	1,439.72
Village industries	1101	0.96	3.21	6.63	3.66	0.02			3,429.91
Handlooms	3377	2.95	7.60	15.69	342.00	2.31	512.26	18.61	4,443.42
Sericulture	493	0.43	5.00	10.32	400.61	2.71	309.96	11.26	986.00
Handicrafts	7067	6.18	4.22	8.71	6400.00	43.22	122.86	4.46	16,746.45
Coir fibre	128	0.12	0.50	1.03	33.32	0.23	39.13	1.43	2,560.00
Total	114314 (35717)	100.00	48.44	100.00	14806.98	100.00	2752.74	100.00	29,769.00
Registered Manufactures	219304 (39247)**		7.00		7830.00		19662.80		9,300.00** (56,070)**

Source : Eighth Five Year Plan, p. 149. Small Scale Industries in India, p. 14 (Dr. D Nagaiya)

Note : For the same year, net domestic product from unregistered manufactures was 30098 and net domestic from product registered manufactures in 39247, while value of output, manufactures registered is Rs. 219304.

TABLE – 10

Small Scale Industries in Backward and Other Districts 1977-78

	Backward	*Others*	*Ratio of others in Backward*
1. Per unit value of gross output	1,72,839	6,62,000	3.83
2. Market value of fixed assets	43,924	1,41,184	3.21
3. Per unit loan outstanding	34,802	1,38,897	3.99
	Registered	Unregistered	Ratio
4. Value of gross output per unit	1.68	0.17	9.88

Source : Patvardhan [Suri (ed.)].

Structural Adjustment and Impact on Unorganised Sector

Structural adjustment in the Indian Economy implies

1. An increasing flow of foreign direct investment alongwith foreign technology;
2. A decline in the role of the State and an increase in the role of market in industrial growth;
3. An increasing reliance on foreign trade as an engine of growth; and
4. A shift away from subsidies and from protection through tariff.

We will examine the implication of each of these for unorganised sector. One could expect that since direct foreign investment supplements domestic investment, its effects should give a stimulus to industries in the unorganised sector through (i) growth effect, (ii) output linkage effects. But such a conclusion is unwarranted when we consider the technology impact in the specific industry and on overall economy. Technology development has been concentrated in the advanced countries. The vast bulk of world's capital goods manufacture is also concentrated here. This means that Third World Countries have no choice but to use technologies of the developed countries. This will be all the more so in the case of foreign direct investment. There is a strong tendency for more capital intensive technologies to be selected. Technology designed in advanced countries does reflect their climatic conditions with a concentration of increased cost when it is transferred. The use of advanced country techniques also means the use of advanced country's organisation. This rules out the possibility of local development and local entrepreneur's talent. Managerial dependence follows from technological dependence. The transfer of technology involves transferring advanced country's investment per head to the underdeveloped economy; but available savings per head is much lower because of the lower labour productivity in the poor countries. As a consequence, most investment resources have to be concentrated in the sector receiving the advanced country technology, so that required investment levels per employee in this sector may be achieved. Since savings per head in India are much lower, only a small fraction of the labour force could be employed in the advanced sector by using the technology designed for US and UK (F. Stewart, Inappropriate Technology and Underdevelopment, Macmillan Press, London, 1978, p. 72).

The heavy investment demands imposed by advanced country technology result in concentration of country's resources in the organised sector to the neglect of the unorganised sector. The organised sector is associated with high labour productivity, and the unorganised sector suffers from lack of resources and poor efficiency as a result of lack of scientific and technological research. The huge gap in labour productivity between the two sectors has a parallel in a gap between the wage levels in the two sectors. The possibility of high wages encourages foreign training facilities. The net effect is disbursal of expenditure on education and training of a few in advanced sector, while neglecting the majority. The educational requirement imposed by advanced technology alters also the style of life in developing countries. Alternative life styles are closely associated with patterns of demand for consumer goods. Two effects ensure out of the transfer of products designed for consumption of much richer society to the poor. Unequal incomes creates markets for high income products, while unbalanced consumption patterns extend these markets.

The links between techniques and other parts of the economy extend to requirements for particular types of transport such as roads, of legal and administrative services and so on, as well as for particular products as inputs.

In brief, the inflow of direct foreign investment is likely to deprive the unorganised sector of resources, skilled workers, etc. It can be seen that a dualistic pattern of development is an inevitable consequence. The origin is to be found in the characteristics of advanced country technology. Concentration of resources in the advanced sector, high labour productivity and high incomes in this sector in relation to rest of economy (Steward, p. 74). The emerging pattern of foreign investment and the capital investment techniques by the MNC's contribute to accelerated growth of dualism in the labour market, reduce the linkage effects between the industrial sector and the rural/agricultural sector and arrest the growth of local autonomous small scale industry [Parthasarathy, G. and Chalam, K.S. (Ed.), "Readings in Political Economy", p.331]. Further, there is an irreconcilable conflict between the social objective of decentralised, participatory and sustainable integration, local development and the pattern of growth achieved when transnationals enter into agro-processing (Parthasarathy, G. "Neocolonialism", Ibid., p. 333).

Subramanyam, who examined the relationship between economic liberalism and development of technological capability of the country finds that the Import of Foreign Technology has an adverse effect on the R & D effort in the country [Subramanyam pp. 13-27; Yoginder. K. Alagh & others (ed.)].

The second implication of structural adjustment is the declining role of the State. In Indian situation, this reflects more in a decline in capital and planned expenditure of the State in Human Resource Development. While the current revenue expenditure continued to be maintained (see G. Parthasarathy, Janus Faced 5th Budget of Manmohan Singh, IDPS, 1995.) such decline in capital expenditure particularly in agriculture has adverse effects on the entire rural sector. As capital formation in agriculture declines, incomes of the masses in agriculture tend to decline particularly in the context of rising capital-output ratios. The falling income of the mass of people in agriculture have adverse effects on the unorganised non-agricultural sector, as the demand for their products shrink. A recent study on the transformation of South Korea (OECD, Paris, 1995) challenges the view that economic success was simply based upon sensible macro economic policies. It argued that the role of government far surpassed that of simply adopting and implementing these policies. It explains why an activist role favouring enterprise, prioritizing education and reducing rural inequalities makes sense in terms of economic efficiency for a country in economic transition. The study concludes that economic transition can be accelerated by such an activist role of the State.

Removal of all trade restrictions and reduction of import duties is considered to bring domestic prices in alignment with international prices. By removing factor price distortions, these are expected to stimulate labour intensive exports. One may argue that liberalisation will benefit the labour intensive unorganised sector as it will be in a position to export its products at competitive prices. The case of garment industry is often cited. While this may be true, this ignores another aspect of the problem. Most of the industries in unorganised sector depend upon raw material supplied by the organised sector. If there is a free export of such products, the prices of raw materials rise. Since the unorganised sector is unable to shift the higher price on to the consumers, the burden of high price of raw material has to be borne by the producer. This will mean further reduction in his meagre earnings. Two feature articles in a popular fortnightly magazine, Frontline, one in the issue of December 6, 1991, entitled "Starvation Deaths in Andhra Pradesh", (p. 47); and another published in a latter issue (Vol. 12, No. 7, March 7-25 April, 1995) under the title Special Feature, "Troubled Tirupur" bring out tellingly how an export-led growth, unmindful of its consequences could ruin the handloom weavers. The journal provided a list of starvation deaths, 31 in Guntur District and 22 in Prakasam District of A.P. The impoverished weaver of Andhra Pradesh has been forced to pay dearly for a range of policies — in particular steps tailored to promote a policy of export oriented growth. Steady export of cotton yarn from 40 million kgs. in 1987-88 to 62 million kgs. in 1988-89 and then to 90 million kgs. in 1989-90 and to 100 million kgs. in 1990-91 resulted in abnormal prices. Another reason behind the rise in yarn prices is an increase in cotton exports. Stocks piled up with master weavers and co-operatives since they could not sell domestically nor export the same. Both the organisations had to count down the employment of weavers, and also pay lower wages. The Government could neither control the prices of inputs like yarn, dyes and chemicals nor organise the market to protect the handlooms from unequal competition with powerlooms and textile mills. On top of all this, the government in acute financial crisis withheld Rs. 20 crore payment. It also cut down its own purchase of cloth from the sector. The APCO, an apex co-operative body has transferred this burden of arrears to primary co-operatives, resulting in domestic decline in production. Further, the continuing cut for the production of Janata Cloth, earmarked exclusively to the handloom sector, has been cut by a hefty 25 per cent.

The weaver has traditionally resorted to the following to cope with crisis — (a) borrowing, (b) migration, (c) occupational diversification, and (d) sale of assets. All these coping mechanisms have been only of limited help. The weaver resorted to sale of cloth at lower prices and the handover of his membership card in the primary co-operative society. The middlemen collects the wage on behalf of the weaver, pays him less and makes a profit. This is the price that weavers pay for primary societies becoming sick and inactive. History repeated again in 1995; this time at Tirupur, a centre for cotton hosiery, Coimbatore District in Tamil Nadu. The first symptoms of trouble came in 1993 when yarn prices began to rise with Union Government's decision to allow exports of cotton and cotton yarn. Early in 1994, yarn prices were up by Rs. 12 per kg. There was enormous pressure on hosiery units with prices going up by 30 per cent. At one shot, the margin scheme came under pressure, production dropped, and the number of shifts came down drastically. The situation worsened when prices rose by another Rs. 12 per kg. For the industry, the situation was fatal. Small units stopped, production and the exports came down slowly by nearly 40 per cent and reduction in jobs followed.

Protection to unorganised sector by way of subsidies, input quotas and reservations have been found necessary, because of handicaps of the unorganised sector in the product, input, credit and labour markets. Further, such subsidies were found increasingly necessary for regionally backward areas which are subject to severe disadvantages due to backwash effects while spread effects are small. Further, while advanced regions have economies of agglomeration investments in backward regions are found to be risky. For this reason, capital instead of flowing to backward areas with high interest rate flows in reverse direction. State intervention by way of subsidies to industries in backward areas are found to be necessary. The ideology of structural adjustment looked with disfavour at all such measures of protection including reservations. Yet popular pressures from handloom weaver organisations have contributed to the continuance of several such schemes, Janata Cloth Scheme, Modified Workshed Housing Schemes, and invariable design collection programmes (see for details, Detailed Reports of Commissionerate of Handlooms, Ministry of Textiles, Govt. of India,). But the impact of the schemes in protecting the handlooms has been negligible in the absence of upgradation of technology, improved labour productivity and adaptation of handloom products to the shifting consumer preferences.

Much reliance has also been placed on agricultural exports in the light of structural adjustment. The GATT provisions, to which India is now a signatory, are expected to contribute to growth of agricultural exports as subsidy revision in the developed countries is likely to raise international prices and make Indian agricultural exports more competitive. While such circumstances may benefit the large farmers among agriculturists, the rise in price of the foodgrains due to structural adjustment will certainly affect the poor, the real wages of casual labour is likely to be pushed down [H.S. Sidhu, p. 153, G.K. Chadha (ed.)].

The issue of reservation to products of unorganised sector is important. They have been stalled by High Court Decisions in the past and it is therefore being pleaded that such reservations should be included in the IX Schedule of the Constitution keeping this out of judicial purview. The IRMA

Report suggests that the consensus in handloom circles is that the existence of a reservation order, even with partial enforcement has a salutary effect (p.12). They also present the view that the entire cotton production should be reserved for handlooms. But the economic consequences of this on the cost and price of cloth, which the IRMA Report did not examine (p. 54), are likely to be adverse.

The Abid Hussain Committee which examined the reservation issue, however, did not view reservations with favour. It preferred promotional measures to reservations. We are inclined to agree with Abid Hussain Committee.

Policy Directions

Structural adjustments programmes are likely to have a significantly adverse impact on employment both within the organised as well as unorganised sectors. The organised sector is likely to witness retrenchment and casualisation of employment opportunities. The unorganised sector will be forced to accept persons released by the organised sector and in the process wage and self-employment opportunities for the unskilled and the semi-skilled are likely to deteriorate further. Industrial firms may shift to capital intensive technologies requiring higher skills and push relatively unskilled to declining traditional industries with prospects of income losses and eventual loss of employment [Ashok Chandra in Rizwanul Islam (ed), p. 91].

Sudipto Mundle (Rizwanul Islam (ed), pp. 164-68) estimated the unemployed as a consequence of structural adjustment at 5 to 8 lakhs for the organised sector. He does not cover the impact of structural adjustment on the unorganised sector. A consequence of structural adjustment is the increase in the number in the unorganised sector. Since the 80s, there has been no additional employment in the private organised sector despite increase in investment. Given this experience, the disinvestment of public sector, and the shift to private sector are likely to close even the meagre opportunities for entry into the organised sector specially for blue collar workers. They will drift into unorganised sector and into self-employment or casual labour. The need for improved access to institutional credit will be greater than in the past. One important aspect of institution building is building of credit institutions to meet the requirements of the poor and unorganised. In this context, the Thrift and Credit Societies organised on group basis for women (see Parthasarathy, "Economic Impact of Women's Thrift and Credit Societies," 1995), have been found to serve a useful function. In the dark environment of credit indiscipline, the Women's Thrift and Credit Societies have emerged as torch-bearers of thrift and self-reliance. In performing this function, they also emerge as training grounds for economic democracy for women. But, their success essentially depends upon commitment with which the sponsoring organisation establishes a system and makes it successful. Government assistance may help, but it is not the key factor. The key factor is the role of voluntary organisation which sponsors the group, nurtures it and makes it a self-reliant Thrift and Credit Society. The role of enlightened citizens in promoting such voluntary organisations becomes important. But, there is a limit to the success of these organisation in the absence of income-generating activities. Income-generating activities for the members have to meet the constraints of marketing [see Parthasarathy "Group Lending by Mahila Mandals in the BCT Area, yelamanchili, Visakhapatnam Dt," (mimeo) 1993]. The tie-up of group activities of women with organised purchasing agencies has been found to be helpful. It is here that government could help promote marketing products of unorganised sector. It should be made obligatory on the part of all public sector employees, who form the privileged section, to purchase part of consumption requirements from unorganised sectors. Similarly, it must be made obligatory on schools to use the products of unorganised sector for uniform material. This may sound unnecessary and wasteful interference with market and consumer preferences. But, where the trade-off is joblessness and starvation for the many petty producers versus a little discomfort to the privileged sections in the organised sectors, this has to be accepted as a measure towards redistribution of incomes from organised to unorganised sectors.

Small and petty producers suffer from constraints of not only marketing, but also production. Water management has to be a group activity even while each peasant cultivates his own plot because of externalities involved. Similar externalities are involved in pesticide spraying. A small peasant with less than a hectare will not gain from pesticide spraying if he alone sprays and the neighbours do not spray. This becomes critical in view of the shift to crops like vegetables, fruits and flowers, in which both water management and pesticide spraying become important. The gains from globalisation could be got from small farmers only with institution building based on group activity.

Structural adjustments have resulted in pressures from certain sections for relaxing all constraints on land market. There is a plea for relaxing ceiling laws and for unlimited flow of private investments into agriculture and land acquisition. This may be considered desirable if the labour has opportunities outside agriculture and land. In the absence of such opportunities, revoking the ceiling law is bound to displace many marginal and small peasants and accelerate the trends towards casualisation of labour. Such trends will result in a situation where less than 25 per cent alone within agriculture (the present position is 25 per cent of the holders belong to the semi-medium, medium and large farms category) could benefit from the changes brought about by structural adjustment. The success of structural adjustment in Korea, Taiwan, People's Republic of China, etc. is attributed to the successful land reforms preceding the New Economic Policy. A widely dispersed agricultural growth benefiting the mass of peasants shifting their consumption patterns to higher levels will be necessary for the emergence and growth of non-farm activities. Even if there is no programme for a fresh piece of land reform, it will be necessary to ensure that current programmes on the statute books are not disturbed. This is also important from the viewpoint of political stability which is necessary for the progress of economic reforms. Given the huge and rising pressures on land, programmes in agriculture alone will not be found to be adequate. They need to be supplemented by development of non-farm activity for the benefit of bulk of marginal farmers and agricultural labourers. The products of traditional industry could be distinguished into the following groups : (1) products with national demand and catering to the elite class, (2) products with local demand and depending on local raw material for their sustenance, (3) product catering to the mass market and competing with the organised sector. The structural adjustments and globalisation are likely to step up the demand for the first type of products. But, this will bring relief to only a small percentage within the unorganised sector. The second type of products depending upon local raw material and catering to local markets will face the competition of the organised sector, especially in the input market. The unorganised sector is not likely to win the race in the raw material market. A similar situation arises in the third type of market also. The unorganised sector might seek to overcome this constraint by arranging tie-ups with the organised sector in production and marketing. As we have seen earlier, such a tie-up system often tends to be exploitative. Non-exploitative relations could be established if group strength of the unorganised sector is promoted through public support. The overall situation of traditional industry is not found to be favourable with structural adjustments. We should expect the current trends of deceleration to continue, within the rural sector. More numbers could be expected to be casualised and drift into urban informal sector.

In the light of not too optimistic position of traditional industries, massive public investments in modern energy, transport and communication infrastructure, public civil engineering projects and social services will be found necessary. This will create massive number of new jobs while at the same time conserving, upgrading and increasing the technological capabilities of workers. But, this needs to temper market fundamentalism and a release from the hegemony of the IMF and World Bank combine (Bhagawan, Economic and Political Weekly, Feb., 18-25. 1995).

Countries with massive proportion of workers in the unorganised sector have to reckon with the fact that the numbers of these are likely to rise as a consequence of structural adjustments. Safety nets and structural adjustment with human face could hardly bring solutions to their problems. A new approach to development in which the petty producers are made the agents of social transformation through their own organisations which will bring them economies of scale of production, technology, credit and marketing will be found necessary. The newly set up Panchayati Raj Institution should help promote this process. It is unfortunate that in the euphoria of liberalisation and globalisation we are made to forget the most fundamental tasks, i.e., institution building for mobilisation of the rural, urban masses within the unorganised sector for growth, employment and poverty alleviation.

References

Breman Jan & Sudipto Mundle (ed.) *Rural Transformation in Asia*, Oxford University Press, New Delhi - 110 001, 1991.

Chadha, G.K. (ed.), *Sectoral Issues in the Indian Economy: Policy and Perspectives*, Har-Anand Publications, New Delhi, 1994.

Chung, H. Lee, *The Economic Transformation of South Korea : Lessons for the Transition Economies*, Development Centre Studies, Development Centre of the Organisation for Economic Co-operation and Development, Paris 1995.

Islam Rizwanul (ed.), *Social Dimensions of Economic Reforms in Asia*, International Labour Organisation, 1994, New Delhi.

Manjit Singh, *The Political Economy of Unorganised Industry : A study of the Labour Process*, Sage Publications, New Delhi, 1990.

Parthasarathy, G. "*Neo-Colonialism, Transnational Corporations and Basic Developmental Issues", Readings in Political Economy*, Chalam, K.S. (ed.), Book Centre, Visakhapatnam, 1991.

Parthasarathy, G. "*Economic Impact of Women's Thrift and Credit Societies*," Institute of Development and Planning Studies, Visakhapatnam, 1995.

Parthasarathy, G, "*Janus-Faced Fifth Budget of Dr. Manmohan Singh*," Occasional Paper, Institute of Development and Planning Studies, Visakhapatnam, 1995.

Rao, S.B., Datar, D.R. & Deshmukh, M.A. (ed.), "*Management of Handloom Co-operatives : Policies, Programmes and Perspectives*," Vaikunth Mehta National Institute of Co-operative Management, Pune-16, 1978.

Schumacher, E.F., *Small is Beautiful: Economics as if People Mattered*, Harper Colophon Books, Harper & Row Publishers, New York, 1975.

Suri, K.B. (ed.), *Small Scale Enterprises in Industrial Development : The Indian Experience*, Sage Publications, New Delhi, 1988.

Sanjiv Misra, *India's Textile Sector : A Policy Analysis*, Centre for Policy Research, Sage Publications, New Delhi, 1993.

Uma Kapila (ed.), "*Economic Status of Handicraft Artisans*," National Council of Applied Economic Research, New Delhi - 110 002. 1993.

Vijayagopalan, S., "*Economic Status of Handicraft Artisans*," National Council of Applied Economic Research, New Delhi - 110 002, 1993.

Yoginder, K. Alagh, Raghuvir, J. Mody & Rohit. D. Desai (ed.), *Sectoral Growth and Change : Essays in Honour of D.T. Lakdawala*, Har-Anand Publications, New Delhi, 1993.

Reports

Central Statistical Organisation, Dept. of Statistics, Govt. of India, New Delhi, "Annual Survey of Industries, 1983-84." 1987.

Central Statistical Organisation, Dept. of Statistics, Govt. of India, New Delhi, "Annual Survey of Industries, 1985-86," 1989.

Central Statistical Organisation, Dept. of Statistics, Govt. of India, New Delhi, "National Accounts Statistics," 1993.

Central Statistical Organisation, Dept. of Statistics, Govt. of India, New Delhi, "Economic Census, 1980, All India Report," 1985.

Reserve Bank of India, "Report on the Currency and Finance — 1992-93," Bombay.

Ministry of Labour, Labour Bureau, Chandigarh, "Report on the Working and the Living Conditions of Workers in the Powerloom Industry in India, 1988," 1991.

Ministry of Labour, Labour Bureau, Chandigarh, "Report on the Working and the Living Conditions of Workers in the Handloom Industry in India, 1986-87," 1990.

Institute of Public Enterprises, Hyderabad, "Technology and Underdevelopment by Stewart, F. in "Technology and Development, Vol. III of Selected Readings for the Course on Policy Planning and Analysis for Civil Servants.".

National Institute of Small Industry Extension Training, (A Govt. of India Society), Hyderabad, "Small Scale Industries in India, Handbook of Statistics," 1989.

Govt. of India, Planning Commission, "Draft Fifth Five Year Plan," 1978-83, New Delhi

Govt. of India, Planning Commission, "VII Five Year Plan," 1990-91, New Delhi.

Govt. of India, Planning Commission, "VIII Five Year Plan Outlay," 1992-97, New Delhi.

Govt. of India, Ministry of Finance, "Economic Survey — 1994-95," New Delhi.

Ministry of Textile, Govt. of India, New Delhi, "Textile Industry in the 1990s Restructuring with a Human Face, Report on the Committee to Review the Progress of Implementation of Textile Policy of June 1980," 1990.

Institute of Rural Management, Anand, "A Study of Interventions in the Handloom Industry — Final report," 1989.

Institute of Development and Planning Studies, "Group Lending by Mahila Mandals in B.C.T. Area, Yellamanchili, Visakhapatnam District, Andhra Pradesh" by Parthasarathy, G., (Mimeo) Visakhapatnam, 1993.